# THE ESSENCE OF GENERAL PHILOSOPHY

# THE ESSENCE OF GENERAL PHILOSOPHY

*By*

**MANMATHA NATH GHOSE**

Thoroughly Revised and Enlarged
By

**DR. JADUNATH SINHA**

BKP

BHARATIYA KALA PRAKASHAN
DELHI (INDIA)

First Edition : 1925
Revised Edition : 2007





*Published by* **C.P. Gautam**
BHARATIYA KALA PRAKASHAN
3421-A, IInd Floor, Narang Colony, Tri Nagar, Delhi-110035.
Phone : 27393083, 32967505 (O), 32492129 (R)
E-Mail : bkp3421@yahoo.co.in

**ISBN : 978-81-8090-170-6**

***Laser Type Setting by***
A-ONE GRAPHICS
Pitampura, Delhi-110088

Printed by :
BDH Printers at D. K. Fine Art Press, Delhi

# CONTENTS

# CHAPTER I

# INTRODUCTION

## The Need and Origin of Philosophy

We are rational beings. We live, but we do not live an unthinking animal life. We live and sometimes think how we live and why we live. We do not swim with the current of life like a straw without thinking whither we go. This reflection on our life and experience is the root of philosophy. In supreme moments of our life when we are overpowered with the mystery of life and 'the heavy and weary weight of all this unintelligible world', our weary soul pants to penetrate the veil of appearances and 'see into the life of things'. In this reflective mood many momentous questions force themselves on our mind and demand a solution—such as "What are we ? Whither shall we go ? What is the meaning of our life ? What is the meaning of this world ? What is the goal of our life ?" etc. It is reflection on these all important problems of our life and experience that constitutes philosophy.

However primitive, crude and uncultured a man may be, in some moments of his life he cannot but ask himself these questions; his very life presupposes an unconscious theory of life and the world, and this unconscious world-view is the germ of philosophy. With the advance of culture and civilization human life becomes more and more complex, and the ever increasing anomalies and contradictions of human experience demand an explanation. It is the intellectual effort on the part of man to harmonize the various phases of our life and arrive at an adequate explanation of the mystery of life in its multifarious aspects—intellectual, aesthetic, moral and religious —that constitutes philosophy.

Man, finite and imperfect as he is, can never solve the riddle of life completely. Human life becomes never complete and perfect; it never presents itself to us in an all-round perfect form; it always reveals to us newer and newer phases and presses upon us newer and newer problems for solution. As human life is never complete, so philosophy or the interpretation of life is never perfect. Philosophy always changes with everchanging human life; actual life and theory of life or philosophy always react upon each other, so that the wider is the life, the deeper is philosophy,—and the deeper is philosophy, the nobler and higher, the life. Thus a complete philosophy is a misnomer; philosophy is always a search after truth an attempt at an adequate explanation of our life and experience.

**(2) The meaning of 'Philosophy'**

The term 'philosophy literally means 'love of wisdom' or pursuit of knowledge. Hence any branch of study was formerly called philosophy, *e. g.* physics, mathematics, theology etc. As men were in the lowest stage of their intellectual condition, they could not differentiate the different departments of the universe and consequently the different branches of knowledge. But with the advance of knowledge they came to distinguish different sciences from one another, and philosophy from sciences, and regarded philosophy as the knowledge of the eternal and essential nature of things

Thus at first philosophy was not distinguished from special sciences; then it was altogether divorced from sciences. But now philosophy, in its restricted sense, does neither mean the study of any particular department of the universe, nor the knowledge of the eternal and essential nature of things alone, but that highest branch of knowledge which aims at harmonizing and systematizing all truths and thus arriving at a conception of the reality as a whole, both in its eternal and phenomenal aspects. Philosophy is the criticism of life and experience.

**(3) The Province or Scope of Philosophy**

By the province or scope of philosophy we mean the range of its subject-matter. Philosophy is an attempt at a rational explanation of the reality as a whole. But we can never directly know the reality in itself; we can know it only as it is revealed to us in our experience; in other words, we know the reality as it appears to us in our experience—we directly know only its appearance or phenomenon. So we cannot know the reality apart from its appearance—the noumemon apart from its phenomenon. (See below Ch. I. (III).) Thus philosophy cannot dispense with the world of our experience.

The reality or the universe, thus, may be studied in its two aspects, the phenomenal and the noumenal. The phenomenon is the appearance of the reality—its manifestation to us in our experience; the noumenon is the reality in itself, behind and beyond our experience. The phenomenal world is the subjectmatter of science, and the noumenal world is the subject-matter metaphysics. Hence science is called phenomenology, and metaphysics called ontology. Philosophy studies the concrete reality, both in its phenomenal or empirical and noumenal or metaphysical aspects, and hence it includes science and metaphysics-phenomenology and ontology both.

And just as sciences fall into three distinct groups, physical sciences or sciences of matter and motion, biological sciences or sciences of life, and mental sciences or sciences of mind, so philosophy too divided into. three distinct parts, the philosophy of matter, the philosophy of life, and the philosophy of the soul. The philosophy of matter and life is called the philosophy of, nature. And besides the philosophy of nature and the philosophy of the soul, there is another branch of philosophy which seeks to know the real nature of the Absolute which comprehends both nature and the soul. Thus there are three branches of philosophy, the philosophy of nature, the philosophy; of the soul and the philosophy of the Absolute. The philosophy of nature, again, is divided into three parts. Cosmogony enquires into the origin of the world; Ontology investigates the ultimate nature or essence of the world; Cosmology, enquires into the constitution and organisation of the world.

Moreover, as philosophy seeks to know the ultimate nature of the reality, it first seeks to justify its claim to do so and prove the possibility of knowledge, as a preliminary step to a strictly philosophical enquiry. This branch of philosophy is called Epistemology. (See below Ch. II, 1.)

Thus philosophy includes the following:

(1) Science or phenomenology.

(2) Epistemology (or theory of knowledge).

(3) Metaphysics or Ontology (theory of being)

(i) Ontology of Nature,

(ii) Ontology of the Soul,

(iii) Ontology of the Absolute.

**Science and Common Sense**

Science deals with the world of common experience. The common sense view of the world is not only derived from unsophisticated sense-experience but also inherited by the individual from his ancestors, imbibed from the social environment. It is vague, superficial unreflective and unsystematic. The facts of our common experience are chaotic and confused, disjointed and isolated from one another. Science seeks to explain them by discovering their causes and laws, and removes all seeming contradictions among them. "Science is nothing but trained and organised common sense."

The characteristics of science are (1) generality, (2) certainty, (3) accuracy, and (4) system Let us discuss these points one by one.

Firstly, ordinary experience or common knowledge is concerned with particular facts; it is limited to the concrete and individual. But science is concerned with the general features and relations of things and events. The aim of science is always to discover the general laws of nature, and apply them to particular cases. The goal of science is generalization.

Secondly, scientific knowledge is certain while common unscientific knowledge is very often uncertain or doubtful.

Scientific knowledge is based on rational grounds, while common knowledge is based on mere opinion or prejudice. Scientific knowledge is proved by experimental methods, while common knowledge is not verified by scientific methods.

Thirdly, scientific knowledge is accurate and precise, while common knowledge is very often inaccurate and inexact. Scientific knowledge is proved by scientific methods, while common knowledge is very often based on conjecture. Science observes facts adequately and precisely, and reports them faithfully.

Fourthly, scientific knowledge is systematic and methodical, while common knowledge is unsystematic and immethodical. The particular facts of common experience are systematized by science. It is based on the facts of common experience. Science organises the isolated facts of common experience and reduces them into a system or organised whole. Scientific knowledge therefore, is systematized common experience. Thus science is organised common sense.

### Philosophy and Common Sense

Everyone, however innocent he may be of scientific lore, has a certain sort of philosophy. He has his views concerning the nature and meaning of life, growth and decay, minds and bodies and their relation to each other, the nature of cause and luck and chance, existence after death, God and His relation to the human individual and to the world, knowledge and belief, truth and error, and the like. Such views are generally based upon vague and unanalyzed inferences, and are usually defined in terms of traditional beliefs. This is a sort of philosophy which we may call the philosophy of common sense." (Cunningham: *Problems of Philosophy,* pp. 69-70.)

The philosophy of common sense is not based on critical reflection. It is derived from authority and tradition, or imbibed from the social environment. It is dogmatic and uncritical. The human spirit cannot rest content with this kind of unsystematic and unreflective philosophy. So, it passes from the philosophy of common sense to the philosophy of the sciences. It builds up the structure of philosophy on the solid foundation of results of scientific enquiry. Science rationalizes common sense, and philosophy rationalizes science.

## Philosophy and Science

Science and philosophy both are based on the facts of our experience, and both of them seek to explain them by discovering their connections and correlations, their unity and harmony. Philosophy has no other subject matter than the world of our experience. It does not deal with any transcendental world, but with the world we perceive, and in which we live, move and have our being, "in passing from the sciences to philosophy, as in passing from common sense to the sciences, we are not entering upon a wholly new and untouched territory; on the contrary, we are still dealing with the same environment and are only pressing on in our efforts to comprehend its meaning." (Cunningham: *Problems of Philosophy,* PP. 76-77.)

If science is a step beyond common experience, philosophy is a step beyond science.

Science organises the particular truth of our common experience, philosophy organises the general truths of sciences. Each science deals with a particular department of the world, and its verdict is supreme within its own sphere. The results of one science may be in conflict with those of another. But the sciences themselves cannot reconcile this conflict. It is the business of philosophy to take up the highest results of the special sciences, and to seek to understand the universe as a whole, by harmonising and organising the highest laws and the most universal truths of sciences. Thus sciences supply the data or materials to philosophy. Philosophy without foundation in science is a sheer dogmatism. Hence science is an interpretation of common experience; and philosophy is an interpretation of sciences.

Particular sciences deal with special groups or particular departments of phenomena. Philosophy, on the other hand, deals with the whole of the universe. "It is not with the ascertainment of particular facts that it is concerned, but with the gaining of a true insight into the general structure of the universe and man's relations to it." (Mackenzie: *Elements of Constructive Philosophy,* p. 15.)

Philosophy is concerned with the synthesis and unification of the ultimate truths of different sciences, and seeks to arrive at an adequate conception of the universe in its totality both in. its phenomenal and noumenal aspects. Thus sciences deal with "definite portion or cross sections of reality" (Paulsen) while Philosophy deals with the whole of the universe as an organic whole of interconnected members. Sciences lose sight of the whole and concentrate their attention upon different parts, while philosophy transcends the limits of sciences and views the universe as a whole, not as a mechanical aggregate of isolated and detached parts, but as an organic whole of inter-dependent reals.

Philosophy transcends sciences also in another way. Sciences are not thorough going. They assume the existence of certain fundamental realities—mind, matter, time, space, etc., and explain the phenomena within their own sphere of investigation in terms of these ultimate assumptions. But philosophy takes nothing for granted.

The task of philosophy is to submit the ultimate assumptions and presuppositions of sciences to a, critical examination andenquire into their validity. Thus philosophy is more penetrating than sciences.

Though philosophy is opposed to science in some respects, they are interdependent on each other in certain other respects. We cannot spin out the web of philosophy by sheer speculation; it must be built upon sciences which supply the data of philosophy. Hence philosophy without sciences is indequate. Sciences, too, are incomplete without philosophy. Sciences are isolated from one another, unless they are co-ordinated and unified by philosophy. Philosophy, therefore, is empty without science and science is blind without philosophy. They are complementary to and interdependent upon each other. "The sciences without philosophy are an aggregate without unity, a body without a soul; philosophy without the sciences, is a soul without a body, different in nothing from poetry and its dreams" (Weber: *History of Philosophy,* p. 2.)

"Philosophy is like science in seeking knowledge which is certain, exact, and well organised. But it is not satisfied with this; it seeks knowledge which is also *comprehensive.* The human mind is not content merely to determine the invariable sequences of phenomena and to formulate their manner of behaviour. It craves some ultimate explanation of things – their first cause, their moving cause, their purpose, their meaning, their value. It is this attempt to *interpret* the world, then, which is one of the tasks of philosophy; while science classifies, formulates, and describes. *The object of philosophy is to take ever the results of the various sciences, to add to them the results of the religious and ethical experiences of mankind, and then to reflect upon the whole. The hope is that, by this means, we may be able to reach some general conclusions as to the nature of the Universe and as to our position and prospects in it."* (Patrick: *Introduction to Philosophy,* pp. 21-22).

"Science really attempts no ultimate explanation of things; it only analyzes and classifies them, determines the conditions under which they occur, and formulates their modes of behaviour. The work of science is as follows:

I. The acquisition of facts
II. The description of facts
  1. Definition and general description
  2. Analysis
  3. Classification
III. Explanation of facts
  1. Ascertaining causes (invariable antecedents)
  2. Formulation of laws (uniformities of behaviour)."
  (*Ibid,* p. 21).

Philosophy is the conscious reflection upon the world as

a whole, particularly as to its meaning, purpose and value. It is the critical examination of the concepts of common sense and science. It is thus speculative and critical. It aims at a World-view. It aims at critical examination of common concepts and concepts of science.

Science takes a *quantitative* view of the world. It is today quantitative rather than qualitative. It ignores the qualities things and events and tries to reduce them to *quantitative formula* and *mathematical equations*. Science measures, weighs computes, and describes results in symbols.

Philosophy takes a *qualitative* view of the world. It is satisfied with quantitative formulae which are mere logical abstractions. It considers the *qualities* and unique features individual things and events and explains their meaning and value. Science considers *facts;* philosophy considers their *value.*

Philosophy aims at a world-view. It is the *integration of* knowledge. But it is not the mere synthesis of the sciences It is the *synthesis* and critical *interpretation* of sciences.

Philosophy investigates the nature of the supreme *ends or values, viz.,* Truth, Good, Beauty, and the Holy, and their relation to the Reality. Philosophy, as the science of values, is called axilogy. This is the most important branch of modern philosophy. It enquires into the nature of human values and their relation to the reality. This distinguishes philosophy from science. Science is not concerned with values. It deals only with facts. Philosophy deals with meaning, purpose and value, of facts. It also deals with the ultimate values, the instrinsic values, which satisfy the deep human aspirations.

Thus philosophy is not simply the, synthesis of sciences. "Philosophy is something far more than the unification of the special sciences; it must satisfy not only our scientific interests but our moral and religious needs, our longings and aspirations; these too are facts, which any system of thought must consider. If we could take *all* these facts and *think them together,* that would be philosophy." *(Ibid,* p. 12).

Philosophy must satisfy not only our intellectual demand for unity and harmony, but also our moral aspiration for the

Good, aesthetic aspiration for Beauty, and religious aspiration for communion with God. It aims at a conception of the Reality which is a completely coherent structure fulfilling the conditions of Truth, Good, Beauty, and the Holy.

**Methods of Science and Philosophy**

Science observes, experiments, measures, analyses, classifies, and explains particular facts by ascertaining their causes and formulating their laws or uniformities of behaviour or by framing hypotheses. Observation and experiment, classification and explanation, analysis and synthesis, induction and deduction are the methods of science. Some philosophers hold that the method of philosophy is *rational reflection* like that of science. They are called *intellectualists*. They insist that "philosophy, like the sciences, must depend upon *intelligence* for the solution of its problems and that, consequently, the method of philosophy is in principle identical with the method of science, the method of *reasoned observation and explanation*. According to the *intellectualist* group, the method of philosophy is purely a *rational* method of procedure and does not essentially differ from the method of science." (Cunningham: *Problems of Philosophy,* pp. 79-80). The *intuitionists,* on the other hand, hold that "the method of philosophy is, or should be, radically different from the reflective method of science. According to the intuitionists the solution of philosophical problems must be attained, not through the activity of intelligence, but through a unique sort of knowing activity which some exponents of the point of view name 'intuition'. From the standpoint of this group, philosophy is essentially *non-rational—not irrational*—in its method; it. is more closely akin to art than it is to science." (*Ibid,* p. 80).

The view of the intuitionists is unsound. First, intuitions vary with different individuals, depending upon different temperaments and even biases and prejudices. These variable intuitions cannot be the basis of philosophy which demands general acceptance. Secondly, intuitionism creates a gulf between science and philosophy. It makes the relation between them unintelligible. It cannot tell us of what possible value the results of scientific knowledge could be to the philosophical enterprise. Thirdly, the intuitionists prove their intuitions by discursive reflection and intellectual arguments which they discredit as abstract and conceptual and hence inadequate to the comprehension of reality. If the method of philosophy, 'intuition,' be wholly *non-intellectual,* it cannot be justified by intellectual arguments. (*Ibid,* pp. 80-81).

"To state the three objections summarily the intuitionist makes of philosophy a body of knowledge that is neither true nor false, because he gives us no standard by which validity can be tested; he makes necessary a sharp break between philosophy and the sciences, and so divides human knowledge into two parts separated by an impassable chasm; and he finds himself at the last forced to contradict himself by appealing to intelligence for justification of the results obtained by that non-intellectual 'intuition' which he holds to be the exclusive and' final source of philosophical knowledge." (*Ibid,* p. 18).

Cunningham observes, "The only method open to the philoso-pher is the method of *reasoned reflection*—the method of-*observing* facts and *interpreting* them through the use of *hypothesis*. For us philosophy offers no short-cut to truth: it attains its end, as does science, by the hard method of *reason,* by *analysis* and *synthesis.*" *(Ibid,* p. 81), "The method of philosophy is the prosaic method of *reasoned reflection*". *(Ibid,* p. 83).

Though the method of philosophy is like that of science *reasoned reflection,* they differ from each other. Metaphysics "is directly concerned with *ultimate reality,* whereas special sciences deal each with some one *particular aspect* of things, and avowedly leave all ultimate questions on one side. Metaphysics deals with the *ultimate problems* of existence in a purely *scientific spirit;* its object is *intellectual* satisfaction, and its method is not one of appeal to immediate intuition or unanalysed. feeling, but of the *critical and systematic analysis of our conceptions*. Thus it clearly belongs, in virtue of its spirit and method, to the realm of science. Yet it differs widely in method from the other types of science. It differs from the mathematical sciences in being *non-quantitative* and *non-*

*numerical* in its methods. It differs, again, from the experimental sciences in that it does nothing to increase the stock of our knowledge of *particular facts* or events, but merely discusses the way in which facts or events are to be *interpreted* if we wish to think consistently. Its question is not what in detail we must regard as the reality of any special set of processes, but what are the *general* conditions to which all reality, as such, conforms." *(Taylor: Elements of Metaphysics,* pp. 5-6).

**Philosophy** and **Metaphysics**

Philosophy is divided into Epistemology or Theory of Knowledge, Ontology or Metaphysics or Theory of Reality, and Axiology or Theory of Values. Thus Metaphysics is a part of philosophy. It is not identical with philosophy. But it is its most vital part. It enquires into the nature of reality, of God and the world of purpose, of causality, and of mind. But at present philosophy has become humanistic. It seeks to appraise rightly the various *values* which are offered to us in this rich and wonderful world. Philosophy offers us a key to the puzzle of the relative worth of things, science, art, poetry, social service, and religion, "In recent years this *humanistic* aspect of philosophy, this attempt to interpret life, to see things in the large, to gain the *right perspective,* has been emphasized much more than the old metaphysical problems, such as the nature of reality, of God and the world, of purpose, of causality of mind." *(Patrick).*

Ontology is the theory of being in general or the systematic knowledge of the absolute reality as contrasted with phenomena or appearances; and as the world is constituted by three factors—mind, matter and God or the Absolute—it asks what mind, matter and the Absolute are in themselves apart from, and independently of their appearances or manifestations, and what are the fundamental conditions of their existence and what kind and degree of reality they possess with reference to one another. Ontology deals, therefore, with the noumenal aspect or inner essences of things, while sciences deal with the phenomenal aspect or outward manifestations or appearances of things.

But as essences are meaningless abstractions apart from their manifestations being the correlative aspects of one and the same concrete reality, philosophy comprehends both science or phenomenology and metaphysics or ontology, to arrive at a rational explanation of the concrete reality as a whole. But though philosophy studies both the phenomenal manifestations and noumenal essences of things, it is mainly concerned with the latter, and studies the former *viz.* phenomena, only as a means to its end, as the phenomena give us a clue to their deep metaphysical implications. So ontology is the most vital part of philosophy, which is divided into three parts *viz.*, the ontology of nature, the ontology of the soul, and the ontology of the Absolute or Rational Theology.

**Psychology, Epistemology and Ontology or Meta-physics**

Psychology is the science of mind or consciousness. The business of psychology is to show how knowledge is, gradually developed in the individual mind. It analyses the states and processes of the full-grown mind into their simplest constituent elements and seeks to explain how the complex states of mind are evolved out of them. Psychology treats of our conscious life merely as a fact; it does not enquire into its validity. It is concerned with the development of knowledge, and not with the nature and validity of knowledge. Psychology assumes the possibility of knowledge and merely traces its growth and development in the human mind.

When psychology has shown how the individual mind acquires a knowledge of the objective world and of itself, the further question arises—How is knowledge possible ?—How is it possible for the subject to know the object ?' Psychology deals with the fact, epistemology with the possibility of the fact. Psychology assumes the existence of the mind and the world, and the possession of knowledge of the latter by the former as given facts.

But epistemology enquires into the conditions under which knowldge is possible. Epistemology means the "Science of Knowledge".. It is an enquiry into the nature, origin, range and conditions of knowledge. It seeks to answer the following questions:

(*i*) Is knowledge of reality possible at all or not ? If so –

(*ii*) What is the nature of knowledge ?

(*iii*) What is the origin and source of knowledge ?

(*iv*) What is the range, extent or limit of knowledge ? and

(*v*) What are the conditions of the validity of knowledge?

What, then, is the relation of epistemology to ontology or philosophy? Epistemology is the theory of knowing, while ontology is the theory of being or reality. Ontology must be preceded by epistemology as we cannot investigate the ultimate nature of the reality that is known, unless we already justify our claim to do so by a prior criticism of the organ of knowledge and prove that knowledge is possible. If we are constituted in such a way that we cannot know the reality – if knowledge is absolutely impossible, it is quite useless to investigate the nature of reality. Epistemology, thus, is the fundamental basis and groundwork of philosophy.

Formerly philosophers dogmatically assumed an ultimate reality or realities and sought to deduce everything of the universe from it or them, without a previous enquiry into the possibility of knowledge. But this is sheer dogmatism. But though epistemology is an indispensable preliminary to philosophy, as Locke pronounced for the first time, it must not be identified with philosophy, as Kant and Fichte did. As a matter of fact, epistemology and ontology are so intimately related to each other, that one cannot stand without the other. A particular theory of knowing leads to a particular theory of being, and a particular theory of being presupposes a particular theory of knowing. In order to ascertain whether knowledge reveals to us any reality we must know what knowledge itself is, and the nature of reality cannot be understood unless we know how it is related to knowledge. The question of the nature and validity of our knowledge and the question of the ultimate nature of what we know are in reality two sides of of the same enquiry – two aspects of the same study.

**Philosophy and Theology**

The Ontology of the Absolute or the philosophy of God is called Theology. Thus 'Theology (theos = God, logos = science or reasoned discourse) is a part of philosophy, which mainly enquires into the existence and nature of God, and His relation to a man and the world. This is called Natural Theology because it investigates the existence and nature of God from the very inner nature of the self and the outer nature of the external world. It is also called Rational Theology because it is based on the use and exercise of the faculty of reason and not on blind faith.

But the term 'Theology' is also used in the sense of Revealed Theology or theology as revealed by God to man through prophets and seers in different positive religions, *e. g.* Hindu Theology. Christian Theology and so on. Though Rational or Natural Theology has no essential relation to Revealed Theology, "still the former must take account of the latter. It must criticise the doctrines of different religions, by rational and philosophical reflection, to arrive at a true conception of the Absolute, by incorporating the truths of all religions into itself, and eliminating the elements of dogmatism. Thus Natural or Rational Theology, which is the highest branch of philosophy, is the truth and essence of all religions.

**Definitions of Philosophy**

Philosophy has three parts, *viz.,* Epistemology, Phenomenology and Ontology But unusual emphasis on the importance of any one of these three parts has led some philosophers to identify philosophy with ontology, some others to identify philosophy with epistemology, and others, again, to identify philosophy with science or phenomenology. But philosophy must not be identified with any of its parts; it is the sumtotal of all its three parts.

1. The following definitions identify philosophy with ontology, without recognizing the importance of science in philosophical investigations.

(i) "Philosophy aims at a knowledge of the eternal, of the essential nature of things." – Plato

(ii) "Philosophy is the science which investigates the nature of Being as it is in itself, and the attributes which belong to it in virtue of its own nature." – *Aristotle.*

2. The following definitions identify philosophy with epistemology, without admitting the possibility of ontology.

(i) "Philosophy is the science and criticism of cognition." – Kant

(ii) "Philosophy is the science of knowledge." – *Fichte.*

3. The following definitions identify philosophy with science. The tendency of contemporary philosophy is more towards phenomenology than towards ontology, as the time-worn distinction between phenomenon and noumenon is obliterated nowadays.

(i) "Philosophy is the science of sciences." – *Comte.*

(ii) "Philosophy is completely unifited knowledge – the generalisations of philosophy comprehending and consolidating the widest generalisations of science." – Herbert *Spencer.*

(iii) "Philosophy is the unification of all knowledge obtained by the special sciences in a consistent whole – Wundt.

(iv) Philosophy is the sumtotal of all scientific

**Philosophy and Religion**

Philosophy aims at a rational conception of the reality as a whole. It seeks to gain a true insight into the general structure of the universe and man's relations to it. It seeks to investigate the nature of matter, life, soul and God, and their inter-relations to one another. Religion consists in belief in a super-human power or powers which control and guide the destiny of man, the sentiments of awé, reverence, love and devotion, and the practical conduct which follows from them. "The great religions of the world express, in general, the efforts of the human spirit to grasp the nature of the universe, to understand man's true place in it, to realize the kind of conduct and the general attitude of thought and feeling that befits that place, and to find the most Suitable means for the cultivation of such modes of thought, feeling and action."

Thus, philosophy and religion have common objects. Both of them try to grasp the nature of the universe, and to understand man's piace, function and destiny in it. But there is a difference between the two. Religion is more or less a matter of feeling and practical experience. But philosophy is a matter of rational reflection. In religion we are absorbed in spiritual communion with the objects of devotion. In philosophy we break the harmony of spiritual enjoyment, and make them objects of critical reflection. Religion is a matter of simple faith and enjoyment. Philosophy is a matter of cold reflection and critical scrutiny. The knowledge that is summed up in creeds is often vague, ligurative, and imperfect, while the knowledge that is summed up in philosophy is clear, rational, and systematic. (Mackenzie: *Elements of Constructive Philosophy,* p. 16.)

"Whilst religion and philosophy have the same objects," observes John Caird, "the attitude of the human spirit towards these objects is, in each case, different. In the one they are present to it in an immediate way as objects of devotion or spiritual enjoyment; they come before it at most only in the form of outward fact or of figurative representation. In the other, they become the objects of reflection or intellectual apprehension, and are finally elevated to the form of pure or speculative thought in philosophy we pass out of the sphere of immediacy, in which the mind is still, in a sense, one with its object, in which subject and object are dissolved in an atmosphere of intuitive emotion. Abandoning the blessedness of simple faith, we enter into that colder yet loftier region in which reason opposes itself to its object, breaks up the natural harmony wherein no contradiction of thought has yet betrayed itself, and advances to the search after a deeper and indissoluble unity. Nor, in asserting this as its prerogative, does philosophy admit of any limits to the range of its activity. Its vocation is to trace the presence and the organic movement or process of reason in nature, in the human mind, in all social institutions, in the history of nations and in the progressive advancement of the world.

Its aim is to discover, not what seems, but what is, and why it is, to bind together objects and events in the links of necessary thought, and to find their last ground and reason in that which comprehends and transcends all—the nature of God Himself." *(Introduction to the Philosophy of Religion,* pp. 1-3.)

Thus philosophy is closely allied to religion, though it; differs from it in its attitude towards its objects.

**Philosophy and Poetry**

Poetry also, like philosophy, seeks to solve the mystery of the universe. Only their methods are different. Poetry depends on emotion and inspiration, while philosophy depends on intellectual. apprehension and critical reflection. Emotion is the organ of poetry. Reason is the organ of philosophy. The poet feels. The philosopher thinks. The poet sets a greater value on the warmth and fervour of the heart. The philosopher sets a greater value on the purity and loftiness of the intellect. The poet grasps the nature of the universe through the heart. The philosopher grasps the nature of the universe through the intellect.

The poet indulges in symbols and images. The philosopher rises above them to the region of pure, imageless thought. The poet gives a symbolic and figurative conception of the universe. The philosopher gives a direct and rational conception of the universe.

The poet seeks beauty in the universe. He seeks beauty in

nature, beauty in man and woman, beauty in the whole universe. He seeks beauty that appeals to the sense, and beauty that appeals to the inner spirit. To him Beauty is Truth, and Truth is Beauty.

The philosopher seeks to harmonize the Ideals of Truth, Good, and Beauty. He seeks to grasp the nature of the Reality as a whole, which is the eternal embodiment of the Ideals of Truth, Good, and Beauty.

Perry distinguishes between the philosopher-poets and the poet-philosophers. Some great poets seek merely to *describe* life; others seek to *interpret* it. The latter are the philosopher-poets. Milton, Dante, Goethe, Wordsworth, Browning, etc., are philosopher-poets. They were, moralists, thinkers, prophets, reflecting the national consciousness of their people. Dante is the supreme philosopher-poet. He tells us in the *Divine Comedy* of the shape and substance of the universe, of the origin of man and his destiny,. and of the origin of evil and its remedy. He tells us how from the heart of the universe there streams forth the divine love, whose purpose is the redemption of man from sin. Milton also tells us of the origin of sin and the redemption of man from sin by the love of God. Goethe speaks of the redemption of man through experience, not through sacrifice and obedience. Wordsworth gives us the message of love for Nature and the healing influence of Nature on man, and awakens us to the call of the spirit. Browning, "the soul dissector," consoles us with his belief in God and love. "The wonderful appeal of all these philosopher-poets reveals the eternal demand in the human heart for a solution of the riddle of the world". (Patrics: *Introduction to Philosophy,* p. 15).

There are philosophical tendencies in modern dramas. "The modern dramatist wrestles with the problems of life. Ibsen and Bernard Shaw seek to emancipate us from outgrown and soul-killing traditions. Their dramas reveal our longings to penetrate life's mysteries and to settle our doubts. The beauty of a drama is dulled when it is too heavily laden with thought. In Bernard Shaw the aesthetic attitude is reduced to its lowest limits and there is little left but a preachment.

Plato and Hegel, on the other hand, are poet-philosophers. ' They give us a true vision of the world and a key to its eternal riddle, which satisfies the intellectual, moral, aesthetic, and religious aspirations of the human heart. They give us a key to the meaning of life and its deep roots in the heart of reality.

Philosophy and poetry both seek to penetrate into the heart of the *ultimate reality.* But poetry appeals to immediate intuition and unanalyzed feeling, whereas philosophy relies on rational reflection and critical analysis.

**Epistemology and Logic**

Epistemology is the theory of knowledge. It enquires into the nature, origin, validity, and extent of knowledge. It is especially concerned with the conditions of the validity of knowledge. It cannot adequately enquire into the conditions of valid knowledge without enquiring, in a general way, into the structure of the reality which it comprehends and represents. So epistemology is closely connected with metaphysics.

Epistemology is the enquiry into the conditions of the validity of knowledge in general. It does not enquire into the nature of the process of inference, the different kinds of inference, and the conditions of their validity. Epistemology is a more general study than Logic. Taylor rightly observes. "The *Theory of Knowledge,* like Logic is primarily concerned with the question of the *conditions* upon which the *validity* of our *thinking,* as a *body of knowledge about reality,* depends. It differs from Logic in not enquiring into the *details of the various processes of proof* but confining its attention to the *most general and ultimate conditions* under which valid thinking is possible, and discussing, these *general principles* more thoroughly and systematically than common Logic usually does. Since the conditions under which truth is obtainable depend, in the last resort, on the character of the reality which knowledge apprehends, it is clear that the problems of the *Theory of Knowledge,* so far as they do not come under the scope of ordinary Logic (the theory of the estimation of evidence), are metaphysical in their nature. The study appears to consist of a mixture of Metaphysics and Logic, the metaphysical element predominating." (*Elements of Metaphysics,* p. 16). Epistemology enquires into the general conditions to which knowledge must conform in order to represent the structure of the reality adequately. Logic is a special enquiry into the *estimation* of *evidence.* It enquires into the various kinds of proof or evidence and the conditions of their validity. But it does not discuss the worth of the evidence for particular scientific theories, but the *general conditions* to which *evidence* must conform if it is to prove its conclusion. Thus Epistemology is a more general enquiry than Logic, its investigations being partly metaphysical and partly logical. Logic is a special: enquiry into the estimation of evidence without discussing the worth of the evidence for particular scientific theories. It investigates the general conditions of the validity of reasoning. Logic generally avoids metaphysical discussions. But it cannot successfully tackle the foundations of reasoning without some, metaphysical discussion.

## Metaphysics and Logic

Metaphysics deals with the reality. Epistemology deals with the general conditions of valid knowledge. Logic deals with the estimation of evidence. It investigates the various kinds of proof and their conditions.

Metaphysics and Logic resemble each other in the *universality* of their *scope* and the *analytical* character of their *methods.* But they differ from each other. "Logic is clearly in a sense a more general enquiry that Metaphysics. For in Logic we are concerned with the *universal conditions* under which thinking or, to speak more accurately, *inference,* is possible.

Now these conditions may be fulfilled by a combination of propositions which are materially false. The same relations which give rise to an inference materially true from true premises may yield a false inference where the premises are materially false. Valid reasoning thus does not always lead to true conclusions. Hence we may say that, whereas *Metaphysics* deals exclusively with the characteristics of *reality. Logic* deals with the characteristics of the *validity inferrible,* whether real or unreal. The distinction thus established, however; though real as far as it goes, is not necessarily absolute. For it may very well be that in the end the conditions upon which the possibility of inference depends are identical with or consequent upon the structure of reality." (*Ibid,* p. 15).

Hegel identified Logic with Metaphysics. Logic is the science of thought. Metaphysics is the science of reality. Hegel holds that thought and reality are ultimately identical. Whatever is real is rational. Whatever is rational is real. The dialectic of thought in the human mind corresponds with the dialectic movement of the Reality or the Absolute Mind. "Hegel held that the successive steps by which the human mind gradually passes from less adequate to more adequate, and ultimately to a fully adequate, conception of the nature of reality necessarily corres-pond, step by step, with the stages of a process by which the reality itself is manifested with ever-increasing adequacy in an ascending order of phenomena. Hence in his system the discussion of the general characteristics of reality and the general forms of inference constitutes a single department of Philosophy under the name of Logic." (*Ibid,* p. 15).

But this view is wrong. Ultimately thought may be identical with reality. But human thought, though coherent and systematic, may not correspond with reality. Internal harmony or coherence is not the only test of truth. So Logic should be regarded as a distinct science separate from Metaphysics. Logic deals with the characteristics of the validity inferable, whereas Metaphysics deals with the characteristics of reality. Logicians have found it impossible to enquire very deeply into the foundations and first principles of inference without being led to face fundamental issues of Metaphysics. Still the details of the theory of evidence are best studied as an independent branch of knowledge. Logic is independent of Metaphysics. Many metaphysical questions have no bearing on Logic. Metaphysics indirectly depends on Logic because its methods must be logical. But it does not consciously borrow its methods from Logic. Metaphysics must depend upon reflection, and metaphysical reflection must be systematic and logical.

## UNIVERSITY QUESTIONS

1. There was a time when men drew no distinction between different kinds of knowledge. How did they come to discriminate philosophy and science from the knowledge of the common man and why did they discriminate science from philosophy ? (1909).

   [See 3, 4 and 5, and fully explain the relation of science to common experience, and of science to philosophy.]

2. What do you undersand by the analysis of experience ?

   Show how the classification of the sciences is based upon such an analysis. (1911).

   [By the analysis of experience we mean the separation of the contents of our knowledge or the facts of our experience. If we analyse our experience, we find two sets of phenomena opposed to each other, *viz.*, the phenomena of nature and the phenomena of mind; the phenomena of nature, again, fall into two distinct, well-marked groups, *viz*, the phenomena of matter or physical phenomena and the phenomena of life or biological phenomena. These three distinct groups of phenomena are taken up by three distinct groups of sciences, *e. g.* the physical sciences, the biological sciences and the mental sciences. Chemistry, physics, mathematics, etc., belong to the first group; biology, botany, zoology, physiology, etc., belong to the second group; psychology, logic, ethics, aesthetics, etc., belong to the third group.]

3. Elucidate the meaning of the following: "Science is interpretation of the world within and without us; Philosophy is an interpretation of that interpretation". (1912).
4. Discuss the scope and standpoint of philosophy. (1915). 5. Explain the meaning of Epistemology, and the relation between Epistemology and Philosophy in general, showing why Epistemology is necessary. (1916).
6. Explain fully the relation of philosophy to the sciences. (1917).
7. State clearly the meaning, province and use of Philosophy and the relation of Philosophy to Natural Science and Theology. (1918).
8. What is the need of the discipline of Metaphysics ? In what sense is philosophy the study of experience as a whole ? (19x9).
9. How does the demand for knowledge lead to the use of standpoints of both Natural Science and Metaphysics ? (1919).
10. What do you understand by Philosophy ? How is it related to Science and Epistemology ? (1920).
11. Explain she distinction between Philosophy and Science. (1909 Hon.) [See 6.]
12. Distinguish as clearly as you can between the scope off Philosophy and that of Science. (1910 Hon.)
13. The philosopher treats of the *real,* the scientist treats of *appearances*. Examine this statement. (1912 Hon.)
14. Explain the relation of Metaphysics to Ethics and Religion. (1912 Hon.)
15. Should Philosophy be based upon Experience ? (1913 Hon.)
16. Is Philosophy, in any sense, 'comprehensive of all particular sciences' ? If so, in what sense, precisely ? If not, how is it related to them ? (1913 Hon.)

17. "The essential characteristic of philosophy, which' makes it a study distinct from science, is criticism.' Explain and examine. (1914 Hon.)
18. Distinguish between Epistemology and Ontology.

    Consider how far the investigation of any of the ultimate epistemological problems may be independent of Ontology and vice versa. (1914 Hon.)
19. The subject-matter of Science and Philosophy is the same, but their standpoints are different. Explain and examine. (1915 Hon.)
20. Exhibit fully the relation between Philosophy, Psychology, and Natural Science, defining and stating the sphere of each and indicating different views. (1918 Hon.),
21. What is Metaphysics ? In what sense is it akin to poetry and religion ? (1921).
22. What is Philosophy ? What is Science ? Explain the scope or province of each. (1921).
23. Define Philosophy, and explain its province and purpose and exhibit the chief points of difference between Philosophy and Science. (1922).
24. Explain the meaning and use of Epistemology, and show how it is related to Philosophy in general. (1923).
25. Explain the difference, if any, between the poetic, the scientific, and the philosophic attitude. (1924).
26. Explain the meaning of Epistemology and Ontology (Metaphysics), and show how they are related to each other as departments of Philosophy. (1926).
27. What do you learn from experience ? Philosophy is described as 'the analysis and rationalization of experience'. Explain the meaning of this, giving illustrations. (1927).
28. What do you understand by Philosophy ? How is it related to science and religion ? (1938).

29. What is Epistemology ? How is it related to Philosophy ? (1929).
30. 'Philosophy is the analysis, interpretation, and criticism of experience'. Explain and illustrate this, and show how far it represents the true method of Philosophy. (1929).
31. What do you understand by Philosophy ? How is it related to Ontology ? (1930).
32. Define clearly the meaning and scope of Philosophy, Metaphysics, Epistemology, and Ontology. (1939).
33. What is Philosophy ? How is it related to Science? In what sense can we define Philosophy as the 'science of sciences'? (1933).
34. 'Philosophy is simply the sum-total of all scientific knowledge'. Explain this definition. Is not Philosophy fundamentally distinct from the Positive Sciences ? (1934).
35. Explain the relation between Epistemology and Philosophy. What precisely is meant by saying that Philosophy is the criticism of experience ? (1935).
36. Explain the aim and function of Philosophy. (1936).
37. Explain clearly the position of Epistemology in relation to Philosophy and Metaphysics. (1936).
38. Philosophy is sometimes defined as criticism of experience. Explain fully. (1945). (See 2.)
39. Discuss the relation of Philosophy to Logic and Epistemology. (1945). (See 9 & 15).
40. Define the scope of Philosophy and distinguish it from that of Epistemology and Logic. (1946). (See 9 & 15).
41. What is the relation of Epistemology to Philosophy ? (1947).

## CHAPTER II

# METHODS OF PHILOSOPHY

### Different Theories

By the method of philosophy we mean the way of investigating the subject-matter of philosophy. It is the procedure of dealing with its data. Different philosophers have adopted different methods which have given rise to different types of philosophy.

### Dogmatism

"Dogmatism is the positive procedure of reason without previous criticism of its own faculty, *i.* e., it is a system which is produced in the direct effort to understand and interpret the world—the effort of a mind which is as yet troubled by no scruples as to its own competence, or as to the efficiency of the methods and principles it uses." *(Edward Caird)*. It plunges headlong into philosophical. investigations, without. first enquiring into the nature, origin, limits and conditions of knowledge. It does not raise the question whether our mind is capable of knowing the reality at all or not, and if it can, to what extent it can know the reality. Dogmatism consists in dogmatically assuming certain fundamental principles as self-evident and axiomatic truths, and deducing conclusions from these unproved premises, without establishing their truth and validity and without proving the very possibility of knowing them by a prior criticism of knowledge.

Dogmatism may take two forms, rationalism and empiricism.

Rationalism dogmatically assumes that sense-experience gives us uncertain and illusory knowledge, whereas we can know the, reality by reason and intuition and spin out a system of philosophy by sheer speculation. Thus Descartes dogmatically assumed matter and mind as two independent substances and God as the absolute substance and deduced everything from these ultimate conceptions. Spinoza dogmatically assumed God as the only substance, and deduced matter and mind extension and motion intellect and will, indeed everything of the universe from this one substance as conclusions from premises. Leibnitz, too, dogmatically assumed an infinite number monads or spiritual atoms governed, by God, the Monad of monads, and deduced 'everything from these ultimate principles. These philosophers believed in the undisputed supremacy of reason over experience, reason having the power of intuiting the first principles.

As rationalism was one-sided dogmatism, regarding the testimony of reason as unquestionable and discrediting the verdict of experience, so empiricism went to the other extreme and dogmatically assumed that the mind is a *tabula rasa* in the beginning, having no innate ideas, and all knowledge comes from experience. This is another kind of dogmatism adopted by Locke, who dogmatically assumed that we can know the reality through experience without proving the possibility and validity of knowledge through experience.

**Failure of Dogmatism**

"The direct dogmatic or uncritical use of the understanding is sure at some point to find itself checked and thwarted by the nature of things. For the simple principles which first present themselves for the explanation of the world, are necessarily imperfect and. one-sided. If they explain phenomena, it is only within a limited range, and when they are extended beyond that range they come into contradiction with facts and even with themselves." *(Edward Caird)*. For instance, the principle of matter can explain all "material phenomena, but it fails to explain the phenomena of life and mind. Thus dogmatism, which uncritically assumes an inadequate principle, and tries to explain the whole universe by it, is bound to fail.

**Scepticism**

Different dogmatic systems of philosophy give different explanations of the universe, which contradict one another. The conflict of opposite dogmas produces a sense of hopelessness, and even, it may be, a conviction that 'whatever can be asserted may with equal reason be denied.' Thus the failure of dogmatism gives rise to scepticism which denies the possibility and certainty of knowledge.

Scepticism may be of a deeper or of a shallower nature. The former we find in Sophism in ancient Greece and the latter we find in the Scepticism of Hume, Mill and others.

The conflict of contradictory opinions on the same subject gave birth to Sophism which enunciated the maxim that "man is the measure of all things."

Modern Scepticism of Hume, Mill and others is the logical outcome of the empiricism of Locke. If knowledge comes from experience, *i. e,,* sensations, it must be confined only to sensations and ideas, and never step beyond them to the realities beyond sensations. Thus sensationism ends in scepticism. [See below Ch. II.]

**Failure of Scepticism**

Dogmatism dogmatically asserts the possibility of knowledge. Scepticism dogmatically denies the possibility of knowledge. Dogmatism sets no bounds to human knowledge, while scepticism sets no limits to human ignorance. But the human mind cannot rest content with such a purely negative way of thinking.

As a matter of fact, a purely negative way of thinking is an impossibility. If I say that all that I know is appearance and that I do not and cannot know the reality beyond the appearance, I must have, at least some knowledge of the reality which enables me to distinguish between appearance and reality. Thus absolute scepticism destroys itself.

### Criticism

The controversy between dogmatism and scepticism presupposes a common principle, but for which the controversy is impossible. Criticism penetrates to this common principle and places both dogmatism and, scepticism in their true places. The critical method incorporates into itself the truths of dogmatism and scepticism and yet is different from both. "It is dogmatic in so far as it recognizes the partial truth of each of the dogmatic theories; sceptical, in so far as it limits each to a part, and dogmatic again, in so far as it discovers the unity which is manifested in their difference and relative opposition." *(Edward Caird).*

Kant introduced the critical method and without dogmatically asserting or denying the certainty of knowledge, enquired into the nature, origin, conditions and limits of knowledge and reconciled the opposite views of dogmatism and scepticism, and held that neither reason is the solo source of knowledge, as, dogmatic rationalism supposed nor sensation, as scepticism and dogmatic empiricism supposed, but both sense and reason are the sources of knowledge, the former giving the matter of knowledge, and the latter, the forms of knowledge.

### Dialectic

The term 'dialectic' literally means arguing for and against, pros and eons in the manner of a dialogue. The dialectic method takes two forms, negative or destructive dialectic and positive or constructive dialectic.

The negative or destructive dialectic is a method of refutation, which was first adopted by Socrates to refute the sophists and hence called the Socratic method. It consists in arguiag pros and cons and exposing the inconsistencies and contradictions involved in an opinion and thus detroying it.

This form of dialectic was revived by Kant in his Transcendental Dialectic of the Critique of Pure Season to expose the contradictions involved in the metaphysical conceptions of the world, soul and God.

The positive or constructive dialectic adopted by Hegel, consists in the two-fold process of contradiction and reconciliation. Being itself contains opposition and contradiction within its own nature: and the force which evolves the world tries to overcome "these oppositions and reconcile these contradictions in its all-embracing unity. "Thus every finite thing, in asserting its own existence, within the whole (its thesis or affirmation of itself), tends thereby to call into existence a contrary or opposite of itself (an antithesis, as it were); and the evolving power of the whole tends to reconcile the opposition by making the opposites co-operate as factors in a higher unity. (synthesis)

Thus synthesis again is itself a thesis calling forth by contrast another antithesis, and thereby a new effort of unification in a higher synthesis and so on. This dialectic process of homogeneity, differentiation, unification; affirmation, negation, reconciliation; thesis, antithesis, synthesis—must be supposed to go on until an absolute unity is reached which will contain all possible differences reconciled within itself." *(Stephen)*.

Human thought, too, is dialectic, since thought and reality at bottom are identical, thought being essentially a reproduction of reality. The word is the dialectic development of the Absolute Idea (God); the human mind is a finite reproduction of the Absolute. Hence the dialectic development of concepts in the human mind is only the subjective repetition of the objective process of dialectic movement of the Absolute Idea in the world or reality itself. The progressive movement of thought through thesis, antithesis and synthesis corresponds to the dialectic development of the world through thesis, antithesis and synthesis. Thus we can understand a thing, *e. g.* A, by contrasting it with its opposite not-A; but we cannot think A and not. A as permanently opposed to each other; the opposition between A and not-A must be reconciled in a higher unity, *viz.* B, which comprehends both A and not-A, within itself. B, again, cannot be understood except in relation to and contrast with not-B, both of which are reconciled in a higher synthesis, *viz.* G. Thus we may go on until we reach an absolute synthesis which reconciles all antinomies and contradictions within itself in its all-embracing comprehensive unity.

**The True Philosopic Method**

Dogmatism and scepticism are both one-sided dogmatisms. Hence neither of them can be the true method of philosophy. Kant's critical method is an improvement upon dogmatism and scepticism but it cannot be taken as the true philosophical method as it is another form of scepticism, denying the knowledge of the thing-in-itself and hence the possibility of metaphysics. Hegel's dialectic method is better than the critical method of Kant, as it removes the opposition between thought and reality, which are at bottom identical, according to him. But the dialectic method is insufficient, as the world in its infinite richness of variety and individual physiognomy, cannot be explained as the dialectic movement of the Absolute Idea through a number of "bloodless' categories or universal notions.

Both the universal and the particular aspects of the world must be taken into account by philosophy. Hence the true philosophic method must not only be reflective or speculative, but also empirical and inductive. The subject-matter of science and philosophy is the same. But the methods are partly different. The method of science is mainly induction based on observation and experiment, but the method of philosophy is inductive and speculative. Philosophy does not directly observe and experiment upon things, like science, but starts with the highest generalisations of special, sciences, as its data, and seeks to harmonize and co-ordinate them, to arrive at a conception of the universe as whole. Philosophy goes higher and higher from the highest conclusions of sciences, by the inductive process of abstraction and generalisation, until it reaches the highest conception of the absolute reality, and then comes down lower and lower, by the deductive process of concretion and specialisation, to re-interpret the facts of our experience in the light of this highest conception. This twofold process of induction and deduction, the upward movement of abstraction and the downward movement of concretion, may be called the empirico-deductive method, which is the true method of philosophy.

**Intuition**

In recent times, the famous French philosopher, Henri Bergson expounds a different view. He makes intuition – not intellect – the organ of philosophy. Intellect gives us a distorted view of the reality. In intuition we feel at one with the reality. In intellectual apprehension we hover about the reality. In intuition we feel the very life-pulse of the reality. The reality is dynamic; it is in perpetual flow and flux; it is all change and becoming. But intellect gives us a static view of it; it makes it fixed and permanent, devoid of life and change.

There is some amount of truth in it. A intellect has got its limitations. It has its own forms and categories. We must rise above them to have an immediate intuition of the reality, We must live the very life of the reality. But the verdict of intuition must be rational. It must not be irrational. If we give ourselves up to uncritical intuition, we may be landed in a dreamland of fancy. Philosohy is not a matter of individual whim or fancy. Its truths demand general acceptance. But they can never meet with universal acceptance, if they are based upon uncritical intuition. Truth is universal. So it must be rational. Even the intuitionist himself justifies the results of his intuition by appealing to rational arguments. So, he cannot rule out reason altogether as an utterly untrustworthy organ of philosophy.

**Intellect**

Bergson holds that intellect falsifies reality. Eeality is incessant change. It is perpetual flow and flux. Intellect breaks it up into isolated parts which are said to be permanent. It cannot grasp the *elan vital* or the surge of life which is the ultimate reality. Intuition is participation in the vital surge. Intuition gives us the true knowledge of reality. Intellectual knowledge is false on the following grounds:

(1) Intellectual knowledge is conceptual knowledge. It is aided by concepts. Concepts are *abstract* and *partial.* They represent only the *common* features of particular things. They do not represent their particular qualities and aspects. Concepts do not yield complete knowledge of individual objects. Intuition gives complete knowledge of them.

(2) Intellectual knowledge is *static.* Things are constantly changing and growing. But concepts"are static and unchanging. They cannot represent the essential element of change and development in things. They picture them as dead and static. Thus conceptual knowledge falsifies reality.

(3) Intellectual knowledge is analytical. The intellect breaks the reality into isolated fragments, and cannot combine them into the *organic whole,* comprehending all its particular features. The intellect can dismember the whole, but cannot restore it from the parts. It breaks, but cannot build. It gives us a fragmentary and analytical view of the reality. It cannot grasp the reality as a synthetic whole.

(4) Intellectual knowledge is *relative.* It gives us similarities and dissimilarities between objects. It gives us knowledge of objects as related to one another. It does not give us knowledge of things as they are in themselves. Intellectual knowledge *is* relative in another sense. It is determined by our selective interest and purpose. It gives us knowledge of an object from a particular point of view. Intellect is a means to action. It is subordinate to the will. The will is guided by a particular end or purpose. Therefore intellectual knowledge is vitiated by subjective interest or purpose. Intuitive knowledge *is* free from these defects. It grasps the reality as it is in itself apart from the individual's subjective interest, and relations of its parts to one another.

(5) Intellectual knowledge gives an *external* view of things. It does not show the inner nature of the reality. It gives us knowledge of things from the outside and tells us nothing of their inner nature. But intuition gives us knowledge of the inner nature of the reality. (Hocking: *Types of Philosophy).*

**Intuition**

Bergson holds that intuition is *'participation'* in the *elan vital* which is the reality. It is through instinct that we feel ourselves to be one with reality; it is through instinct that we appear to ourselves to enter into the flow of life and to live it. Bergson gives the name *'intuition'* to instinct in this relationship. "Instinct", says Bergson, is sympathy. If this sympathy could extend its object and alsoreflect upon itself, it would give us the key to vital operations." Now intuition is instinct conscious of itself; it is instinct that has become disinterested, self-conscious, capable of reflecting upon its object and of enlarging it indefinitely. Intuition grasps the reality as a whole. It is by intuition that we enter into and appreciate the meaning of the reality as an indivisible whole. It is through instinctive sympathy or intuition that we are able to enter into the ceaseless flow of the reality which is our life and to grasp its nature.

I Intuitive knowledge is concrete and whole, not partial and abstract. It is dynamic, not static and dead. It is synthetic, not analytic. It is absolute, not relative. It gives an internal view of the reality, not an external view of it.

**Intellect and Intuition both necessary**

Bergson takes a wrong view of intellectual knowledge. He discredits intellect and extols intuition too much. He justifies the claim of intuition by appealing to rational arguments. Thus he appeals to intellect to justify the claim of intuition. Philosophy is bound to rest on intellectual knowledge. Its method is rational reflection and critical analysis. It cannot give a reasoned view of the reality based on intuition. In fact, intellect and intuition both are necessary. Intuition gives a world-view in a flash; and this is justified by intellectual considerations. Intellect follows the lead of intuition. Intuition oversteps the bounds of intellect. But intuition can never supplant intellect. The reality must be intelligible. It must be capable of being understood by the intellect. It must admit of analysis and synthesis. The defects of intellectual knowledge are not inherent in the nature of intellect. They can be removed by intellect itself.

## UNIVERSITY QUESTIONS

1. Show how in the development of philosophic thought there is a natural transition from Dogmatism to Scepticism and from Scepticism to Criticism. (1910).
2. Explain the difference between the Dogmatic and Critical methods in Philosophy. Name and give some account of any leading dogmatic and any leading critical thinker explaining clearly in what their dogmatism or criticism lies. (1913).
3. Explain fully the meanings of Dogmatism and Scepticism in Philosophy, and also the meaning of Criticism and its bearing on the two methods. (1918).
4. Estimate the relative merits of Dogmatism, Empiricism and Scepticism as methods of philosophizing. (1920).
5. Fully explain what you understand by Criticism as a method of philosophy, and also as a doctrine of the origin of knowledge. (1911 Hon.)
6. Dogmatism and Criticism: Explain precisely the nature of these two methods, and give examples of these methods from, the History of Philosophy. (1916).
7. Explain fully the meaning of Dialectic, and exhibit clearly the different applications that have been made of Dialectic in Philosophy, and the results arrived at by this method. (1918 Hon.).
8. What is the place of Dogmatism, Scepticism, and Criticism in the development of the problem of knowledge ? (1921).
9. What are Dogmatism and Scepticism in Philosophy ? What

objection is there to each, and what do you consider to be the best way of avoiding them ? (1921).

10. What is meant by Method in Philosophy ? Explain the meanings of Dogmatism and Scepticism in Philosophy, and show to what consequences each of them leads. (1923).
11. Explain the meaning of Dogmatism, Scepticism and Criticism, and show their relation to each other as methods of Philosophy. (1926).
12. What do you understand by the Critical method in philosophy ? How is it related to that of Dogmatism ? (1928).
13. What is meant by a method of Philosophy ? What are the methods of Dogmatism and Scepticism, and what is their use in Philosophy ? (1930).
14. State fully the implications of the Dialectic Method and show the use made of it in the analysis of philosophical knowledge. (1932).
15. Explain clearly the meaning of the terms 'Dogmatism' and 'Criticism' as methods of philosophical thought. (1934).
16. What is meant by Criticism as a method of Philosophy ? How is it related to Scepticism ? (1935).
17. Discuss how far the Critical method in philosophy removes the defects of Dogmatism.

## CHAPTER III

# JUDGMENT AND INFERENCE

### The Nature of Thinking

Logic is the science of thinking. Thinking furnishes the mind with truth or knowledge. It is the conscious process by which knowledge is built up. It is a process rather than a dead thing. It does not resemble mechanical processes such as attraction and repulsion. It is a living process subject to growth and evolution. Thinking is a conscious function, or mode of acting which develops according to the general laws of organic evolution. The process of thinking undergoes development in the individual and in the race. There is no fundamental difference in kind between the various processes of thinking. Judgment, conception and inference appear as stages in the one intellectual process in course of its evolution.

### The Law of Evolution applied to Thinking

Differentiation, integration and determination are the laws of evolution. We have discussed them in connection with Herbert Spencer's theory of evolution. Evolution is unfoldment. It is transition from the homogeneous to the heterogeneous. The organism is at first a mass of simple homogeneous protoplasm. Then it becomes heterogeneous, and is composed of parts such as bones, muscles, tendons, etc. There is a gradual differentiation of structure and function. Different organs are evolved with different function. Thus the process of evolution involves differentiation both of *structure* and of *function,* in passing from the homogeneous to the heterogeneous" (Creighton & Smart: *An Introductory Logic,* p. 369). But differentiation, or increase in diversity, is only one aspect of evolution. Integration is its other aspect. As we pass from a lower to a higher stage, the various parts of an organism become more interdependent on one another, Integration or unification goes along with differentiation. The parts become essential to the whole and to one another, and together form a *real or organic whole,* as distinguished from a mere aggregate. Evolution involves differentiation of structure and function as well as integration or unification whereby the parts are brought into closer and more intimate relation to one another. Evolution is transition from the indefinite and incoherent to the definite and and coherent.

In is not difficult to apply this general law of evolution to the thinking process. Thinking, in its first stage, both in the individual and in the race, is simple and undifferentiated. The earliest and simplest thinking tends to take things in a lump, without making any distinctions. The infant does not distinguish one person from another at first. Gradually he differentiates them from one another by comparing them with one another, analysing them into their qualities, and finding out their similarities and differences. "Now it is clear that intellectual development, growth in knowledge, must in the first place involve *differentiation.* What is complex must be analysed or separated into its various parts. Things which are different must be distinguished and clearly marked off from one another. The development of thought implies, then, as one of its moments, discrimination or analysis – what we previously called differentiation." *(Ibid,* p. 371).

Integration also finds a place in the development of thought, and goes hand in hand with differentiation. The child and the uneducated person fail to distinguish different things or parts of a thing from one another, and also fail to interconnect different parts of their knowledge with one another and form a well-organised system of knowledge. Integration, unification or systematization is an important characteristic of, evolution of the process of thinking. Completely unified knowledge is the goal of intellectual development.

The more complete and difficult kinds of thinking have

evolved from simpler types of thinking, and not from something: different in kind. Hence what is true of simple types of thought is essential to the thinking process as such. So we should start with the simplest type of thinking.

**Judgment as the simplest type of Thinking**

Judgment is the simplest kind of thinking. It is the starting point of thinking. It is essentially an activity of the mind. Thinking involves intellectual work. It involves interpretation of sensations, putting together of ideas, and reaching a conclusion. "Thinking is simply the way in which the mind puts two and two together and sees what the result is. It implies that the mind has waked up to the significance of things and has interpreted them for itself." *(Ibid,* p. 373). Judgment, in its simplest; form, is perceptual; it involves interpretation of meanings of sensations, *e. g.,* 'grass is green'. The term 'judgment' is used for both the act itself and its result. It is the mental process of putting two or more ideas together as well as its result. Proposition is the verbal expression of judgments

**Judgment and Concept**

Judgment is the elementary process of thought. It is the starting-point of all knowledge. It is expressed in a proposition. A proposition consists of three parts, *e. g.,* the subject, the predicate, and the copula. In the proposition 'grass is green,' 'grass' is the subject green' is the predicate, and 'is' is the copula. A judgment, therefore, is defined as the act of joining together two ooncepts or ideas. The judgment given above presupposes the existence of the concepts of 'grass' and 'green'. Therefore it is held by some that concepts are formed before judgments are made.

This view is wrong. The process of forming concepts is essentially a process of judgment. The concept of 'grass' is formed by a series of perceptual judgments. The concept of 'green' also is formed by a series of perceptual judgments. Conception does not involve a kind of intellectual activity different from that involved in judgment. Conception or the process of forming concepts also involves judgments. "The new judgment is a further expansion or development of a previous set of judgments represented by the concept. The concept, then, stands for the series of judgments already made. The concept has no meaning apart from the series of judgments it represents. And as thinking goes on, and new judgments are made, its nature is constantly changing. In short, concepts are not dead *things* but living *thoughts* in constant process of development." *(Ibid,* pp. 377-78). Conception is not prior to judgment. In making new judgments we have to start with judgments already made. Concepts already formed are the results of a series of judgments. These are the data of new judgments. "The progress of knowledge is not from the unknown to the known, but from a state of partial and incomplete knowledge to one of greater perfection. Thus the judgment 'gold is malleable' adds to, or develops further, our existing knowledge of gold, as represented by a series of judgments previously made regarding it." *(Ibid,* p. 379).

Judgment is the first act of thinking. We cannot get behind judgment. It is the simplest form of thinking. It cannot be reduced to a simpler process of thought. "Consciousness must be regarded as having from the first the form of a judgment." *(Ibid,* p. 379). It of the form of some reaction, however weak, upon the content, resulting in knowledge. Even the newly-born infant reacts, or judges vaguely, in this way. But the primitive judgments are vague and confused, while later judgments are more coherent and complete. "Growth in knowledge is simply the process by means of which these vague and inarticulate judgments are developed and transformed into a more-complete and coherent experience." *(Ibid,* p. 380).

**The Main Characteristics of Judgment**

In the first place, all judgments are *universal* in the sense that the conclusion they reach is true for every one. Whatever the subject and the predicate may be, a judgment *e. g.,* 'grass is green' is true for all minds. "It is by Judging, or putting things together for itself, that the human mind gains knowledge. Knowledge is not something merely individual in character. When I judge that 'two and two are four,' or that 'iron has magnetic properties', the judgment is not merely a statement of what is going on in my individual consciousness; but it claims to express something true for other persons as well as for me. It professes to deal with facts that are true, and in a sense independent of any individual mind. The judgments by which such conclusions-are reached are universal, then, in the sense that they are-asserted as true for every one and at all times." *(Ibid,* p. 382). All judgments are also objective in the same sense. They are not merely subjective processes of the individual minds, but true for them alone. They are true for all minds and hence objective. The only alternative to this position is pure individualism and scepticism.

In the second place, all judgments are *necessary.* "By this- we mean that when a person judges, he is not free to reach this or that conclusion at will. As an intellectual being, he feels bound to judge in a certain way." *(Ibid,* p. 383). Judgments are necessary, because certain reasons necessarily lead to certain conclusions. There is no choice in the matter. "No judgment can claim to be necessary in its own right. Its necessity comes from its connection with other facts known to be true. Or in logical terms, we may say that it comes from reasons or premises supporting it." *(Ibid,* p. 384). Therefore judgment necessarily develops into inference. It supports its conclusion by reasons. Thus "necessity is not a property belonging to any judgment in-itself, but something arising through its dependence upon other judgments. In other words, *necessity* is always *mediate,* not immediate." (*Ibid,* pp. 985-86). In explaining facts we refer to other facts or principles. And, at last, we assume certain *fundamental first principles* or *necessary truths*.

In the third place, judgment involves *analysis* and *synthesis*. Judgment proceeds by analysis of things into parts and synthesis of parts into wholes. Analysis and synthesis go together. New qualities and relations are discovered in things known, and integrated into the system of knowledge. Analysis or discrimination is always present in judgment. It also goes along with synthesis or union. "Every judgment affirms the *unity* of the different parts or aspects of a thing; and this is of course synthesis." *(Ibid,* pp. 388-89). Judgment is a process of synthesis and analysis both. There is no incompatibility between analysis and synthesis. We may analyse a watch into its parts, *e. g.*, springs, wheels, hands, etc., in order to understand it. But we cannot understand the watch until we see how one part fits into another, and all combine together into one whole. Analysis and synthesis go together here. They do not take place in succession. The detection of the various parts and the perception of their connection go hand in hand. In order to understand the watch, we take it to pieces and put them together at the same time. But the two moments of analysis and synthesis are not always equally prominent. Sometimes one and sometimes the othe prominent. Analysis is prominent in the judgment water is composed of hydrogen and oxygen'; synthesis is prominent in the judgment 'springs, wheels, and hands, etc., make up a watch.' Thus analytic and synthetic judgments are not different in kind, as they are supposed to be by some logicians. "Judgment is a single act of intelligence which at once discriminates and brings into relation different aspects of the whole with which it is dealing." (*Ibid,* p. 391). "In a judgment, a subject is only a subject *through* its relation to a predicate. The proposition may be divided inbo parts but the judgment is a single thought-activity, and cannot be divided." (*Ibid,* p. 391).

Lastly, judgment constructs a *system of knowledge*. "Judgment works both analytically and synthetically: it discovers new parts and distinctions and at the same time brings the parts into relation and thus builds up a whole." *(Ibid,* p. 391). Analysis is differentiation. Synthesis is integration. "Each judgment is a step in the process of building up a *system* of knowledge. A system is a whole composed of various parts. But it is not an aggregate. In an aggregate no essential relation exists between the units of which it is composed. In a heap of grain, one may take away any part without the other parts being at all affected thereby. But in a system each part has a fixed and necessary relation to the whole and to all the other parts." *(Ibid,* p. 392).

Judgments constructs a *system* of knowledge. It is not merely a process of adding one fact to another. "Judgment combines the new facts with which it deals, with what is already known, in such a way as to give to each its own proper place in relation to and interdependence with the others. Different facts are not only brought together, but they are arranged, related, systematized. No fact is allowed to stand by itself but has to take its place as a member of a larger system of facts and receive its value and meaning from this connection. Of course, a single judgment is not sufficient to bring a large number of facts into relation in this way. But each judgment contributes something to this end and brings some new fact into relation to what is already known." (*Ibid,* p. 393).

"Judgment is the process by which knowledge grows into a system. It is by judging that we attempt to bring the various parts of our experience into relation with one another." "Truth is one and indivisible. It must be possible ultimately to harmonize all facts in one all-embracing system of judgments." (*Ibid,* p. 395).

**Types of Judgments**

There are judgments of quality, judgments of quantity, judgments of causality, and judgments of purpose. The judgments of quality are the first efforts of intelligence. The young child takes notice of the simple *qualities* of things. He cannot discriminate the various parts and relations of the objects perceived, but takes notice of the most obvious qualities of things. An adult notices not only the qualities of things but also their quantities. He forms judgments such as 'rose has fragrance,' 'this rose is more fragrant than that,' etc. He comprehends *degree* or *intensity* which the same quality manifests in different instances. Quantitative judgments belong to a higher stage of intellectual development than qualitative judgments. Then judgments of *causal connection* appear in the field. They seek to show how the various changes which go on in things are causally connected with other things or events. They discover causal connections among things and events. They lead us beyond particular objects to a knowledge of the ways in which they are connected with other objects. They seek to discover connections and relations among facts of experience.

Therefore they belong to a higher stage of intellectual development than judgments of quality and quantity. Causal judgments, however vague and unsatisfactory, are higher than judgments of quality and quantity. The law of causality expresses the fact that things are related as causes and effects. "Judgment is a process of constructing a *system,* of showing how the various parts of knowledge fit into one another, and are mutually dependent upon one another. The tendency of thought to connect things *causally,* then, is simply one of the fundamental forms in which its tendency towards a system expresses itself. In employing the causal category judgment has become more explicit and conscious of itself than it was in quality and quantity." (*Ibid,* pp. 419-20). Later appear judgments of *purpose or teleology.* They are also called judgments of *individuality.* They seek to understand the *organic unity* and *wholeness* of things, and the common *purpose* or *end* subscribed by the parts. Thus we regard a plant as an organic unity of parts co-operating to realize a common end. We regard a person as a conscious system of ends. Judgments of causal connection relate events as causes and effects. A change in a thing is explained by a change in some other thing. The causal explanation is a never-ending process. It seeks an endless series of causes and effects. It cannot find a cause which is not the effect of some other cause. Therefore causal explanation leads to an infinite regress. But judgments of purpose seek the explanation of changes in an individual organism in itself, not in any other thing. From the causal point of view, "everything is externally determined; its cause, or principle of explanation, lies outside of it in something else." *(Ibid,* p. 429). From the *ideological* point of view, the organism is *self-determinate;* its cause, or principle of explanation lies within itself. "The mark of *individuality* is the power of origination, or *self-determination.* If, then, there exist any genuine individuals, they are something more than causally determined phenomena. And a man, social institutions such as a church, the state, and so on, may be regarded as examples of individualities of greater or less degree of concreteness." *(Ibid,* p. 429). Hence teleological judgments belong to a highe stage of intellectual development than causal judgments.

**Judgment and Inference**

Inference is a completely developed judgment. Inference is more complex than judgment. "As thinking develops from the form of simple judgment to that of inference, it displays progressive differentiation and integra-tion." *(Ibid,* p. 431). Judgment, in its simplest form, can hardly be said to have any parts; it is a single act of intelligence. (1) Inference, on the other hand, involves *steps* or *stages* in thinking—a passage of the mind from one fact to another. (2) Moreover, inference differs from judgment in exhibiting the *grounds* upon which its statement rests. Judgment does not seek the support of reasons for a statement. It does not attempt to gain support for a statement *e. g.,* 'the ground is wet' by pointing out the connection of this fact with other facts. A simple judgment makes a statement on the basis of sense perception. But "to infer is just to show the necessary connection of facts—that from the presence or absence of certain things the presence or absence of certain other things necessarily follows." *(Ibid,* p. 432). Sometimes we infer a truth from known facts. Sometimes we infer reason from a fact. Inference is based on the assumption that the future must always resemble the past. The Uniformity of Nature is the ground of inference. "When a judgment develops so as to become *conscious* of its *reasons,* it has already taken on the form of inference. This is the usual procedure of knowledge. We begin by believing without reason, or we assume that certain things are true, and try to find reasons for our belief. The conclusion, which is of course logically last, is usually first for us, and we set out from it to find the grounds, or the premises." *(Ibid,* p. 434). *Judgment conscious of its ground is inference.*

**The Nature of Inference**

There is no hard and fast line of demarcation between judgment and inference. We are said to infer when we do not simply accept a fact on the basis of perception or memory, but show that it necessarily follows from some other known fact or facts. Inference requires (1) that certain *data or premises* already *known* should be accepted as true, and (2) it requires an *insight* into the *necessary connection* of some *new* fact or set of facts with what is *known* already. "What we very often do in inference is to show the reasons or necessity of some fact that we have previously accepted without knowing why. No matter whether we go from premises to conclusion (from the reasons to the fact), or in the opposite direction, from the conclusion to the premises, we are said to infer whenever we find the ground for the existence of one fact in the nature of another fact." *(Ibid,* p. 437).

There is no inference unless the result reached is different from the starting point. But how do we proceed from the known to the unknown ? We can do so on the strength of the element of *identity* between the premises and the conclusion. There is always some aspect or feature in which the premises are identical with the conclusion. "All inference takes place within a *system,* where the parts are so held together by a *common* nature that you can judge from some of them what the nature of the others must be. Suppose you were given the leaf of a plant. If you had some systematic botanical knowledge, it might be possible to infer the species of plant to which the leaf belonged. That is, from the nature of a part, the nature of the whole to which it belongs could be determined. The part represents the whole—in some sense contains it implicity." *(ibid,* p. 440). Judgment seeks to construct a system of knowledge. Inference pushes on the work of constructing a system further. "If each thing were known by itself, if the parts of our knowledge did not fall together into systems where each part of some extent determines the nature of the other parts, no inference would be possible. It is because the various pieces of knowledge are never independent of one another but form an organic whole, like the members of a living organism, that certain facts follow, as we say, from certain other facts. Otherwise we could only guess, or infer vaguely on the expectation that the future will resemble the past. Even this expectation, however, has no rational basis unless the world does form some kind of a *coherent system.*" *(Ibid,* p. 441). The more completely our knowledge in any field is organised, the better can it be used as a basis of inference. As knowledge grows, it shows an increasing degree of integration.

"Inference is simply a deep *insight* into the *necessary connection* of things. It is an act of thought which discovers the essential relations between things which at first sight appear to have no connection with one another. It is a *reasoned judgment, i. e.,* a judgment which has become *conscious* of the *reasons* for the connections which it affirms." *(Ibid,* pp. 442-43).

Bosanquet rightly points out that *novelty* and *necessity* are the characteristics of inference. "We have not got inference unless the conclusion (i) is *necessary* from the premises, and (ii) goes *beyond* the premises. To put the paradox quite roughly – we have not got inference unless the conclusion is (i) *in* the premises, and (ii) *outside* the premises." *(The Essentials of Logic,* p. 137). The conclusion *follows* from the premises and yet goes *beyond* them. It must contain an element of *novelty.* It must be new to the premises. And yet it must be *necessary, i. e.,* it must follow from the premises.

**Deduction and Induction**

We may start with certain principles already known, or assumed to be true, and proceed to show that some result necessarily follows from them. This kind of inference is called *deduction.* It proceeds from premises to conclusion. In deductive reasoning, a particular fact is always brought under a general law or principle already known or assumed to be true. Socrates is known to be mortal, because as a man, he falls under the general law that all men are mortal. Deduction proceeds from a general law or principle to its consequences. It applies a general law to particular facts or instances.

In induction, on the other hand, we start with particular facts and try to discover from them the general law or principle which unites them. Inductive inference is a process of reading a general law out of the particular facts. "It is an insight into the *whole* or *system,* based upon a careful examination of the *parts.*" *(Ibid,* p. 444). It discovers the ground or explanation of the connection among particular facts observed in a general law or" principle.

It is wrong to speak of deduction and induction as two *kinds* of reasoning quite distinct and independent of each other. "The essence of inference consists in the fact that it exhibits the manner in which particular facts are connected together into a system or whole. And this end is achieved by both deduction and induction. In the former case the *general law* of connection—the nature of the *system* within which the particulars fall—is *known,* and we argue from this as to the nature and relations of the various parts falling within it. Deductive inference shows the way in which a general principle or law of connection runs through a group of facts and constitutes them a real or organic whole. The same insight is insight reached by inductive inference, although the starting point is entirely different. Induction begins by observing that certain phenomena are frequently conjoined and attempts to discover some law or principle which will make the fact of their connection intelligible." *(Ibid,* p. 445).

Induction is said to be an inference from particular facts to a general law. But it is more correct to say that inductive inference gives us an insight into the necessary connection of the particular facts observed, and enables us to understand the general principle that units them together. We not only obtain a general law through an inductive inference but also a perception of its concrete application to particular phenomena. For example, we not only know the law of gravitation through an inductive reasoning, but also its application to particular facts, *e. g.*, bodies falling to the earth. Thus induction and deduction are not two different *kinds* of inference. Inference is always an act of thinking which tries to find out how particular phenomena are necessarily connected according to some general principle. Sometimes it starts with the general law of connection and tries to discover the nature of some particular fact. Here the method of reasoning is deductive. Sometimes an act of thinking starts with particular phenomena observed and tries to discover from them the general law of their connection.

Here the method of reasoning is inductive. "But from whatever point we set out, and whatever may be the immediate object of the inference, the result is always the same—*an insight into the necessary connection of facts according to some general principle.* And both in ordinary life and in scientific procedure, induction and deduction are constantly employed together as mutually supplementing each other in the work of organising experience-" *(Ibid.,* p. 446-47).

## UNIVERSITY QUESTIONS

1. Explain the nature and characteristics of Judgment. (1945). (See 5).
2. Explain fully the nature of Judgment. How would you distinguish Judgment from Inference ? (1946). (See 5 and 7).
3. Explain the nature of Judgment. (1947). (See 5).
4. Distinguish between Deduction and Induction. What is the common element in them ? (See 9).

## DIVISIONS OF PHILOSOPHY

Philosophy has mainly two parts, epistemology and philosophy proper, which again, is divided into three parts, the philosophy of nature, the philosophy of the soul, and the philosophy of God. The philosophy of nature is divided into three parts, the philosophy of the origin of the world called" Cosmogony, of the ultimate nature of the world called Ontology, of the number of fundamental principles constituting the world called Cosmology.

PHILOSOPHY

| Epistemology | | Philosophy (proper) | |
|---|---|---|---|
| | Philosophy of Nature | Philosophy of the Soul | Philosophy of God or the Absolute |
| Cosmogony | Ontology | Cosmology | |

# CHAPTER IV

# EPISTEMOLOGY

## (1) The Nature and End of Epistemology

'Epistemology' literally means the science of knowledge. (episteme= knowledge; logos = reasoned discourse). It does not deal with the process and growth of knowledge as psychology does, nor with the ultimate nature of the object that is known, as ontology or philosophy does, but it is an enquiry into the nature, origin, conditions and limits of konwledge. It seeks to answer the following questions: Is knowledge of the reality possible at all or not ? What is the nature of knowledge? What is the source or origin of knowledge ? And what is the range, extent or limit of knowledge ? And within these limits what conditions are to be fulfilled in order that knowledge may be valid ?

## (2) The Problem of the Origin of Knowledge

The problem of the origin of knowledge is the most vital problem of epistemology. This problem has been answered in different ways by different schools of thinkers, nationalism holds that all true knowledge is innate and *a priori* intuited by reason alone. Empiricism holds that all knowledge is *a prosteriori i.e.* comes through experience alone. Criticism or the critical theory of knowledge reconciles these two opposite theories and holds that knowledge is the resultant of two factors, *viz.,* reason and experience both, reason giving us the forms of knowledge, and experience supplying the matter of knowledge. The evolutional theory of knowledge holds that the forms of knowledge are not derived from reason but were acquired from experience by our ancestors, and the products of the accumulated experience of our ancestors have been transmitted to us by heridity, and hence though originally acquired by ancestral experience, have come to be innate and *a priori* in us—thus all knowledge is ultimately *a posteriori* (evolutional empiricism). According to the Dialetic view of knowledge, knowledge cannot come from experience alone; it is, not doubt, the joint product of sense and reason, as Criticism (Kant) maintains, but it is not a mechanical resultant of two disparate factors, *viz.*, reason and experience, forms and matter of knowledge, but it is an organism in which the forms and the matter of knowledge are component factors in an organic whole.

**(3) Rationalism, Apriorism, or the 'a priori' theory of knowledge**

According to rationalism or the a *priori* theory of knowledge all true knowledge must come from reason and intuition. Descartes is the father of rationalism. According to him, there are certain fundamental notions or ideas in the mind which cannot be derived from experience, but are innate in the mind implanted by God at the time of birth. Hence the innate ideas, *e. g.* the ideas of infinity, eternity, perfect being, causality and so on, are unquestionably true. The development of true knowledge consists in the deduction from these self-evident innate ideas, as propositions are deduced from axioms and definitions in Geometry. Thus Descartes applies the mathematical method to philosophy, and Spinoza applies the geometrical method. Hence this form of rationalism has been called Mathematical Rationalism (by Paulsen), since it applies Mathematics to philosophy.

Empiricism or the *a posteriori* theory of knowledge:

**(4) The Empiricism of Locke**

Empiricism is a reaction against rationalism. Locke, the father of empiricism, revolted against the Cartesian doctrine of innate ideas, and advocated the doctrine of empiricism. Thus Locke had two tasks, a negative task and a positive task. His negative task was the criticism of the theory of innate ideas, and his positive contribution was the introduction of empiricism.

**Locke criticizes the theory of Innate Ideas as follows:**

Firstly, if there were any innate ideas in the mind, they would be equally present in all minds. If there were any innate principles, they would be universally assented to. But Locke contends that there are no such universally present ideas; there are no principles that are universally admitted. Children, savages and idiots are quite unconscious of the so-called innate ideas and principles.

Secondly, if there were innate ideas in the mind, they would be of the same nature in all minds. But the so-called innate ideas, *e. g.* of God, morality and so on, differ in different societies, in different religions, and in different countries.

Thirdly, the first facts of knowledge are not abstract general principles, but particular instances of experience. The so-called innate ideas are abstract general principles. Hence they must be the acquisitions of our later experience. The child knows that sweet is not bitter, long before he understands the logical principle of contradiction. Therefore, the so-called innate ideas are derived from experience.

Thus, according to Locke, there are no innate ideas. The mind was a *tabula rasa, i. e.* an empty tablet in the beginning. All knowledge comes from experience (empiricism). Experience, again, is two-fold: (i) sensation, giving us knowledge of external objects; and *(ii)* reflection, giving us knowledge of the internal' states of the mind. All knowledge is made up of experience and elaborations of experience. There is no contribution from reason. Hence Locke enunciated the dictum, – *"There is nothing in the intellect which was not previously in the sense."* This is called the *a posteriori* theory of knowledge, since according to it, all knowledge is posterior to experience. [See criticism below.]

**(5) Hume's Scepticism: another form of Empiricism**

Scepticism is the natural outcome and logical consequence' of a thorough-going empiricism.

Firstly, if knowledge comes solely from experience, then it is wholly made up of sensations and ideas, and cannot extend to anything beyond sensations. We can reason from past sensations to future sensations, but never to anything beyond sensations.

Secondly, though sensations are discrete from one another, they are associated with one another by the laws of contiguity, similarity and causality.

Thirdly, if it is said that sensations are the effects produced in the mind by external objects, Hume replies that by a cause we do not mean a power or force which produces the effect, but it is merely an invariable antecedent of an event. By causality Hume means a customary sequence of ideas or an invariable succession of phenomena.

Fourthly, if experience is the only source of knowledge, it can never give us universal and necessary knowledge. Probability is the guide of life.

The so-called material things are to us clusters of actual and possible sensations; and the mind is a series of feelings, and ideas. Thus the empiricism of Locke ends in the sensationalism and scepticism of Hume.

## Criticism of Empiricism and Scepticism

Firstly, according to Hume, all knowledge comes from sensations. But merely atomic sensations, which are discrete and isolated from one another "with no inner bond of connection, cannot account for the unity of knowledge. The laws of association cannot constitute the inner bond of connection among the sensations, as Hume supposes; discrete sensations cannot account for the Jaws of association.

Secondly, if experience is the only source of knowledge, it cannot give us universal and necessary knowledge. But knowledge of things involves and presupposes certain universal and necessary forms or notions, *e. g.*, those of causality, substantiality, space, time and so on, which cannot be derived from experience, but must be supplied by reason from within.

Experience cannot give us universal and necessary truths; they must be supplied by reason. And the merely contingent and particular truths of experience cannot carry out the purpose of our life.

Thirdly, experience gives us only sensations, but sensations are meaningless, unless they are interpreted by the intellect. We can have knowledge of things only by understanding or interpreting the meanings of sensations; and the meanings of sensations can be interpreted by reason or the intellect, which compares one sensation with the other sensations, differentiates or distinguishes it from the disparate sensations, and assimilates it to the like sensations, and refers it to a substance or an object in nature, in a particular point of space at a definite point of time. These acts of differentiation, assimilation, and association and supplying the notions of substance, causality, space, time and so on, can be done only by reason or the intellect. Hence—

Leibnitz amended the empirical dictum of Locke in this way: "There is nothing in the intellect which was not previously in the sense—*except the intellect itself*'. Exprience must be interpreted by reason or rationalized before there can be knowledge.

Leibnitz holds that truths of facts are derived from experience, while necessary truths are derived from reason. Leibnitz does not hold, like descartes, that the mind comes into the world with certain innate ideas, but that it has certain predispositions or aptitudes. Ideas are only implicit in the infant mind, as **a** statue might be said to be implicit in a block of marble. Leibnitz differs from Descartes in holding that ideas do not pre-exist in the mind actually, but they exist in it virtually or potentially, which are brought out by experience. Thus Leibnitz tried to reconcile empiricism with rationalism.

**(7) The Critical Theory of Knowledge—Kant**

Kant took up the thread of the doctrine of Leibnitz. The critical theory of Kant reconciles the opposite theories of rationalism and empiricism and holds that knowledge is neither wholly *a priori,* as rationalism holds, nor wholly *a posteriori,* as empiricism holds, but consists of both *a priori* and *a posteriori* factors. Kant distinguishes between the forms and matter of knowledge, and holds that the material factor is supplied by experience and the formal factor by reason. The materials of knowledge are sensations or what Kant calls the 'manifold of intuitions' imposed on the mind by the external reality;Things in themselves affect us somehow, and produce impressions, or in Kantian language, 'intuitions' in our mind. These intuitions or sensations are chaotic and meaningless, unless they are interpreted by the mind; and the mind interprets them by applying its forms and categories to them, and thus builds out of this chaos of sensations the cosmos, of intelligible knowledge. The mind imposes upon the materials, viz. the 'manifold of intuitions' its forms of perception, *viz.,* space and time, and thus arranges the sensations in a spatial and temporal order; then it applies the categories of the understanding, viz., substance, causality etc. to the spatially and temporally arranged sensations; and then the mind co-ordinates and systematizes our experience, according to the three regulative Ideas of Season, *viz.,* and God.

Hence, according to Kant, the Understanding makes Nature, *i. e.,* the world of our experience is a *construction of our own* understanding out of the materials supplied from without by experience – according to its own forms and categories. But since sensations which form the materials of knowledge are the subjective states of our own mind, and the forms of knowledge are supplied by reason from within, our knowledge is phenomenal: we cannot know the things in themselves, since they are beyond the range of our experience, and beyond the application of our own forms and categories.] Kant's critical theory of knowledge has been called by Paulsen Formalistic Rationalism, since it holds that reason supplies the forms of knowledge.

**(8) The Evolutional theory of Knowledge (Evolutional Empiricism)**

**Herbert Spencer –**

Kant tried to reconcile the *a priori* with the *a posteriori* factors of knowledge in his Formalistic Rationalism. Herbert Spencer tried to reconcile them in another way, not by adopting the theory of rationalism, but by a modification of empiricism by the doctrine of heredity. According to him, both the forms and matter of knowledge are ultimately derived from experience (empiricism); but the froms or the necessary factors of knowledge, *e. g.* our belief in the law of causality, uniformity of nature etc. have come to be innate in us. They were derived from accumulated and uncontradicted experience by our ancestors in innumerable generations, and have been transmitted to us, according to the law of heredity, and so, though originally *a posteriori* in our ancestral experience, have become innate and *a priori* in us, by heredity (evolutionism). Hence it is called Evolutional Empiricism.

**(9) Criticism of Evolutional Empiricism**

Firstly, the evolutionist theory is, no doubt, of great importance in explaining the growth of knowledge, but it must begin by presupposing experience. Ancestral experience is as much in need of explanation as our own experience. The evolutionist theory explains certain features of the development of experience, but not experience itself. Hence this theory involves all the defects of empiricism.

Secondly, experience, whether individual or collective, can never give rise to *a priori* ideas, or universal and necessary forms of knowledge, for experience gives us only particular and contingent truths.

Thirdly, no knowledge is possible without the application of the *a priori* forms and categories of the mind. "Hence ancestral experience, too, presupposed the *a priori* ideas, instead of evolving them.

Fourthly, evolutional empiricism is based upon the doctrine of the transmission of acquired characters by heredity, which is discredited by many distinguished modern biologists, *e. g.*, Weismann etc.

Hence Kant's Critical theory of knowledge is a better explanation of the origin of knowledge, than either rationalism or empiricism, in any of its forms, though evolutional empiricism explains certain features of the *growth* of knowledge.

**(10)The Dialectic Theory of Knowledge–Hegel.**

Kant regarded knowledge as made up of two component factors, *viz.*, forms and matter of knowledge; but knowledge cannot be the mechanical resultant of two heterogeneous factors, coming "from two distinct sources, *viz.*, reason and experience. For why should the matter of knowledge given by experience submit to the forms of our own mind ? How can we impose our own forms and categories upon the materials of sensations produced by things-in-themselves in us ? Kant could not answer this question,

Hegel carried out the Kantian theory of knowledge to its logical consequence, and held that the forms and the matter of knowledge are not quite foreign to each other, but the forms of our own mind are already imbedded in experience. The world is the objective manifestation of the Absolute Spirit. God has thought out the world according to the same forms and categories as we apply to our experience. The categories of our mind are also the categories of the Divine Mind; hence the *a priori* categories of our mind not only apply within the range of experience or phenomena, but also apply to the so-called things-in-themselves beyond phenomena, thought and reality being at bottom identical.

**The Problem of the Nature of Knowledge**

The problem of the nature of knowledge has been answered by Idealism and Realism in their various forms. (Realism holds that knowledge is an exact copy or representation of reality, which exists independently of mind. Idealism holds that there is no extra-mental reality, everything knowable being a content of consciousness. According to Ideal-Realism, the real is ideal and the ideal is real–the external world is the objective manifestation of the Absolute and hence ideal innature, and the ideas of the human mind are the representations of the real things in Nature, since the human mind is a finite reproduction of the Absolute Spirit.

**Realism: Naive or Popular**

According to realism there is an extra-mental reality, which is outside and independent of mind; and knowledge is an exact copy or representation of this reality. But realism takes two forms, naive or popular ralism and scientific or critical realism.

According to Naive or Popular Realism, our ideas are exact copies of external real things and their qualities. Hence all the qualities of matter are real and objective existences in Nature, seated in things themselves. Thus colour, smell, sound, heat and cold are as much absolute and objective qualities of things as extension, impenetrability, motion and the like.

But all the qualities of matter are not equally essential and real as naive holds. Of the qualities of matter some are essential to the very conception and existence of matter, *e.g.,* extension, impenetrability, shape, size and the like; where-as the other qualities, e.g., colour, smell, sound and temperature are inessential and variable qualities of_matter. So all of them cannot be regarded as equally objective qualities of matter.

**(13) Realism: Scientific–Distinction between Primary Qualities and Secondary Qualities**

Scientific or Critical Realism draws a distinction between primary and Secondary qualities and holds that the former are real and objective qualities of matter, where as the latter are only subjective states of our mind. This distinction goes back to the Greek atomists, and has been adopted by Descartes, Spinoza, Hobbes and Locke clearly stated the distinction and put forward the following arguments on its behalf:

Colour, taste, smell, heat and cold vary under different conditions, in the same object to different individuals and to the same person at different times. What is sweet to one, is bitter to another; what is relishing to one, is distasteful to another. Hence these qualities, argues Locke, are not objective extra-mental qualities of things, but only subjective modes of our sensibility.

A mango is not sweet in itself, but has a *power* of producing sweet taste, when it comes in contact with the tongue. Colours, sounds, odours, tastes and temperatures cannot exist apart from our sensibility. Tŏ speak of colour, if there is no eye, is absurd; sound, if there is no ear to perceive it, is inconceivable; taste without any tongue to taste it, is unthinkable. Take away the sensations which we have of these qualities; let not the eyes see light or colours, nor the ears hear sounds; let not the palate taste, nor the nose smell, nor the skin feel heat or cold; and all colours, sounds, tastes, odours, and temperatures will vanish and cease to exist. So these qualities do not belong to the bodies themselves, but are nothing but sensations produced in us by the primary or real qualities of bodies, that is, by the bulk, figure, and motion of insensible parts; these are called by Locke secondary qualities of matter, whereas extension, impenetrability, solidity, bulk, figure, motion etc., are called primary qualities.

Colour, smell, taste, sound and temperature are not absolute objective qualities of things in nature, but they are merely subjective states of our mind corresponding to which there are certain powers in nature. But extension, impenetrability, motion, shape, size and the like are universal and permanent qualities which belong to all physical bodies under all circumstances, and hence must be regarded as actual objective qualities of matter. Thus, according to Scientific Realism, our ideas are the representations of actual realities, only in respect of the primary qualities of matter. The external world outside of our mind is neither light nor dark, neither silent nor resonant, neither hot nor cold, but is extended and impenetrable."

**(14) Idealism**

According to Idealism, our ideas are not copies or

representations of extra-mental realities. It takes various forms among which subjective, idealism, phenomenalistic idealism and objective idealism are three main forms. But we shall discuss objective idealism under another heading, *viz.,* ideal-realism.

The Critical Realism of Locke ia a step towards Idealism; it is half-realism and half-idealism–realism, in respect of the primary qualities, and idealism, in respect of the seçondary qualities. But we cannot draw such an arbitrary distinction between the primary qualities and the secondary qualities.

Scientific realism does not stand the scrutinity of reason. The fact that constitutes the basis of the distinction between the primary and the secondary qualities is the truth that some qualities of material bodies are more permanent or universal than others. In regarding the primary qualities as objective, and the secondary qualities as subjective, we commit a fallacy. We mistake, as Marvin points "out, exceptional or variable existence for 'subjective existence' and constant, permanent or universal existence for 'objective existence.'

The facts do not justify the denial of the objective existence of the secondary qualities. If the primary qualities are regarded as objective, the secondary qualities too must be regarded as objective; or if the secondary qualities are regarded as subjective, the primary qualities too must be regarded as subjective. The former view has been taken up by modern realists; the latter view was taken up by Berkeley, the father of modern idealism.

The same-arguments as were advanced by Locke against the objectivity of the secondary qualities can equally be employed against the objectivity of the primary qualities.

Firstly, if the secondary qualities, colour, smell, etc. cannot exist except in relation to our sensibility, *e, g.,* eyes, nose etc., and hence are merely subjective modes of our consciousness, the so-called primary qualities, too, e.g., extension, solidity etc., cannet exist except in relation to our sensibility and hence are merely sujbective states of our mind. The same sense-organs that reveal to us the extended moving things, also reveal to us the coloured things and so on. "Without the sense of sight and touch, we could no more talk of extension and solidity than of sounds -without hearing" (*Paulsen*).

Secondly, if the secondary qualities of matter are nothing but merely subjective states of our mind since they vary under different conditions, the so-called primary qualities, too, are nothing but merely subjective modes of our consciousness since they too vary under different conditions, *e. g.*, the size of a thing varies from different distances.

Thirdly, as the primary and the secondary qualities can never be perceived apart from each other, they must share the same fate; and if the secondary qualities are nothing but ideas of our mind, the primary qualities, too, are subjective states of our mind.

Fourthly, the secondary qualities of colour, smell etc. are supposed to be different molecular arrangements of the particles of matter by critical realism. But quality can never be derived from quantity, and the so-called primary qualities are empty abstractions apart from the secondary qualities.

### (15) Subjective Idealism or Mentalism—Berkeley

Berkeley developed the empiricism of Locke to its logical conseauence in idealism. Matter is nothing but a cluster of qualities; and all the qualities of matter, both primary and secondary, are nothing but subjective states of our mind. Hence Berkeley argues that the existence of a thing consists in its being perceived (*esse est percipi i. e.* existence = perception): if all knowledge comes from experience, as Locke holds, we know nothing but the ideas of our mind as what we perceive is an idea of the mind. Thus the conception of extra-mental matter is a dogmatic and superfluous assumption. The external world does not exist, and consequently the qualities of the world, both primary and secondary, are the subjective ideas of the mind. The world outside us is neither hot nor cold, neither bright nor dark, neither sweet nor sour, neither fragrant nor otherwise, and it is neither extended nor impenetrable. The worlds and its qualities are nothing but the perceptions or ideas of our minds. But the ideas of things are not created by our own minds, but communicated to us by God. Berkeley, thus, admits the existence of mind alone, of the finite minds and of God, but not of the external world.

**(16) Sensationism and Scepticism – Hume**

Hume carried the empiricism of Locke to its furthest logical consequence. Locke admitted the existence of matter, mind and God; he held that we know matter through external perception, and hence it is real, but he relegated the secondary qualities of matter to the subjective region of mind. Berkeley went a step further and regarded the primary qualities, too, as subjective ideas of our mind and thus resolved matter into a system of ideas. But he admitted the existence of the finite minds and God. Hume went a step further and held that if knowledge is wholly made up of sensations, we cannot know anything beyond sensations. Thus the so-called material things are nothing but clusters of actual and possible sensations, and the mind is nothing but a series of mental states, and we cannot know the existence of God, since He is beyond our sense-experience. Thus empiricism ends in sensationalism and scepticism.

**(17) Phenomenalistic Idealism or Phenomenalism – Kant**

According to Kant the mind is not a passive principle which receives knowledge from sense-impressions, but it is an active organising principle which constructs the world of our experience, out of the materials of our sensations, produced in us by the extra-mental reality, according to its own forms and categories, *e. g.*, space time, substance, causality, etc. Things-in themselves somehow affect our minds and produce impressions in them. These impressions are a mere manifold; they are arranged in time and space by the mind and subsumed under twelve thought-categories, substance, causality etc., and are thus organised into a coherent system of knowledge. And as the forms and categories of our mind are *a priori* notions of purely mental origin, they apply only within the range of our experience, but not to things-in-themselves. Thus our ideas are not true representations of things-in-themselves, but only of their phenomenal manifestations.

This doctrine is called Empirical Realism, since according to it, our ideas truly represent the phenomena only, and it is also called Transcendental Idealism, since it admits the existence of a transcendental reality or a reality beyond our experience (Transcendentalism), unlike Empirical or Subjective. Idealism, and holds that our ideas do not represent or correspond to the things-in-themselves beyond experience (Idealism); it is also called Phenomenalistic Idealism, since according to it, our knowledge is confine to phenomena only, and does not extend to the things-in-themselves beyond phenomena.

**(18) Absolute Phenomenalism or Solipsism – Fichte**

Fichte carried Kant's phenomenalistic idealism to its logical consequence in his extreme form of subjective idealism or solipsism. Kant maintained that causality is a category of the understanding and as such cannot apply to things-in-themselves, but only to phenomena within the range of our experience. But nevertheless he maintained that things-in-themselves are the *causes* of our sensations. Fichte removed this contradiction in Kant by holding that things-in-themselves can in no way affect our mind. How, then, can we infer even the mere fact of their existence. We have no reason to assume their existence. Thus according to Fichte, we are confined within the circle of our own ideas, and cannot go beyond our ideas to any transcen dental reality. "My world of ideas constitutes the only reality, beyond that there is nothing." This doctrine is called Solipsism.

Fichtean idealism is kindred to Berkeleyan idealism Both of them agree in denying the existence of the external world; according to both, the external world and its qualities are nothing but ideas of our minds. But there is a difference. According to Fichte, I create my ideas and my world of ideas constitutes the only reality – there is nothing beyond it. But according to Berkeley, my ideas are produced in me by God. Berkeley, therefore, admits the existence of God or the infinite mind as well as that of other finite minds. Fitchtean idealism is solipsism, pure and simple, which holds that I and my ideas alone constitute the reality. This is one tendency in Fichte's Philosophy.

### (19) Ideal-Realism or Real-Idealism or Objective Idealism or Absolute Idealism

But solipsism is an intolerable position. The subjective idealism of Berkely and Fitchte cannot satisfy the human mind since it denies the objective existence of the world. So Hegel introduced his doctrine of Ideal-Realism or Real-Idealism, which incorporates into itself the truths of realism and idealism both.

How can the ideas of our mind represent the reality beyond our ideas ? And how can we know the reality by means of the categories of the understanding which are merely subjective forms of our own consciousness only ? Berkeley reduced reality to thought and thus could not answer the first question. Kant set up an absolute opposition between thought and reality, and so could not answer the second question.

Berkeley was right when he held that there can be no object apart from the subject—nothing can exist without being perceived, but he was wrong when he reduced the object to an idea of the mind. If the object cannot exist apart from the subject, *i.* e., except in relation to a mind, the subject, too, cannot exist apart from the object; the duality, but not the dualism of the subject and the object is the indispensable condition and presupposition of experience. The absolute spirit evolves the world which is its manifestation; and it also reproduces itself in finite minds; so the finite minds and the world are not entirely foreign to each other; the former can know the latter, because the latter is the manifestation of spirit or Universal Reason. The Absolute manifests itself as a system of finite objects in the world, on the one hand, and as a system of finite minds, on the other, so that the former are not unintelligible to the latter. The world, thus is both real and ideal – real, being external to finite minds, and ideal, being the manifestation of the Absolute Spirit. This is the doctrine of Hegel who removed the defect of Berkeleyan subjective idealism by establishing ideal-realism or real-idealism. Kant was right when he held that discrete sensations – the 'mere manifold of intuitions' cannot account for the unity of coherent and intelligible knowledge, but they require certain synthetic principles of the understanding in the shape of forms and categories to combine them into a coherent order. But he was wrong when he regarded knowledge as the joint product of the matter of knowledge and the forms of knowledge supplied by sense and reason respectively. If the matter of knowledge *(i. e.,* discrete sensations) is foreign to the forms of knowledge (*i.* e, forms of perception and categories of the understanding), then neither the latter can be imposed on the former, nor can the former yield to the latter, and thus knowledge becomes impossible. Hegel, truly pointed out that our categories of knowledge are not merely the frame-work of thought, but also the frame-work of reality; they not only apply to phenomena within the range of our experience, but also to the reality beyond our experience, for ultimately thought and being – knowledge and reality are identical. Thus Hegel logically turned the phenomenalistic idealism of Kant into ideal realism or real-idealism.

### (20) Relativity of Knowledge: Agnosticism

By Relativity of knowledge we mean that we cannot know an object in itself, but only as it is related to the mind or the subject that knows it, and to other objects. The main arguments in favour of the relativity of knowledge are the following:

Firstly, consciousness presupposes the duality of the subject and the object. We can know an object only as we distinguish it from our mind; thus we can know an object only as distin-guished from the subject; we can never separate the subject from the object; we can never come in direct contact with reality in itself since it exists apart from, and independently of our minds; the object cannot be known as it is in itself apart from its relation to the subject, but only in relation to the subject. Hence we know the object only as coloured and modified by the subjectivity of our mind. To think is to condition, to relate, to limit. Thus knowledge is relative.

Secondly, we know an object as we distinguish it from other objects which limit its determinate existence; and these objects too are known in their relation to other objects; thus we cannot know objects in themselves, but only the relations among them. Hence our knowledge of objects is relative and conditional.

**(21) Criticism of the doctrine of Relativity of Knowledge**

Firstly, the conception of the object existing in itself apart from the subject ia an unreal abstraction. The object is not only perceived in relation to the subject, but it also exists only as it is perceived by some mind. The object exists outside and independent of the finite minds, but not of the Absolute Mind. Thus an object is real only in relation to the mind; and hence our knowledge of the object, too, is real only relation to the mind.

Secondly, an object, existing in itself, apart from its relation to the other objects is a mere fiction of our imagination. The existence of an object depends upon its relations to the other objects. Consequently, when we know an object only in relation to the other objects, we know the object as it really is. If it is said that we know only relations among objects, but not objects themselves, it is indulging in an unmeaning abstraction. Relations are meaningless apart from the terms of relations. Thus when we know the relations among things, we do not know the relations among zeros or nonentities, but relations among given facts. Hence knowledge is not relative.

## Berkeley's Subjective Idealism

### (a) Transition from Locke to Berkeley

Berkeley took up the empirical doctrine of Locke and developed it into his doctrine of subjective idealism, spiritualism or immaterialism. Accordidg to Berkeley, all knowledge comes from experience. Locke already proved the subjectivity of the secondary qualities of matter. Berkeley applied the same arguments to the primary qualities and proved that the primary qualities are as much sensations of the mind as the secondary qualities. Thus he made Locke's doctrine more consistent, by depriving matter not only of the secondary qualities, but also of the primary qualities. But, then, Locke's material substance remained.

Berkeley proved the non-existence of the material substance and he found a clue to his argument in Locke's explanation of the conception of material substance. "What is material substance ? Why are we compelled to assume the existence of the material substance ? Locke holds that we perceive a number of certain ideas going constantly together; they cannot subsist by themselves. So we are compelled to assume the existence of material substance. We are *somehow obliged* to suppose 'we know not what'. Locke holds that we are constrained by reason to assume the existence of material substance. It is an intellectual necessity. But he cannot give an adequate explanation of that reason.

### (b) Berkeley's Spiritualism or Immaterialism

This explanation of Locke prepared the way for Berkeley's doctrine of immaterialism. Berkeley holds that material substance is not perceived; therefore, it does not exist. The existence of a thing consists in its being perceived. We perceive certain ideas, *e. g.*, colour, taste, extension etc., constantly going together and so erroneously suppose that there is a material substance behind them, without perceiving the contradiction involved in our supposition. These ideas do exist in a substance in so far as they are perceived by it. But it is not a material substance; it is the mind or spirit that perceives them. In this way Berkeley proved the non-existence of matter external to the mind, and obliterated the distinction between primary qualities and secondary qualities, regarding both of them as sensations of the mind. *Esse* is *precipi:* the existence of a sensible object consists in its being perceived by a mind. The sensible qualities exist in so far as they are perceived; and as they are perceived by a mind they are *ideas* existing in that mind. Thus sensible qualities are ideas of the perceiving mind; they can never exist in the so-called material substance whick is non-existent.

But what is the *cause* of these sensations ? It cannot be matter since matter is non-existent. It cannot be the finite spirit itself which experiences these sensations, for sensations are dependent of its will—they are forced upon it from without, But spirit alone is a cause. Therefore, God must be the cause of our sensations. Thus Berkeley recognizes the existence of the finite spirits and God. He reduces the so-called material world into a system of ideas in the finite minds excited by God or the Infinite Spirit according to certain fixed laws.

Thus Berkeley admits the existence of spirits and ideas, and nothing else. He reduces human knowledge to the knowledge of spirits and perceived appearances or ideas that, in themselves, are unsubstantial and powerless. Berkeley reduces the material world to sense-appearances or ideas. He never denies the reality of a single phenomenon which is presented to our senses. He denies the existence of the so-called material substance which is never perceived. "When we say that we see or touch a material object, all that we ought to mean is, that we perceive appearances in sense which have a practical meaning, in as much as our pleasures and pains largely depend upon them. When we are actually percipient, we have as much evidence of their reality as we have of our own. In being percipient we are conscious of ourselves, and, simultaneously with this, of the passive and dependent appearances which our senses reveal. Strictly speaking, we are *conscious* of the former (the self) and *percipient* of the latter (appearances or ideas)". *(Fraser)*. "So Berkeley melted the material world into what is actually presented or presentable to our senses." *(Fraser)*. This is his doctrine of subjective idealism, immaterialisrn, or spiritualism. He reduces the material world to phenomena or appearances presented to our senses, or subjective ideas perceived by the finite minds. So his doctrine is called subjective idealism. For the same reason, his doctrine is also called immaterialism, since he denies the reality of material substance. His doctrine is also called spiritualism, since he belives only in the reality of spirits, finite spirits and the Infinite Spirit, and their ideas.

### (23) Criticism of Berkeley's Subjective Idealism by contemporary realism

(1) Berkeley asks: What is the meaning of the *existence of* sensible things ? They *exist,* that is, they *are perceived* by mind. Their *existence* consists in their *being perceived.* Their *esse* is *percipi.* We can never think of the absolute existence of unthinking things without relation to a mind, or unperceived by a mind.

The dependence of the *object* on the mind's knowing it has been criticized mercilessly by different schools of realists of the present day. The object *exists;* it is *independent* of the mind and its knowledge of it; its existence is not affected by the mind's knowledge of it; it is not a *content* of consciousness. (Perry). *Esse* is *percipi:* it means that being *is,* and therefore it *is perceived.* If there were no being or *object* it would not be perceived. Its being does not consist in being perceived as Berkeley erroneously supposed; it is perceived because there is *being* or existence of the object. *(Moor).* Thus the neo-realists believe in the *existence* of the object and its *independence* of the knowing mind.

The objective idealists (Hegelians), on the other hand, argue that knowledge presupposes the *duality* of the subject and the object both of which are real. Just as the subject cannot be reduced to the object, so the object also cannot be reduced to the subject, or ideas of the mind. The subject and the object are equally real. They are correlative to each other.

We cannot but believe in the *existence* of the object and its *knowability* by the mind. Otherwise all knowledge and philosophy would be impossible. But from this we cannot argue that because the object is knowable, or is actually known by a mind, it must be an *idea* of that mind, a *content* of its consciousness. Berkeley has never proved it. He has simply assumed it. Beyond this we cannot pursue the question any further here.

(2) Further, Berkeley argues that whenever we perceive an *object* ('blue'), we perceive a *sensation* of the object *at the same time.* We can never separate the two from each other in actual perception. So they must be *identical* with each other. The *sensible object* ('blue') must be identical with the *sensation* of it ('sensation of blue'). "It is impossible for me to see or feel *anything* without an actual *sensation* of that thing, so it is impossible for me to conceive in my thoughts any *sensible thing* or object distinct from the *sensation* or perception of it. In truth, *the object and the sensation are the same thing* and cannot therefore be abstracted from each other." *(Berkeley).*

According to Berkeley, 'blue' and 'sensation of blue' are identical with each other, because they can never be perceived apart from each other. But *inseparability* in perception (or conception) does not prove *identity.* If A and B cannot be perceived or conceived apart from each other, it does not prove that they are identical with each other. *Variety in sensations* cannot be accounted for without *variety in objects.*

(3) It is generally believed that all sensible objects have a natural or *real existence,* distinct from their being perceived by the mind. Berkeley argues, What are the forementioned (sensible) objects but the things we perceive by sense ? And what do we perceive besides our own ideas or sensations Berkeley is right when he says that the *sensible* things are those *objects* which are *perceived* by us. But from this he jump to the conclusion that the *sensible things* are *ideas* or *sensations* of the perceiving mind inasmuch as what are perceived by us are our own ideas or sensations. But Berkeley never proves "that whatever are perceived by us are our own sensations or ideas. He simply assumes it. And on this link of his arguments binges the whole superstructure of his philosophy.

The neo-realists, on the other hand, argue that the mind *immediately* perceives *objects* not through the medium of ideas. What is the use of positing *ideas* as a *tertium quid* between the mind and the objects ? The mind knows them directly and immediately. Berkeley cuts out the objects. The neo-realists cut out ideas. Both are advocates of the *presentative* theory of perception but in different ways.

(4) Berkeley criticizes Locke's *representative theory of perception* as follows: If *ideas* are copies or images of extra-mental *objects,* they are *like* the objects. If ideas are *like* objects, the objects must be *ideas*. "An idea can be nothing but an idea; a colour or figure can be like nothing but another colour or figure." "An idea can be like nothing but another idea." If there is likeness between ideas and their objects they must be identical in nature, and the objects must be nothing but ideas. This argument is wrong. *Likeness* does not necessarily mean *identity* in nature. There may be likeness between two things belonging to *different* orders.

Again, Berkeley argues: Are the so-called external objects perceivable or not ? If they are *perceivable,* then they are *ideas* of the mind. Here, again, Berkeley assumes what he has to prove. He never proves that what are perceived or *perceivable* by a mind are *ideas* of the perceiving mind. He is begging the Question.

Johnston truly observes: "Berkeley's doctrine is defective by reason of its lack of psychological analysis; it is too undiscriminating and too facile, and it does not account for the complexity of the process of perception. He never attempted any exhaustive analysis of the actual process of perception. He draws no distinction between *sensations and sensible qualities:* and he even identifies *sensations* and *sensible things* or objects. For him the word *idea* means at one and the same time a *sensation* in the mind and a *thing* presented to the mind." There is a distinction between what the mind *means* or intends in perceiving, and the actual experience which it has as a particular psychical existent. "The former is called 'thing' or 'object', the latter 'experience' or act." Again, in mental experience there are 'presentations' in the language of Stout. "It is characteristic of presentations to be presentative of something beyond themselves. Presentations are always contents of immediate experience; but they are not the things that they present. They perform the function of presenting objects that are not themselves contents of immediate experience...Berkeley makes no analysis of this kind. What he calls *ideas* bear much resemblance to *presentations,* but in distinction from them they are presentative of *nothing* apart from themselves. Ideas for Berkeley are both presentations and what presentations are presentative of. He does not distinguish carefully between the actual process of perception, the particular experience in tha psychic individual, and the thing or object perceived. His theory suffers seriously from absence of psychological analysis."

(*The Development of Berkeley's Philosophy,* pp. 150-54.)

**(24)Was Berkeley a Solipsist ?**

According to Solipsism!, I and my ideas are real; I am certain of my own existence and of my ideas. I do not know anything beyond myself and my ideas. "Each person is shut up to himself alone, *solus ipsel'* [ Hooking: *types of Philosophy,* p. 266. ]

Berkeley is not a solipsist. He believes that experience is a result of an. external activity, not of my own solely. He depends on God to escape from the magic circle of the self. He holds that the sensations in my mind depend on God; they are excited in me by God according to certain fixed laws. Again, certain sensations are produced in me by other finite spirits; and my belief in their existence and my communion with them are guaranteed by my faith in God. Thus the conception of God saves Berkeley's philosophy from lapsing into *Solipsism.* "His doctrine is not really solipsistic, for he explicitly holds

(a) that the world contains, in addition to me and my ideas, other finite spirits with their ideas, and

(b) that I am not the. source of my presentations, but am

dependent for them on God, who causes them to occur in a fixed and regular order." (*The Development of Berkeley's Philosophy,* p. 205).

## UNIVERSITY QUESTIONS

1. "There is nothing in the intellect which was not first in sense." Examine this statement. (1909).
2. How does the relativity of knowledge affect its validity ? (1909).
3. 'All knowledge begins with experience, but all knowledge is not derived from experience.' Fully elucidate the contents of this proposition. (1910). [See 2 and 6].
4. "There is nothing in the mind which was not first in the sense" – Criticise the statement as a doctrine of the origin of knowledge. (1912).
5. Discuss the question as to whether the world we know is real or only phenomenal. Explain carefully what you mean by "real" in this connection. (1912).
6. Distinguish between *a priori* and *a posteriori* in reference to knowledge. Give examples of principles often held to be *a priori*. Is it possible to explain, the principles you give in the *a posteriori* way ? Discuss the relation and relative importance of Experience and Reason as factors of knowledge. (1913).
7. What is meant by "innate ideas" ? Give briefly the arguments for and against their existence. (1914).
8. Explain and examine the distinction between the primary and the secondary qualities of matter. (1915).
9. State and examine the doctrine that all knowledge is relative. (1915).
10. Explain the meaning of Epistemology, and the relation between Epistemology and Philosophy in general, showing why Epistemology is necessary. (1916).
11. Explain the meaning of *a posteriori* and *a priori* in relation

to knowledge, with full illustrations. What thinkers consider knowledge, to be wholly *a posteriori* ? Do you agree with them ? Give your reasons. (1916). [See Empiricism, Rationalism and especially Criticism, 2, 4, 5 and 6.]

12. Give a detailed and critical exposition of Realism and Idealism as metaphysical doctrines. (1917).
13. What is the source and criterion of knowledge, according to Empiricism and nationalism ? (1919).
14. Does Idealism resolve physical phenomena into mental phenomena, make the objects that it knows, come into being' and finally obliterate the distinction between subjective and objective ? (1919).
15. Determine the relative claims of Idealism and Realism as philosophical systems. (1920).
16. What do you understand by Epistemology ? Distinguish between, and discuss the claims of, Apriorism, Empiricism and Criticism as Epistemological doctrines. (1909 Hon.)
17. Give a critical review of Scientific Realism as a theory of the constitution of the world. (1909 Hon.).
18. What do you consider to be the true basis of the distinction between the primary and the secondary qualities of matter ? How is the relation between the two concerned in the mechanical theory of nature ? (1910 Hon.).
19. What exactly are the points involved in the question of the validity of knowledge? Clearly state the solution of the question as given by Rationalism ? (1910 Hon.).
20. What is empiricism ? What do you consider to be its chief difficulties as a theory of knowledge ? (1912 Hon.).
21. Define subjective idealism, and apply your definition to determine Berkeley's position. (1912 Hon.).
22. What is realism ? Is every form of idealism opposed to realism ? Discuss this. (1912 Hon).
23. Is scepticism the necessary logical development of

empiricism ? (1913 Hon.).

24. Distinguish between the standpoints of Scepticism and Agnosticism, and discuss their tenability. Why was Hume called a Sceptic, and Spencer an agnostic ? (1914 Hon.).
25. Define the *idealistic* position. State and examine some of the typical forms in which it has appeared. (1914 Hon).
26. Write short notes on the following:Empiricism, Phenomenalism, Subjective Idealism (1915 Hon.).
27. Explain the difference between *a priori* and *a posteriori* elements of knowledge, giving examples of each kind. Some thinkers say that knowledge contains no *a priori* elements: give your own opinion on this subject, with your reasons. (1922).
28. Distinguish between Ealism and Idealism in Philosophy, and state which of them gives the better explanation of the world, giving your reasons. (1923).
29. State and examine the view that all knowledge is derived from sense-perception. (1924).
30. What is meant in Philosophy by Realism and Idealism ? State briefly the grounds on which each of these theories is based. Give your own opinion regarding them. (1925).
31. What do you mean by experience and reason ? How are they related as factors of philosophical knowledge? (1930).
32. Evaluate the meaning and importance of the different theories that have been held with regard to the origin of knowledge. (1932).
33. 'There is nothing in intellect which was not in sensation, except the intellect itself.' Develop fully the implication of this statement for a theory of the origin of knowledge. (1933).
34. Explain and examine the following statements:
    a) The real is independent of all minds.
    b) The real has no existence apart from minds. (1933).
35. Explain the meaning of idealism in Philosophy. Explain

realism and idealism as metaphysical theories. (1935).

36. Explain the main theories of the origin of knowledge. (1945)
37. Explain the philosophical implications of Intuitionism as a theory of the origin of knowledge. (1946).
38. Give a comparative estimate of Idealism and Realism as types of philosophical thinking. (1946).
39. Distinguish Realism and Idealism as enterpretations of the world of knowledge. (1947).

## II

## CATEGORIES OF KNOWLEDGE

### (25)The meaning of categories of knowledge

The term 'category' means what is predicated or affirmed of something. The simplest form of knowledge is expressed in a judgment. A judgment consist of a subject and a predicate. Different judgments have different predicates. But there are certain predicates which are present in all judgments. These universal notions involved in all judgments are called the categories of knowledge.

Different philosophers have given different lists of categories. Aristotle has mentioned ten categories, *e. g.*, substance, quantity, quality, relation, where (space), when (time), position, possession, action and passion. Kant has given the following list of twelve categories under quantity, quality, relation and modality:—

| I. Quantity. | II. Quality. | III. Relation. | IV. Modality. |
|---|---|---|---|
| 1. Unity. | 4. Reality | 7. Substantiality and inherence | 10. Possibility and impossibility. |
| 2. Plurality. | 5. Negation. | 8. Causality and dependence | 11. Actuality and non-existence. |

| | | | |
|---|---|---|---|
| 3. Totality. | 6. Limitaion. | 9. Reciprocity or Community | 12. Necessity and contingency |

Hegel mentioned seventy categories; Schopenhauer reduced all the categories into causality. But most are agreed in holding space, time, substance and causality as the fundamental categories of knowledge. Whenever we think of a thing, we think of it as a substance existing somewhere in space and at a certain point of time having the power of produeing changes in other things.

As regards the categories of knowledge, there are two questions

(1) a psychological and epistemological question, viz,, how do we get the ideas of these fundamental notions? and

(2) an ontological question, viz., what is the real nature of these categories ?

**(26) Space: (A) Its Nature**

We may describe space by its following characteristics:

1. Space is infinite. For if it were not so, it would have a limit. It would be either a body or a void, therefore, again in both cases space ! It is also infinitely divisible; for if it were not so, it would have no parts and therefore no particular figure would be drawn in it.
2. But still it is not built up of its parts – it is not a mere sumtotal of finite parts; for finite quantities, however indefinitely added, can give only a finite quantity, however indefinitely large. It is therefore a single whole, out of which particular spaces are drawn by limitation.
3. It has three dimensions – length, breadth and depth or distance. Linear space has only length; superficial

space both length and breadth; and solid space, length, breadth and depth or distance.

4. The most essential and differentiating attribute of space is co-existence. All the points, lines, figures and things in space co-exist with one another.

## 1. Objective Space

The popular view of space is that it is an objective reality existing outside and independent of mind—an empty receptacle in which all things are contained. The relation between space and material objects is that of a container to the contained, This is the view of Newton and of common sense Realism and Intuitionism.

Descartes regarded space or extension not as an objective reality or substance but as an attribute of matter. Space or extension is the essence of matter: matter without extension *(i. e.* an atom) is impossible and extension without matter *(i.e.* empty space) is impossible. To be material is to be extended; unextended matter is inconceivable.

Spinoza also regarded space or extension as an attribute not of matter, as Descartes supposed, but as one of the infinite attributes of the one Substance, viz., God.

Criticism of the objective view:An object, existing independently of mind is an impossibility. (See above subjective idealism and objective idealism). So space cannot be regarded as an independent and extra-mental reality.

## II. Subjective Space

Leibnitz regarded space not as an objective entity, but as confused perception, on our part, of the order of monads. According to Leibnitz, the monads, the ultimate constituents of the universe, are non-extended spiritual atoms. Space is not real, but only a phenomenal appearance *to us* of the co-existence of monads, owing to the inherent limitations of our nature.

The empiricists, Berkeley, Hume, Mill and others regard space as purely an abstract idea generalised from the ideas of co-existence derived from tactuo-muscular sensations. The idea of empty space is derived from the sensation of unresisted movement, and that of filled space from the muscular sensation of resisted movement.

According to Kant, space is neither an objective entity, independent of mind, nor an abstract concept generalised from motor experience. It cannot be derived from experience as experience presupposes it. The very idea of movement and co-existence involves and presupposes the idea of space. So, space is an *a priori* notion of the mind, a form of perception, *our way* of representing things in their mutual externality to each other. The noumenal world of things-in-themselves is not a spatial world.

### III. Space both subjective and objective

According to Hegel, space is not only an *a priori* form of the finite mind, but also a form of the Divine Mind, of which nature is an objective expression. God has thought out the world according to the form of space; the human minds are finite reproductions of God; so the finite mind too interprets the world according to the form of space. Hence space has not only a subjective existence in the finite minds, but also an objective existence in nature. Things exist in nature as external to one another; this mutual externality of things presupposes the unity of Divine Consciousness which relates things to one another, distinguishes them from, and opposes them to another and comprehends them in its all-embracing unity.

## (B) The Origin of the idea of Space

I. Intuitionists (Reid, Martineau, and others) hold that space is an independent reality which we can directly perceive by intuition.

II. Empiricists and Associationists (Berkeley, Hume, Mill, Bain etc.) hold that we derive the idea of space from motor experience (tactuo-muscular sensations). We experience muscular feelings by the movements of our limbs; from these motor experiences we abstract a general possibility of movement; space is nothing more than this possibility; free and unresisted movement gives the idea of empty space.

James and his followers seek to derive the idea of space from the quality of extensity, massiveness or voluminousness of sensations.

III. Kant holds that the notion of space is not derived from experience as experience presupposes it. "Movement does not explain space: space explains movement;." Space is an *a priori* notion of our mind, a form of perception. Kant establishes the apriority of space by the following arguments: Firstly, *(i)* we can think away one quality after another of an object, but we can never think away its position in space. Space is a necessary condition of thought. Secondly, (ii) Geometry' deals with the idea of space (figures etc.). The propositions of Geometry are universal and necessary judgments. But experience can never give us universality and necessity. Hence space cannot be derived from experience, but must be regarded as an *a priori* form of perception.

Kant proves the apriority of space by the following arguments:

1) Space is not an abstract idea or conception derived from experience by generalisation. According to the empiricists, the idea of space is derived from the perception of *outwardness* of things. But Kant rightly contends that the perception of the *outwardness* of things already involves the idea of space. The idea of space cannot be derived from experience, for space is the presupposition of all experince.

2) The notion of space is *a priori,* for we can in imagination divest a thing of all its attributes, we can even think away things altogether and annihilate them in thought, but we cannot think away space itself.

3) Space is infinite. And what is infinite cannot be perceived or experienced. Hence we know it *a priori,*

4) The most decisive proof of the *apriority* of the idea of space is furnished by Geometry. Geometry is the science of space as it deals with figures. Now, Geometrical truths are *universal* and *netessary* in character. But experience, being restricted to a limited number of cases, cannot give us universal and necessary knowledge. If our notion of space were derived from experience, the truths of Geometry would not be universal and necessary. Hence the notion of space must be regarded as an *a priori* form of perception.

Thus according to Kant, space is neither a thing, nor an attribute existing in the world of things-in-themselves; it is not a relation or order existing among things in the world; it is an *a priori* form of perception, according to which we arrange the manifold of impressions produced by things-in-themselves in our minds into a spatial world; the world of things-in themselves is not a spatial world.

IV. According to Herbert Spencer and other Evolutionists, the idea of space was originally derived from motor experience by our ancestors, but the accumulated experience of our ancestors has been transmitted to us according to the law of heredity, and has become innate and instinctive in us.

V. Kant is right so far as he goes. Space is, no doubt, a form of perception in the finite mind; but we can perceive Space in space, only because there is space in nature—because God has thought out the world according to the form of space, Space is mutual externality of objects in nature, and it is possible because of the presence of the Eternal Spirit in nature which relates them to one another. This is the view of Hegel and Green.

**Time: (A) Its Nature**

We may enumerate the-following characteristics of time:

1. Time is infinite in both directions. For, if it were not so it would have a beginning and an end. Both would be Points of time, and would consequently be within time and not outside of it.

2. It is also infinitely divisible, for otherwise there would. have been no parts or moments of time.

3. It is still not made up of its parts or moments added together; for mere addition of finite parts, however indefinitely carried out, cannot give what is infinite. Time is, therefore, a single whole out of which particular times are derived by limitation.

4. It has only one dimension.

I. Intuitionists and Realists hold that time is an objective reality, independent of mind, which contains the successive events of nature.

II. Empiricists and associationists hold that time is not an independent objective reality, but an abstract concept of the mind generalized from the ideas of succession of events. It is only a subjective form of sequence.

III. According to Kant, time is neither an objective reality, nor an abstract concept generalized from the experience of succession or sequence. The notion of time cannot be derived from the ideas of succession of events, as the experience of succession *i. e.,* apprehension of events in the order of *before* and *after* presupposes the notion of time. Hence the notion of time is not derived from and posterior to experience, but prior to all experience. It is an *a priori* form of perception, an *a priori* notion which the mind evolves from within itself in order to represent to itself the succession of events.

IV. According to the Dialetic view of Hegel, time is, no doubt, an *a priori* form of the human mind but it is so, only because it is also the form of the Divine Mind of which the external world is an objective expression. Hence time has not only a subjective existence in the human mind, but also an objective existence in nature.

**(29) (B) The Origin of the Idea of Time**

I. According to Intuitionism and Realism, we can directly perceive time, which is an independent reality, by intuition.

II. According to Empiricism, the notion of time is an abstract idea generalized from the experience of successive events. Perception gives us the idea of the present. Memory gives us the idea of the past, anticipation gives us the idea of the future. We derive the abstract idea of time from these experiences by generalization. [See Psychology, conception of time.]

III. According to Kant, the idea of time cannot be derived from ' experience as experience presupposes it, but it is an *a priori* notion of the mind, a form of perception, which is prior to all experience.

IV. According to Herbert Spencer and his followers, the idea of time, though originally derived from experience by our ancestors, has become innate and *a priori* in us, according to the law of heredity.

V. According to Hegel, time has not only a subjective existence as an *a priori* form of the human mind, but also an objective existence in nature as a form of the Divine Mind, which manifests itself in nature. Kant proves the *apriority* of the notion of time by the following arguments:

1) The idea of time cannot be derived from experience; for all experience presupposes the notion of time; experiences must come either *successively* or *simultaneously,* and the ideas of succession and simultaneity imply the idea of time. Therefore, it must come from within the mind itself which recognizes them as successive or simultaneous.

2) We can think away one event after another in time, but we cannot think away time itself;, we connot annihilate time in thought, though we can very well think it emptied of contents or events. So the notion of time must be *a priori* or prior to all experience.

3) Time is infinite in both directions, and as such it can not be perceived or experienced. It follows, therefore, that we know it independently of experience *i.e., a priori*.

4) The most decisive proof of the *apriority* of the notion

of time is furnished by Arithmetic. Arithmetic is the science duration, the successive movements of which constitute number Arithmetical truths are universal and necessary in character. But they would not be so, unless the notion of time were *a priori*. They cannot be derived from experience which gives us only (particular and contingent truths.

**(30) Substance: Its content.**

1) Substance is that which is permanent in the midst of changes—that which remains essentially the same throughout all the successive changes of state which it undergoes in course of time, and sustains and holds these changes together, gives them a certain continuity, connection and unity. Thus substance is that fundamental reality which manifests and realizes itself in and through successive changes commonly called attributes, but remains essentially identical through them all.

2) Substance, regarded as a permanent entity amidst all changes, implies also the notion that it is a centre of effort, energy and activity. For its permanence implies a continuous effort of self-assertion and self-preservation, which consists in resisting and overcoming the external forces acting upon it.

**(31) (A) The Nature of Substance**

By substance we mean the permanent principle of identity in the midst of change and difference.

**I. Rationalistic account**

According to Descartes, substance is that which so exists that it needs nothing else in order to its existence. It is evident that so denned there can be only one substance, *viz.,* God. But Descartes inconsistently recognizes the existence of two other created substances, which depend on God, but are absolutely independent of each other, viz., mind and matter. The essence of mind is thought, and that of matter is extension, Descartes is a dualist.

Spinoza accepts the Cartesian definition of substance and logically concludes that God is the only substance. Mind and matter, or thought and extension, are not substances but the *attributes* of God, the only substance. Spinoza is a monist.

Leibnitz agrees with Descartes and Spinoza in thinking that substance does not depend for its existence upon anything else; but according to him, there are an infinite number of substances absolutely independent of each other. These substances are spiritual atoms, called by Leibnitz monads. Thus Leibnitz is a pluralist.

### II. The Empirical occount

According to Locke, the father of empiricism, the only source of knowledge is experience; we know the different attributes of matter through sense-experience, but these attributes cannot be conceived to exist by themselves. Hence Locke supposes that there is an unknown and unknowable substratum underlying and supporting qualities revealed in sensations. Substance means, in the case of matter and mind alike, simply 'we know not what'. Sensation convinces us that there are solid extended subs-tances: and reflection, that there are thinking ones." *(Locke).*

According to Berkely, *esse est percipi,* the existence of a thing consists in its being perceived; so substance, in order to be real must be perceived by the mind; hence Locke's unknown and unknowable substratum is a meaningless abstraction.

Substance, so far as matter is concerned, is nothing but a cluster of sensations. But Berkely recognized the substantiality of mind.

Hume argues, if a material object is nothing but a cluster of sensations, why should we recognize the substantiality of mind ? We never perceive the permanent self which does not change at all. All that we perceive is a flux of mental states. Hence, there is no such thing as substance at all, mind or matter. Mill, too, regards substance as a "permanent possibility of sensations" in the case of matter, and of ideas and feelings, in the case of mind.

**III. According to Kant** substance is neither an objective entity, nor merely a cluster of sensations and ideas, but it is an *a priori* category of the understanding, which is involved and presupposed in our experience of change. We cannot understand changes, unless we refer them to a permanent substance which itself does not change; hence the notion of substance is an *a priori* category of the understanding, according to which the mind interprets sensations and its ideas. In Kant's language, the principle of substance may be stated thus – "In all changes of phenomena the substance is permanent and the quantity of it in nature is never either increased or decreased."

**IV. According to Hegel,** substance is both subjective and objective, ideal and real, ideal as an *a priori* category of the human mind, and real, as already existing in nature, being the category of the Divine Mind.

**(B) Substance and its relation to quality** Substance, then, is the permanent principle of unity in the midst of changes'. Changes are possible only in relation to a permanent substance that does not itself change. But substance is not the unknown and unknowable substratum of qualities, but something which reveals itself to the mind through its attributes or qualities. Just as qualities cannot be conceived apart from substance, so substance cannot be conceived from its qualities. Substance is not a blank predicateless entity lying behind and beyond phenomena, but it is the principle of unity which remains identical with itself in the midst of changes and supports and unifies its qualities.

**(C) The Origin of the Idea of Substance**

**I. Popular Realism**

We derive the idea of substance from direct perception – internal and external. We know the substantiality of mind through internal perception, and that of matter through external perception.

**II. The Empirical account**

According to Locke, we cannot perceive substance in the external world; we perceive only the qualities of matter; but these qualities cannot be conceived to exist by themselves. Hence we are driven to suppose a substratum as their basis, which is unknown and unknowable.

According to Berkeley, there is no substance in the material world; in our experience we find that certain sensations of touch and sight etc., are always presented together; so we think that they are produced by an outward material substance, though as a matter of fact, there is none. But Berkeley holds that we have a *notion* of mind as a substance.

According to Hume, there is neither a material substance nor a mental substance. The notion of substance is only a figment of imagination. The belief in a permanent substance underlying the attributes is generated by repeated experience association. When we experience a cluster of sensations always together, they are grouped and associated in the mind, this repetition of experience and association produces in us the belief in a substance. The mind is never perceived as a permanent substance, but only as a flux of mental states. The illusion of personal identity is engendered by the rapid succession of ideas.

**III. According to Kant,** we cannot derive the idea of substance from experience as experience presupposes it. It is an a *priori* category of the understanding, which the mind evolves from within itself in order to understand and interpret sensations.

**IV. According to Herbert Spencer** the idea of substance was originally derived from experience of our ancestors, but the accumulated experience of our ancestors being transmitted us by heredity, the idea has become innate and *a priori* in us.

**V. According to Idealism and Intuitionism,** we get the idea of substance through our internal perception; we perceit the mind as a permanent principle of unity which remains identical with itself in the midst of changes. The mind is the standard or type of substance; we first get the idea of substance only in ourselves in our own self-consciousness and self-activity, and then transfer this notion of substance to the external objects by analogy. "We may take it as established that the self or subject as 'thinking, active principle' or spirit is the source of this concept of substance." *(Ward)*.

## Causality: (A) Its Nature

### I. The Popular and Scientific view

The popular view of a cause is that it is a power or force, which produces or originates the effect. Physical science improves upon this popular view and interprets causality in the light of the doctrine of Conservation of Energy. By Conservation of Energy we mean that the total amount of energy in the universe is constant; it is neither increased nor decreased; but it undergoes modification in different forms. One kind of; energy (*e.g.* heat) can be transformed into another kind (*e.g.* light) without any loss of quantity. Thus the cause (one kind of energy) though qualitatively different from its effect, another kind of energy), is quantitatively equal to it. Thus physical science reduces all causality to transference and transformation or redistribution of energy.

### II. The Empirical account

According to the empiricist, all knowledge is derived from experience. We never apprehend a force or power or energy in our sense-experience; we know nothing of production and necessary connection between cause and effect. All that we experience, merely a succession of phenomena. Now, if in our experience one phenomenon is uniformly or invariably followed by another, the ideas of them become associated in our minds so that whenever, we think of the former, we cannot but expect the latter. Thus causality is nothing more than uniformity of order among events, and the cause is nothing but the invariable antecedent of an event. This is Hume's definition of a cause.

But, in that case, day would be the cause of night, as it is invariably followed by night. So J. S. Mill defined a cause as an unconditional, invariable antecedent of an event.

**Criticism**

(1) A cause cannot be regarded as merely an invariable antecedent of an event. Day is invariably followed by night, spring by summer, winter by spring, but still the invariable antecedents are not regarded as causes. Thus mere invariability of sequence does not constitute our idea of causality.

(2) J S. Mill, in defining a cause as an unconditional, invariable antecedent, *i.e.,* antecedent which, without any further condition is followed invariably by the effect, surreptitiously introduces the notion of efficiency and necessary connection into the idea of causality, inasmuch as if sequence of events would constitute causality, invariability of sequence would be sufficients but unconditionality of an antecedent implies something else than mere succession, it means efficiency and necessary connection. [*Vide* Inductive Logic. ]

(3) The empirical view cannot account for the necessary connection between cause and effect, as experience can never give us necessity.

**III. The nationalist or a priori theory**

Kant denies ontological reality to causality. There is no causality in the reality in itself behind and beyond phenomena. It is real only within the range of experience. It is an *a priori* category of the understanding which the mind evolves from within itself, in order to understand and interpret our experience.

**IV. The Intuitionist view**

According to the Intuitionists (*e.g.* Martineau and others) causality does not consist in mere uniformity of sequence, as empiricism holds, nor is it an *a priori* category of the understanding having no objective counterpart in nature, as Kant supposes. It is a power or force which produces the effect. Thus the intuitionist view agrees with the popular view.

We get the idea of production in our own self-consciousness and self-activity in volition; the only causality and efficiency we directly perceive is our own causality in ourselves, *ie.,* mental causality; then we transfer the idea of causality to nature. What, then, is the nature of causality in nature ? A cause, *e.g., a* produces a particular effect; *viz., b,* and not *c* or *d.* But why should a particular cause produce a particular effect to the exclusion of others ? Origination and direction of energy is made possible only by the mind; the choice between alternative possibilities is the essence of the will. Hence all causality is will-causality. This is the view of Martineau and others. "The idea of cause is regarded as conditional on the subject's own activity." *(Martineau).* "When in ordinary thinking we say A causes this or that in B we project or analogically attribute to A what *we* experience in acting, and' to B what we experience in being acted on." *(Ward).* V. *The Idealistic view:*

The Idealists (*e.g.,* Hegel and his followers), too, hold that all causality is will-causality. There are incessant changes in nature. But why should things change at all ? It cannot be a matter of chance or blind necessity. There must be a reason for it. All change is directed towards an end or purpose, and consists in the struggle towards a better state. Causality in nature is the putting forth of energy for the overcoming of defects in order to realize an end or purpose; a future end can realize itself in the present only as an idea. Hence "all energy of change is mental energy, or will-force realizing idea," and all causality is will-causality.

Thus, according to Hegel, causality is not only a category of the human mind, but also a category or framework of reality, which is the objective expression of the Absolute.

### (B) The Origin of the Idea of Causality

### I. Popular and Realistic view:

According to Realism, we get the idea of causality through external and internal perception. We can see that motion passes over from one thing into another, in the external world and this is causality. We get the idea of mental causality in volition and attention.

### II. The Empiricist view

According to Empiricism and Sensationism, we get the idea of causality from sense-experience. We find in our experience that one event is always followed by another event. When we observe this sequence repeatedly in our experience, these ideas are closely associated in our minds, so that whenever we observe the antecedent we expect the consequent to follow. This habit of expectation grows with the repetition of experience, due to association of ideas. There is no necessary connection between cause and effect, but only a subjective bond of association between the ideas of the invariable antecedent and the invariable consequent. Thus our idea of causality is derived by generalization from particular cases of invariable sequence.

#### Criticism

(i) The idea of causality is a universal and necessary condition of thought. So it cannot be derived from sense-experience, as experience can never give us universal and necessary knowledge.

(ii) The idea of causality is supposed to be derived by induction or generalization from particular cases of invariable succession. But induction itself is based upon the Law of Causality; hence it is arguing in a circle to derive causation from induction and induction from causation.

### III. Evolutional Empiricism

According to Herbert Spencer and others, the idea of

causality was derived from experience by our ancestors, but has been transmitted to us by heredity and has become innate and instinc tive in us. The idea of causality was *a posteriori in our* ancestral experience. but is a priori in us.

**IV. The nationalist or a priori view**

Kant who holds the succession theory of causation, however, says that it is a necessary truth that events must have a regular, uniform, and irreversible order so that one antecedent event must always be followed by the same consequent event. This is not a mere probable inference from past experience as described by Hume, but a necessary truth, otherwise the world as a system of events would become impossible.

Hence, according to Kant, we cannot derive the idea of causality from experience as experience presuppose it. the idea of causality is an *a priori* notion or categori of the under standing which is presupposed in our experience.

**V. The Intuitionist and Idealistic view**

According to Hegel, causality is not only a necessary form of thought, as Kant holds, but also a form of the reality, as thought and reality are at bottom identical. According to Martineau and others, we derive the idea of causality from our own self-consciousnes and self-activity in volition, and then transfer the idea of causality to physical events by analogy. Thus the notion of causality is derived from our own self. This is the view of the Intuitionist and the Idealist both.

## UNIVERSITY QUESTIONS

1. What is space ? (1909).
2. Give a full analysis of the notion of Substance and explain its relation to quality. (1911).
3. Give a philosophic explanation of the idea of Substance. (1912).
4. What do you consider to be the most adequate meaning of term Substance ? (1915). (1945).

5. What is meant by Causation ? On what does the possibility of defining it depend ? (1914).
6. Explain the meaning of Cause and Causality in nature, also that of Energy and Conservation of Energy, and the rela-tion between Energy and Causality. (1918).
7. How does mental causation differ from physical causa-tion ? Explain. (1912).
8. What do you consider to be the true nature of space and time? (1919).

   Clearly explain the content and origin of any one of tha following ideas: to Space, (b) Time, (c) Substance. (1920). (1945).
10. Explain the meaning of Categories in the theory of knowledge. If they are subjective, how can they form elements in the knowledge of reality ? (1913 Hon,)
11. Analyse the conception of *Cause* as employed by modern science, and discuss the sufficiency of causal explanation in an explanation of reality. (1913 Hon.)
12. State and examine Mill's theory of causation.(1915 Hon.)
13. Explain fully the content and origin of the idea of Time, and explain and examine the theory which makes Time 'subjective' and the theory which makes it to be 'objective', showing the bearing of each on the theory of the world. (1918 Hon.)
14. Explain fully the meaning of substance (in Philosophy) and the origin of the idea of substance; and explain the relation of Attribute to Substance. (1916 Hon.)
15. Discuss the problem of Causality in its popular, scientific, and philosophical sense. (1921).
16. State your own view with regard to the nature of Causality and state a theory different from your own, with criticism. (1921).
17. Analyse the idea of Causality, and discuss the question

whether the belief in the law of Causality is of *a posteriori* or *a priori* origin. (1923).

18. What, in Philosophy, is meant by Substance ? Explain how the idea of Substance is obtained. Illustrate your meaning by examples. (1925).
19. Show how you acquire the ideas of space, motion, and position in space, illustrating your meaning by examples. (1927)
20. What do you consider to be the true nature of space and time ? (1928).
21. Consider fully the nature of Causality. (1929).
22. What is the true meaning of Space and Time ? How do we get these ideas ? (1930).
23. What do you understand by a Category of Knowledge ? Explain fully the nature of Causality as a Category. (1931).
24. What do you understand by 'Causality' as a Category of Knowledge ? What is its real nature as an objective fact ? (1933). (1947).
25. Compare Hume's theory of Causality with Kant's. (1934).
26. Analyse the idea of Causality. Examine the treatment of the Category of Causality by Hume and Kant respectively. (1935).
27. Discuss fully Hume's theory of Causation, and state your own view with regard to the nature of Causality. (1936).
28. Is Space objectively real ? (1946).

## III

## POLARITY OF KNOWLEDGE

Our experience involves, besides the categories, several pairs of complementary ideas, each of which suggests the other by dialectic necessity. Such dialectic contraries are the following:

### Subject, Object, and the Absolute

Knowledge always implies the distinction between the

subject and the object, the knower and the known, the self and the not-self. There can be no knowledge without a subject or thinking mind knows, and an object that is known. This correlativity of subject and object is not only a logical necessity of thought, but also an ontological one. In other words, we can not only conceive of an object without conceiving it as being thought by subject or mind, and we can not only conceive of a subject or mind without conceiving it as thinking an object, but also no object can exist without being thought by some mind and no subject can exist without thinking an object. The very exis tence of the object depends upon the existence of the subject and vice *versa*.

The duality but not the dualism of subject and object is the indispensable presupposition and necessary condition of all knowledge. Hence recognizing that the object exists in distinction from and relation to the subject, we cannot reduce the subject or mind to the object or a phase of matter, as materialism does. And recognizing that the subject exists as only it returns upon itself from and realizes itself in the object, we cannot reduce the object to a mere phase in the life of the subject, *i. e.,* to state of the mind, as subjective idealism does. But recognizing them in their true light, as invisible and yet necessarily opposed, as incapable of identification and yet necessarily related, the subject and the object, the self and the not-self, mind and matter, must be regarded as correlative (but not identical). moments in the life of a higher principle, viz., the Absolute Spirit which manifests itself as subjects or finite minds, on the one hand, or objects or material things, on the other, and overcomes and transcends the opposition and comprehends them in its all-embracing unity of self-consciousness. *(Caird)*. The ultimate principle is neither a mere subject apart from the object, (subjective idealism) nor a mere object apart from the subject (realism), but Subject-Object or the Absolute Spirit which bifurcates itself into the subject and the object and comprehends them in its unity of self-conseiousness in which thought and reality are identical (*i. e.* absolutely correlative).

"The ultimate basis of consciousness,", observes John Caird, "is not the consciousness of self, for the individual's consciousness of self would have no meaning, if it did not rest on a more universal consciousness which lies beneath it. The consciousness of self is given only in relation to the consciousness of that which is not self. We cannot separate, in any act of thought, the two factors or elements—the object perceived or thought of, and the subject or mind which thinks it. We may distinguish, but we cannot divide these two, or for a moment conceive an object or thing in itself apart from a thinking subject, or again the latter in abstraction from object thought of. Subject and object are correlative as indivisible as the notions of outward and inward, motion and rest, parent and child etc. But the very fact that the two elements are inseparably related proves and rests on the consciousness that there is a unity which lies beyond the distinc-tion. In relating my individual self to an outward object, I at the same time necessarily presume that the two, I and the object, are not distinguishable as terms in the relation, but that there is a wider unity in which they are both alike embraced. In other words, the distinction between self and not-self, between the individual mind and the world of outward objects, is a distinction which thought, by the very fact that it can make it; shows that it can transcend, and has already virtually transcended. The consciousness which apprehends both self and its object cannot be confined only to one side of the contrast. When, we think, we rise above our individual existence as limited by the outward world, to an existence which is not so limited, which comprehends both all individual selves and the world, we do not think, that is, as individual beings, but as passing over to and sharing in a universal thought or reason We cannot think, save on the presupposition of a thought or consciousness which is the unity of thought and being, or on which all individual thought and existence rest."

**Phenomenon and Noumenon**

A Phenomenon means an appearance or a manifestation.

We know things through the medium of our senses. We cannot know things, in their true nature as they are in themselves, but only as they appear to our senses only, as they produce feelings and sensations in our minds. Likewise we cannot know our own self as it is in itself, but only as it appears to us in feelings and ideas. The feelings and sensations, thus, may be regarded as phenomena in which both mind and matter manifest themselves to us.

But appearance implies something which appears or manifests itself; a phenomenon implies its correlative noumenon. By noumena we mean things-in-themselves behind and beyond their appearances to us. Noumena are objects of *nous* or reason. (Plato and others).

Phenomena and noumena are correlative to each other; they are the outer and the inner aspects of the concrete reality. Phenomena and noumena, though distinct from each other, are not opposed to each other; they are two correlative aspects of the concrete reality. The reality viewed in itself is a noumenon and viewed in relation to us, a phenomenon. Hence phenomena and noumena must not be regarded as so separate from each other, that the one can be known without the other. Sceptics, agnostics and phenomenalists (Hume, Herbert Spencer, Kant etc.) commit a mistake in supposing that we can know only sensations and phenomena, but not anything beyond sensations and phenomena, because whenever we know an appearance or manifestation (phenomenon), we also know the essence (noumenon) through this manifestation. Phenomena and noumena, thus, are meaningless abstractions apart from each other. Pringle Pattison rightly says: "The Phenomenon *is* the noumenon so far as it has manifested itself."

## The Relative and the Absolute and the Conditioned and the Unconditioned: Agnosticism

Our knowledge of the world implies other correlative and complementary ideas such those of the Relative and the Absolute, the Conditioned and the Unconditioned etc. We find in our experience that everything in the world depends for its existence and continuance upon other things external to it, and thus upon conditions lying outside and beyond it. As for example, a plant depends upon, the soil, water, air etc. in the environment; we depend for our existence and continuance upon our parents, friends and relations *(i. e.* the social environment) and upon the air, water, light, food etc. of the external world (physical environment). Thus all the objects of the world depend for their existence upon certain conditions and relations, and are consequently called the conditioned and the relative.

But when we think of things as conditioned and relative, this thought forces upon us, by dialectic necessity as its complementary any correlative, the idea of the unconditioned and the absolute. What, then, is the nature of the Unconditioned and the Absolute ?

**The nature of the Unconditioned and the Absolute**

Hamilton, Mansel and others regard the Unconditioned and the Absolute as the opposite of the Conditioned and the Relative, which transcends all conditions and relations and hence is above and beyond the world of conditions and related things. The Absolute means a self-existent and self-complete reality which has no relation to anything without or within itself. It has no relation to anything at all, within or without it, and is conditioned by nothing without it, but it is above all conditions.

Hamilton holds that the Absolute is the Unconditioned and. the negation of all conditions. But to think is to condition; therefore, to think the Absolute is to condition the Unconditioned which is self-contradictory. "Thought is possible only as the relation of the thing thought of to the thinker, and an object of thought can only be known or enter into consciousness, in relation to the thinking subject. All human knowledge therefore is necessarily relative. The Absolute we can never know." *(Introduction to Philosophy of Religion,* p. 13)

Mansel also holds that the Absolute is beyond all condition; and limits. But to think is to distinguish, and to distinguish is to limit. We can know a chair because we distinguish it from a table and other things which limit it. But the Absolute is not limited by anything other than itself. Therefore the Absolute cannot be thought of. It is unknown and unknowable. Herbert Spencer also holds the same view.

**Criticism of Agnosticism**

Hamilton, Mansel and Herbert Spencer conceive the Absolute as unrelated to thought or consciousness, and then charges thought with inability to comprehend the Absolute. In fact, Thought and Being are ultimately identical. Knowing and Being are inseparably related to each other. When we segregate being from knowing, reality from thought, what remains is not an unknowable something or Absolute, but an utter non-entity. "The endeavour to conceive of an Absolute being or reality existing apart by itself and having no relation to thought is the quest after a chimera." *(Ibid,* p. 21.) "The Absolute is not simply the negation of thought, but rather that which comprehends all finite things, and thoughts; only because it is itself the Unity of Thought and Being." (*Ibid*. p. 23.) It is the very nature of the Absolute to realize itself, the thought or self-consciousness of finite intelligence. And it the very nature of the finite spirit to find the highest and fullest ralization of its own freedom and life in the Absolute.

If the Absolute is beyond the world of conditioned and related things, it cannot be regarded as the ground and cause of the finite and limited world. In this way the world cannot be explained. So it must be regarded as a necessary factor in the life of the Absolute, its objective expression and manifestation. The Absolute, thus, does not wholly transcend the world of finite and conditioned things, but is immanent in it as its ground and origin, and at the same time transcends it, as it is never fully revealed and exhausted in the world of finite things. The Absolute, or the Unconditioned, thus, is not a reality which is beyond all conditions, but it is the self-conditioned reality comprehending all conditions and relations within itself.

Agnostics hold that we know only phenomena or appearances, but not things-in-themselves or noumena. Kant is the exponent of this view. But to hold that we know only the phenomena and not the noumena is self-contradictory. Whenever we know phenomena as phenomena, we tacitly know something about the noumena; if we do not know anything about the noumena, how can we assert that wa cannot know them ? "The assertion that man's knowledge is limited to the finite and relative would have no meaning save by a tacit reference to the infinite and absolute object to which his knowledge does not extend. When we say that a thing is only a phenomenon or appearance, a quality or attribute, we of course imply that there is something which is not mere appearance but reality, not a mere quality but a substance, with whose deeper nature we place the former contrast. In order to pronounce that we know only phenomena must needs be aware that there must be something other phenomena, we must know at least of the existence of things-in-themselves, realities lying beyond phenomena, from the knowledge of "which, in the full sense of the word, our intelligence is debarred. If we know no other than finite and phenomenal existence, then we should never know or be able to characterise them as finite and phenomenal. To pronounce, in short, that our knowledge is, in any sense, limited, we must have access to some standard to which that limited knowledge is referred, we must be aware, at least, of the existence of a something beyond the limit, which is to our intelligence gence inaccessible." (John Caird: *Introduction to the Philosophy of Religion,* pp. 14-15.)

### The Finite and the Infinite

#### (a) The Nature of the Infinite

The ideas of the finite and the infinite correspond closely to those of the relative and the absolute, the conditioned and the unconditioned, being the same object of thought regarded from different points of view. There are two questions as regards the finite and the infinite: (l) a psychological one as to how we get the idea of the infinite, and (2) an ontological one as to the nature of the infinite.

**1. The negative conception**

The idea of the Infinite is merely a negative idea, and the infinite is supposed to be the negative of the finite.

According to Locke, the idea of the infinite is merely a negative idea which is derived by negation of the finite. According to Locke, experience is the only source of knowledge; there is to innate idea of the infinite, as Descartes supposed. Experience cannot give us anything that is really infinite. In our experience, we-perceive things and events limited in space and time. We can never think of space beyond which there is and space; we cannot think of any time beyond which there is no time. This inability of the mind to conceive any limit to space and time gives rise to the negative idea of the infinite. The infinite, thus, is the negative of the finite, *i.e*,. the not-finite.

A cording to Hamilton and Mansel, the ideas of the infinite and the absolute are mere terms indicating the negation or absence of the conditions and limitations under which thought is possible. To think is to condition and limit; so to think the infinite or the unlimited is impossible. The infinite cannot be known through reason, but can be known through faith or belief.

But besides reason, Hamilton recognizes another source of knowledge under the name of belief. He says, "The sphere of our belief is much more extensive than the sphere of our knowledge; and therefore when I deny that the Infinite can be known by us, I am far from denying that it is, must, and ought to be believed by us. Belief is ultimate, knowledge only derivative; knowledge itself finally rests on belief: natural beliefs are the sole warrant for all our knowledge. And as we have beliefs which tell us that we know, and without which we could not be assured of the truth of our knowledge, so we have and are warranted in having, beliefs beyond our knowledge, belief respecting the Unconditioned."

According to Max Muller also, the idea of the infinite is a negative one and the infinite is the opposite counterpart of the finite *i. e.,* the not-finite. "Limitation and finitude always implies a something beyond. Beyond every limit we must always take it for granted that there is something else. The reason why we cannot conceive an absolute limit is because we never perceive an absolute limit or, in other words, because in Perceiving the finite we always perceive that beyond the finite, that is, the Infinite." Thus Max Muller conceives the Infinite as something beyond the finite or the not-finite.

**Criticism of the negative view**

If the infinite is beyond the finite, it is limited by the finite and thus becomes itself finite. If the infinite is beyond the finite it cannot be the origin, ground and explanation of the finite, and the relation between them is an external and mechanical one. we suppose that the infinite though beyond the finite is not limited by it, then the finite too is not limited by anything and becomes itself infinite.

The infinite of Locke, Hamilton and Max Muller is not truly the Infinite, but only the Indefinite, a bare abstraction of thought derived by the negation of all limits or absence of the conditions of thought. The true Infinite is not beyond and opposed to the finite, but is the concrete unity which comprehends both the finite and the not-finite or the indefinite and reconciles them.

The idea of the infinite cannot be a negative idea derived by the negation of the finite. It is the most positive conception implied in and presupposed by our knowlege of the finite as such. We cannot know the finite things as finite unless we have a positive though implicit idea of the infinite. The infinite thus is the *prius* of the finite; the finite are the limitations of the infinite. The infinite is not the negation of the finite.

**II. The positive conception**

Descartes and Spinoza hold that we have an innate idea of the Infinite in our minds, which is not a negative idea. The Infinite is the positive ground and explanation of all finite things and beings.

Herbert Spencer holds that the idea of the Infinite is a positive one (Cf. Descartes and Spinoza), which is an indispensable presupposition of our idea of the finite as such. The Infinite is not a mere negation of the finite, as Locke, Max Muller and Hamiltion supposed, but is the affirmative or positive basis of the finite of which we know that it is in the form of a vague and *indefinite* consciousness, but do not know what it is. Thus Herbert Spencer holds the positive view of the Infinite but denies definite knowledge of it.

We may compare the view of Herbert Spencer with that of Max Muller. "There is a general basis of agreement between them and also a difference of considerable importance. Max Muller and Spencer agree in conceiving the infinite as the correlate and counterpart of the finite. But the former thinks of it as a Beyond, to which the mind always reaches out from the limits of the finite, while the latter thinks of it as the pre-supposition from which all the determinations of the finite start. To the former the infinite is the *posterius* of all positive knowledge, like the indeterminate space which stretches beyond every limit. To the latter it is the *prius* of all positive knowledge, like the space which is presupposed in the definition of spatial figures. To the former the infinite is never given except as the negation of every thing that is positively known. To the latter it is always given in a primary positive consciousness which we must have before we can know anything else. The former takes his stand on the finite as the affirmatively determined reality which, however, in its limited character, always implies something beyond that we cannot so determine, while the latter takes his stand on the infinite as the affirmative basis of all our knowledge, knowledge that is conceived as the process of limiting the infinite by negatives."

(Edward Caird: *The Evolution of Religion, Vol. I,* Lecture IV.)-"An abstract, self-referent Infinite", as Principal Caird remarks, "must, equally with an abstract, self-referent Finite, " yield to another and higher idea. The Infinite of religion cannot be a mere self-identical Being, but one which contains, in its very nature, organic relation to the Finite, or rather, it is that organic whole which is the unity of the Infinite and Finite. In other words, an Infinite which does not extinguish the Finite as its bare contradictory or negation, must contain in itself the determination of the Finite."

(*Introduction to the Philosaphy of Religion,* P. 238.) According to Hegel, the true Infinite is not merely the negative of the finite (as Locke, Hamilton and Max Muller suppose), but the positive basis or ground of the fiinite. It is not merely an indeterminate background of the finite as Spencer holds, but it is a self-determining principle which manifests itself in all the determinations of the finite, it is an inexhaustible power or energy which realizes its infinite potentialities in the finite objects and minds, but is never exhausted in them infinite, thus, does not exclude the finite, but includes and explains it; the infinite is expressed in the finite, which is a necessary factor in the life of the infinite. The infinite without the finite would be an abstract power and unrealized potentiality not a rich and concrete reality.

**The origin of the idea of the Infinite**

**I. The negative view**

According to Locke and Max Muller, we get the negative idea of the infinite by thinking away all limits to space and time.

According to Hamilton and Mansel, the negative idea of infinite is obtained by the negation or absence of all condition of thought.

**II. The positive view**

According to Descartes and others, the idea of the infinite

is a positive one, and it is innate in the mind, prior to all experience."

According to Herbert Spencer, the idea of the infinite is a positive one, and we have a vague and indefinite consciousness of the infinite as the positive, but indeterminate background of our consciousness of the finite as such.

According to Hegel, the thought of the finite as such forces upon us, by dialectic necessity, the definite (but not complete) thought of the infinite, which is a positive conception and is supposed in our consciousness of the finite.

**(B) Consciousness or Knowledge of the Unconditioned or the Absolute and the Infinite.**

**I. Agnostic view**

If the Unconditioned or the Absolute excludes all conditions and relations, and if the Infinite is beyond the finite, then the Absolute and Infinite is unknown and unknowable. This is the view of Agnostics, Hamilton, Mansel and their followers. They advance the following arguments on behalf of their doctrine:

Firstly, to know an object, we must distinguish it from other objects external to it, by which it is conditioned and limited. But there is no other object than the Absolute and Infinite; it is not limited and conditioned by any other object. Hence it is impossible for us to know the Absolute and Infinite.

Secondly, we cannot know an object unless we assimilate it to other like objects. Just as we cannot know an object, unless we distinguish it from other disparate objects, so we cannot know it, unless we assimilate it to other similar objects. Assimilation is as much a condition of knowledge as discrimination. But there is not more than one Absolute and Infinite; so it cannot be known.

Thirdly, knowledge is nothing but a function of life, and life is nothing but the adjustment of the inner relations to the outer relations, the adaptation of the organism to the environment. Consciousness is evolved as a matter of necessity for the better adjustment of the organic forces to the outer forces of nature. But as there can be no adaptation of the psycho-physical organism to the Absolute and Infinite, there can be no consciousness of it. *(Herbert Spencer).*

**Criticism of Agnosticism**

Firstly, distinction or discrimination is, no doubt, an indispensable condition of knowledge. Though there is no other object *external* to the Absolute and Infinite, there are many finite objects and selves *within* the Absolute and Infinite. Hence though we cannot distinguish the Infinite from any other object *outside* it, because there is no such object, we can distinguish the Infinite from other finite objects and minds *within* the Infinite, and thus we can have a consciousness of the Infinite.

Secondly, though there is not more than one Infinite, so that there may be assimilation of the one to the other or others, and though the infinite is one and unique, it can be known through reason by the dialectic necessity of thought, not as the opposite counterpart of the finite, but as the origin, ground and explanation of the finite.

Thirdly, that consciousness is a function of life, which is evolved as a matter of necessity for the better adaptation of the organism to the environment may be regarded as a psychological and biological truth; but it can never be regarded as a philosophical truth. So the third argument of the agnostic is groundless.

(See also the criticism of Relativity of Knowledge. Ch. I,)

**UNIVERSITY QUESTIONS**

1. What is your idea of the Infinite ? Can you explain how you get that idea and what place it occupies in your views about Nature and Mind ? (1910).
2. Is the world finite or infinite ? How do we get our idea of the Infinite and what is the proper significance of the idea ? (1911). ]

3. Explain the meanings of, and difference between ditioned and Unconditioned in philosophy, On what grounds me say that it is impossible to know anything about what is unconditioned ? Give your own opinion with reasons. (1918).
4. Discuss the meaning and mutual relation of the terms Infinite, Absolute, Unconditioned. (1913 Hon.)
5. Analyse the conceptions of the Finite and the Infinite. Does the former imply the latter and *vice versa* ? Is the Infinite anything more than the Indefinite ? (1915 Hon.)
6. Unconditioned and Conditioned, Absolute and Relative: explain precisely the contents of these ideas and their relations to each other. What arguments can be advanced against the possibility of knowing the Unconditioned ? Examine these arguments, and sketch briefly the history of the question. (1916 Hon.)
7. Explain what is meant by infinite and finite, and how we acquire the idea of infinity, showing whether it is of *a priori* or *a posteriori* origin. (1927).
8. What is meant in Philosophy by the Relative and the Absolute ? *World, Soul, God:* are these relative or absolute ? Give your reason in each case. (1922).
9. What do you understand by the term Absolute ? What are the principal forms of Absolutism ? (1924).
10. Explain what is meant by infinite and finite, and how you acquire the idea of infinity, showing whether it is of *a priori or a posteriori* origin. (1927).

    State precisely the significance of the Relative and the Absolute as evolved by the dialectic necessity of knowledge. How does this analysis stand to the doctrine of Relativity of ? (1932),

## CHAPTER V

# PHILOSOPHY OF NATURE OR THE WORLD IN GENERAL

### Introduction

Epistemology is a preliminary to philosophy. Unless we are sure of our capacity of knowing the reality, we cannot enter on the discussion of the nature of reality. Now, we have learned the nature, origin, conditions and limits of knowledge. We have refuted the agnostic and sceptic view that the reality can never be known. Now, the question is: What is the nature of the reality that is known ? The reality may be studied in its three aspects, Nature God. We reserve our investigation of the nature of the Soul and God. In this chapter we propose to discuss the nature matter and life which are found in the world. We see many material objects arounds us. We must try to investigate the ultimate nature of *matter* which is the stuff of these material objects. We see also many animate objects in the world, *viz.*, plants and animals. We must try to understand the ultimate nature of *life* which vitalises these living objects. The problems of matter and the problems of life are the general: problems of the Philosophy of Nature.

## I

## THE PROBLEM OF MATTER AND MOTION

### The Nature of Matter: Its Primary and Secondary Qualities:

The objects of the world are mainly divisible into two classes, *viz.*, mental and material. The essential attribute of mind is thought or consciousness' Matter exists in space whereas mind is unextended. Matter is unconscious, whereas mind is conscious. What then is matter ? We consider the substance to be material, which has the attribute of filling space and resisting motion through space, –*i. e.,* which has the attributes of impenetrability and inertia and other attributes which rise out of these as consequences.

Thus matter has *(a)* for its primary qualities, the attribute of filling a certain extent of space, *i. e.,* extension, the attribute of excluding other bodies from the space it occupies, *i.* e., impenetrability or inertia, and the attribute of shifting from one position to another, or mobility. When it is compound or made up of many atoms, it manifests also (b) some secondary qualities such as colour, sound, smell, temperature which arise from the different positions, arrangements and motions of its constituent atoms and molecules. We have already discussed the question whether primary and secondary qualities are equally real or not.

Thus, the secondary qualities of matter are regarded by physical science as derivatives of its primary qualities, *viz.,* impenetrability and mobility, inertia and motion.

But we may go further than this, and hold that the above two primary qualities of matter, *viz.,* inertia and motion are only two different modes of one more ultimate quality, *viz.,* energy or power which manifests itself as inertia or fixed energy, and motion or free energy.

Thus, either we may regard inertia and motion as quite different from and foreign to each other, or we may regard them as different modes of one ultimate energy. The first view is entertained by the atomists, and the second, by the advocates of energetics. Let us consider these two conceptions of matter more elaborately.

**Theories of Matter: (A) Atomic Theory**

According to Atomism, material bodies are composed of

atoms or minutest particles of matter which can no further be divided into smaller fragments. These atoms are absolutely indivisible particles of matter without any structural complexity. They are devoid of any inherent force or motion; they are altogether passive and inert. They are without any pores, and consequently, they are absolutely incompressible and impenetrable. The essential property of these atoms is inertia or impenetrability. Though they have no intra-atomic motion, or motion inherent in them, they have the power of shifting from one position to another in space, when motion is put into them from the outside. Thus though there is no intra-atomic motion, there is extratomic motion. These atoms are devoid of secondary qualities, *viz.*, colour, sound, smell, taste, and temperature which arise out of the different positions, arrangements and motions of the constituent atoms of material bodies. The world is nothing but a heap of atoms in their various combinations and collocations.

**Criticism of the atomic theory of matter**

This theory makes matter altogether passive and inert and consequently, it cannot explain, in any way, active energy or motion. Atoms have no inherent motion in themselves; it will have to be put into them from the outside. Hence, many scientists regard an atom not as an inert particle of space-filling substance, but as a mode of energy. (See the Dynamic theories of matter below.)

The atomic theory is purely an abstract, and hence an utterly inadequate theory of matter. As triangles and circles are abstract concepts of Geometry, and what are real are triangular and circular things, so atoms are abstract theoretical concepts af Science; what are real are not atoms, but atomic things. Thus the atomic theory can neither be an adequate description nor an explanation of the concrete world.

The atomic theory seeks to derive the secondary qualities of colour, small, sound and temparature from the different configurations of the primary qualities, *viz.*. shape, size and so on. But qualities can never be derived from quantities. The qualities of things can never be the mere arithmetical sum-total of quantitative characteristics or atomic properties.

**(B) Dynamic theories of matter**

The difficulties mentioned above led to the dynamic theories of matter, which regard unextended atoms not as absolutely hard and inert bits-of matter, but as unextended centres of force or energy, and thus obviate the difficulties of the dualism of matter and motion by the monism of energy.

(1) Boscovitch and Faraday hold that the ultimate units of matter are not bits of inert and impenetrable substance, as the atomists suppose, but mare centres of force or unextended mathematical points from which attractive and repellent forces operate according to fixed laws through an all-pervading ethereal fluid.

According to this theory, the so-called atoms are not absolutely hard and unalterable, but are centres of force and as such elastic and compressible. The elasticity thus ascribed to atoms can, to a certain extent, account for the motion and interaction of things.

(2) Sir William Thomson (Lord Kelvin) holds that atoms are mere vortex rings or whirlpools in an all but perfect fluid called ether which is absolutely frictionless and unresisting without any inertia. A vortex in an all but perfect fluid might by rapidity of revolution, possess such self-sufficiency and durability as to be impenetrable and indestructible as an atom. Helmholtz mathematically investigated the properties of such vortex-rings and sought to prove the tenability of Lord Kelvin's hypothesis.

(3) Ostwald and many others hold that the so-called atotm is immensely more complex than Faraday's centres of force or Kelvin's votex-rings; it is a magazine of forces in a state of equilibrium of infinite complexity and capable of being liberated and of passing over into free force of motion. An atom, thus, is

an infinitely complex system or reservoir of equilibrated forces or forces in equipoise. (Stephen: *Problems* of *Metaphysics),*

(4) Bohr holds that an atom is dynamic, the ultimate elements of which are electrical charges. An atom is composed of the *proton,* a positive charge, and the *electron,* a negative charge. "Each atom has a positive nucleus, encircled by one or more negative electrons." An atom is like a planetary system. Its nucleus corresponds to the sun. The electrons correspond to the planets.

Thus, the advocates of the dynamic theories of matter, *e. g.,* Faraday, Kelvin, Ostwald and others resolve matter into energy The essential qualities of matter are resistance or impenetrability and mobility or capacity of motion. These attributes of, impenetrability and mobility are nothing but different modes of one ultimate substance, *viz.,* energy. Thus impenetrability is the energy with which a material object resists other things and excludes them from its own portion of space; and motion is the energy with which a material object changes its position in space and in doing so dislodges other things from their positions in space. Thus there are two modes of energy, fixed energy or matter, and free energy or energy as motion.

**(a) Fixed energy or energy as matter** A part of the world's energy is stored up in a state of fixed equilibrium which constitutes the essence of matter and manifests itself in inertia and impenetrability.

**(b) Free or liberated energy or energy as motion** A part of the world's energy is still free and acts upon atoms from the outside and impels them from place to place, constituting what we call moving force and is manifested either in actual motion (kinetic energy) or tendency to motion (potential energy).

**Conservation of Mass and Motion**

Energy manifests itself in the physical world in two ways, as

(i) fixed or stored energy or the equilibrated forces which constitute elements of matter, and as (ii) motion and tendency to motion. Thus, by conservation of energy we mean conservation of mass and motion, in other words, the indestructibility of matter and motion.

**(a) Conservation of Mass or Indestructibility of Matter**

By the conservation of mass we mean that the total amount of mass or quantity of matter in the world is constant, *i, e.,* can neither be increased nor decreased. A material body may dis-appear in one form and reappear in another, but its quantity can never be changed. If we burn up a candle in a closed jar. it will disappear as such but will re-appear in another form. Carbon and hydrogen are the main constituents of a candle. When we burn it, carbon is oxidised by the air and is converted into carbon-dioxide, and hydrogen, with the oxygen of the air, forms water, the quantity remaining the same.

In the first place, the doctrine of the conservation of mass cannot be proved experimentally. Experiment requires a standard of measurement, and the standard, in order to be trustworthy, must be uniform and invariable. But to have a uniform standard we must assume the conservation of mass. For all the things of the world together with our standard of measurements may change in mass without at all interfering with the result of our experiment. Hence, Herbert Spencer takes it to be an *a priori* principle.

Secondly, it is only a relative, not an absolute doctrine. We cannot say that the mass' of any object in the universe shall remain absolutely constant apart from its relation to other objects. The mass of an object will remain constant only relatively to the masses of other objects.

Thirdly, the principle of the conservation of mass cannot apply to the whole of the universe, but only to the particular objects of the universe. The so-called mass or matter is fixed or stored up energy. Some portion of this fixed energy or equilibrated forces may be liberated and pass over into free energy or energy of motion, and thus decrease the total quantity of matter in the universe. Conversely, some portion of free energy may be fixed and sealed up in the form of atoms and thus increase the total amount of matter in the world. In other words, as intra-atomic energy may pass over into extra-atomic energy, and *vice versa,* the total amount of matter in the universe can never remain constant.

### (b) Conservation of Motion (generally called Conservation of Energy)

By this doctrine we mean that the total quantity of motion in the universe is constant, it is neither increased nor decreased. But one kind of motion may be converted or transformed into. another kind without any increase or loss of quantity. Thus, motion, heat, light, magnetism, electricity, chemical affinity may pass one over into the other; all available energy may pass into potential energy; but during the transformation, no quantity of energy is absolutely lost.

By the doctrine of Conservation of Energy we mean the conservation of matter and motion both. But generally we mean by it conservation of free energy or motion.

### Criticism of the doctrine of Conservation of Energy

In the first place, the doctrine of conservation of energy cannot explain the qualitative changes of energy. It simply asserts that one kind of energy may be transformed into another, but its quantity remains the same. But it cannot say why and how one kind of energy is converted into another.

In the second place, the doctrine of conservation of energy is not an absolute doctrine. It simply asserts that different forms of energy are converted into one another without any increase or loss of quantity, but it cannot positively assert that the total amount of energy in the universe is constant, *i. e.,* is neither increased nor decreased. None can weigh the whole amount of energy in the universe. So we should better call this doctrine the correlation of forces, than the conservation of energy.

In the third place, the doctrine involves the metaphysical

difficulty of the transference of motion or passing over of energy from one thing to another. Suppose A strikes against B and communicates its motion to B, *i.e.,* motion passes from A to B. In what condition does the motion exist in its passage from A to B ? Let M stand for motion; M is detached from A and then is attached to B. If, in its transition, it exists in itself without any support, it is a non-entity, because there can be no motion without mass, as there can be no length without breadth in a concrete object. Then, if one body cannot communicate its motion to another body from a distance, one must come into contact with the other. There are similar difficulties in the contact of one thing with another. Hence, the doctrine of conservation of energy may be better called the doctrine of correlation of forces, which maintains that all the things in the are so correlated and co-ordinated as factors of one system, that the increase of activity in one thing will give rise to a corresponding diminution of activity in another, so that no transference of motion is needed from one thing to another.

## II

## THE PROBLEM OF LIFE

The material world is a world of *mechanism* with no power of self-preservation and self-development. But the world of living beings is a world of *organisms* which are self-sustaining and self-regulating entities. Hence we must distinguish a mechanism from an organism.

### The Nature of a Machine or Mechanism

A machine or a mechanical system is an aggregate of material parts, so adjusted to one another in shape, size and position as to produce through their interaction and co-operation, one joint result setting something else in motion.

The characteristics of a mechanism are the following:

1) A machine is an aggregate of parts externally fitted adapted to one another, having no internal reciprocal influence upon one another.

2) (Thus, a machine is an artificial whole, which has no

central power of self-preservation and self-evolution; it has no internal unifying and self-regulating principle. In it the whole does not precede and vitalize the parts, but the parts preca the whole.

3) Consequently, a machine is worked and regulated not by itself but by an external agent -which puts motion into it from the outside end sets it in motion.

4) A machine, thus, does not serve its own end; it has no end of its own; it is worked by an external agent and realizes an end external or foreign to itself.

**The Nature of an Organism**

A living organism is not a mere aggregate or a mechanical combination of parts externally adapted to one another to subserve an end foreign to it, but it is a real and systematic unity of parts or organs which are evolved and sustained, and so adapted to one another by a central unifying and regulating power as to co-operate as factors of this higher unity and realize a common end which is immanent in it.

The characteristics of an organism are the following:

"The most striking characteristics of living things can best be told by aid of the word 'self: they are self-building, self-repairing, self-regulating, self-reproducing." (Hocking: *Types of Philosophy,* p. 52.)

In an organism, the parts are not externally fitted to one another, as in a mechanism, but are evolved by a central organising power from within and thus are internally adapted to one another.

"In all organisms," says John Caird, "there is involved the new conception of *systematic unity.* With certain apparent exceptions, the unities of the inorganic world – those unities which are produced by mechanical and chemical forces – are either mere unities of aggregation, in which the parts are related to each other only externally, and the whole is indifferent to the parts; or unities in which the whole is produced by the annulling of the individual existence of the parts or elements, of which it is composed. The parts of a stone are only repetitions of each other, and are accidentally combined in a mass which is held together by external or mechanical force.

If any part is struck off, the diminished mass remains a unity as complete as the original whole. But a living organism is not a mere aggregation of independent parts, but a systematic unity of members, each of which has its individual place and function.

If any one member be severed from such a system, both the whole and the lopped-off member cease to be unities and become fragments; they descent into the lower stage where there is no unity but that of mechanical aggregation. The totality here is something more than the sum of its parts; there are infused into the parts the invisible elements of order, proportion, diversity of form, distribution of function according to a general idea or end. And so, if your break up the organic structure into isolated parts that which constituted the essential existence of the organism is gone." (*Introduction to the Philosophy of Religion,* pp. 98-99).

(2) An organism is not worked and regulated by an external agent which puts motion into it from the outside, but ith as a power inherent in it, which is a self-evolving and self-sustaining unity.

"If the organism is to be called an engine,then it is a self-stoking, self-repairing, self-preservative, self-adjusting, self-increasing, self-reproducing engine. It is a teleological engine, whose every activity in some sense serves the end of the organized whole." (*Problems of Philosophy*, pp. 236-37).

An organism is not made, but grows. It is not a "manufactured article" in which the parts are mechanically combined to produce artificial whole, as in a mechanism, but it is a real, systematic unity of parts in which the whole precedes and vitalizes the parts, so that the whole is necessary to the parts and the parts to teh whole and to one another. An organism does not serve an end foreign to it, like a mechanism, but realizes its own end immanent in it.

"In organic structures," says John Caird, "we find not only the idea of system, but also the idea of system which is *self-developed*—in other words, not only of a unit of diversified parts or elements correlated by one principle, but ofa unity which is due to the self-activity of that principle. We can conceive in mere inorganic matter a systematic order imposed from without and maintained simply by the action of inorganic forces. Evern human construction, such asa house or piece of mechanism, is an order of this kind, for it is the arrangement of dissimilar parts for the realization of a common idea or plan.But inall such constructions, the idea or plan is something foreign to the Nature of the separate parts or materials by means of which it is realized; and in order to produce it, these parts must surrender or be deprived of their individual existence and value. The stone, the wood, the lime, which compose the hpuse have nothing in themselves which makes it necessary that they should be combined in the house.

"In a complex living organism it is quite otherwise. Here we come upon the conception of unity of which the idea or end is not arbitarily imposed from without, on certain independent materials, but it is the result of an internal spontaneity or self-activity, working out diversities of member, form, function, from its own inherent self-producing energy, and, form at the same time, in the act of differentiating, reintegrating its diversities into the common unity. Here also, instead of the end being outward and accidental to the means, it is their own immanent end; instead of the parts being used up for the production of the end, we have membered totality in the production and maintenance of which the parts have their own natural fulfilment or realization." *[Ibid,* pp. 99-101.]

An organism, to realize its own end, can exercise certain powers which are wanting in a mechanism. It can select and assimilate its materials from without to itself and, to a certain extent, counteract the hostile forces of nature for the maintenance of its own life.

An organism has the power of self-reparation which is wanting in a machine. If in an organism, *e.g.*, a plant, some part is injured, it will repair itself in course of time. But the defect of a machine cannot be removed by itself.

An organism, unlike a mechanism, has the power of self-reproduction. An organism (*e.g.,* a plant or an animal), can reproduce another organism *(i.e.,* a plant or an aninal), when it attains maturity, but one machine cannot by itself produce another machine.

"A living body is an *organism,* and the peculiar feature of a living organism is the possession of a group of unique properties, of which the two most conspicious are *irritability* and *reproduction*. Living organisms are responsive to stimuli and they have the power of self-perpetuation. But organic bodies possess also other distinctive properties, such as growth, by the assimilation of food, adaptation and self-adjustment to the environment, self-maintenance and self-protection." [Patrick : *Introduction to Philosophy,* p. 97.]

**Mechanism and Organism compared**

**(a) Resemblance**

*(i)* Both a machine and an organism are composed of parts which are adapted to one another.

*(ii)* Both in a machine and in an organism the parts are so adjusted to one another as to produce a common result and realize a common end.

**(b) Contrast**

*(i)* A machine is made, while an organism grows.

*(ii)* In a machine the parts are extremely fitted to one another; in an organism the parts are externally adapted to one another.

*(iii)* A machine is an artificial whole, in which the parts are necessary to the whole, but the whole is not necessary to the parts. An organism is a real system in which not only the parts are necessary to the whole, but also the whole is necessary to the parts. In a

machine the parts precede the whole, white in an organism the whole precedes and vitalizes its parts.

*(iv)* A machine is worked by an external agent which puts motion into it from without; an organism has an inherent unity.

*(v)* A machine serves an end foreign to itself; an organism realizes its own end immanent in it.

*(vi)* A machine has not the power of self-preservation and self-development; an organism has the rower of self-preservation and self-evolution through assimilation of materials from without and development from within. But a machine grows by the mechanical process of addition to it from the outside, *i.e.* accretion from without.

*(vii)* An organism has the power of self-reparation and self-reproduction which are lacking in a machine.

Hence an organism contains something quite new in it, which cannot be accounted for by mere mechanical forces. So, an organism should not be regarded as a complex mechanism. Life is the sustaining principle in an organism which is wanting in a machine. What, then, is the nature and origin of life ?

**The Nature of Life : Mechanism and Vitalism.**

**(1) The Mechanises view**

The mechanist and the materialist suppose that an organism is nothing more than a very complex mechanism and life is nothing but the combination and interaction of physical and chemical forces which bring together the molecules constituting the protoplasmic cell and differentiate it into many cells and co-ordinate these into organs to make up an organism. Thus, life is nothing but the mechanical resultant of all the physico-chemical forces of the particular cells and organs in an organism. There is no special 'vital force.' This theory is called *Mechanism.* It holds that life is a complex physico-chemical force.

Cunninghum says, "The mechanist holds that the living organism is only a physical-chemical machine and that its be-haviour can be resolved by analysis into physico-chemical processes. For him there is no fundamental difference between them which he admits is that of complexity, the organic forms being much more complex in their structure than the inorganic."

**(2) The Vitalist's view**

"The vitalist objects," says Cunninghum, "to this position, and urges that the organism is not a physical-chemical machine differing from the inorganic only in complexity of structure. He insist on the contrary, that organic forms are radically different in kind from inorganic forms, that there is in the organism something new which is not found in inorganic or non-living matter." This theory is called *Vitalism.* It holds that life is a new power, a vital principle, a special force sharply distinguished from all forms of matter and mechanical forces. Life is a non-material force or entity called a "vital principle." Driesch is an exponent of this view. He believes that life is due to the presence of a non-material factor, which he calls *Entelechy,* and sometimes *Psychoid.* He tends to believe that it is a mental power which organises the body.

Thus the vitalist holds that the phenomena of life cannot be explained by purely mechanical laws. The more thoroughly we seek to investigate the phenomena of life, the more we are con-vinced that they are infinitely more complex than they are supposed to be, and they defy all mechanical explanation in physico-chemical terms. For, the simplest cell, the formless structureless, microscopic protoplasm already shows all the essential features of lifenutrition, growth, self-preservation and self-reproduction. All these processes are wanting in a mechanism. So, an organism cannot be reduced to a mechanism and life to physico-chemical forces. There is a special vital power which is above the mechanical forces.

"Life, therefore, is not explained," as Dr. Stephen aptly remarks, "by merely pointing out the mechanical processes in-cluded among the manifestations of life. It is not the mechanism that makes life; life is that higher form of power which makes, applies and co-ordinates the forces that; operate mechanically. We can see that the mechanical forces have no self-unifying, self-co-ordinating power in themselves; without the higher co-ordinating power of life they fall asunder, and the materials on which they operate, the C, H, 0, N, of the body, are at once dissipated into the earth and air. The physical forces of nature by themselves tend towards nothing but a dissipation of motion and an accumulation of matter in its crudest form, which mean death;- the forces of life tend towards differentiation and co-ordination." *(Problems of Metaphysic,* p. 233.)

*The Mechanist's objections against Vitalism considered:*

First, vitalism contradicts the doctrine of conservation of energy. If there is such a thing as a special vital force, it must be on the same level with the physical and chemical forces of the organism.; and therefore there must be a continual transference from the physical form to the vital and from the vital to the physical, and consequently, there will be a constant increase and decrease of physical energy in an organism. But according to the doctrine of conservation of energy, the quantity of physical energy operating in a body is exactly proportionate to the amount of materials assimilated from without and no increase or decrease can be accounted for in this way. So there is no place for a special vital force in an organism.

**Criticism**

Firstly, the precise amount of physical energy latent or operative in an organism can never be determined precisely, nor therefore its incrsase nor decrease.

And further, the vital power is not a force on the same level with the physical forces, but its nature is to, select, control and regulate their directions as means to its own end.

Secondly, many organic products (*e. g.* bile etc.) once thought to be products of living organisms, and therefore of a special vital power, can now be artificially product by a combination of physical and chemical forces in the laboratory.

**Criticism**

A living protoplasm cannot be manufactured in a laboratory. "The protoplasm which can be analysed and of which the chemical constitution is known, is not living but dead protoplasm, whilst that protoplasm which can be designated living though containing similar elements with that which is not living, manifests qualities or functions that are totally new, and which, therefore, cannot be ascribed to its merely chemical or physical composition." (John Caird: *Introduction to the Philosophy of Religion,* p. 96.)

The new phenomena in a living organism require a new factor, *viz.,* life, and life cannot spring from non-living matter. Life is a superior power which controls and guides the purely mechanical forces. So, life cannot be reduced to physicochemical forces.

Herbert Spencer defines life as "the continuous adjustment of internal to external conditions". The power of adjustment undoubtedly belongs to life. "Life is self-adjusting, self-maintaining, self-preserving, and self-perpetuating. There is nothing like this in the mechanical world. Machines do notadjust, maintain, preserve, or perpetuate themselves." *(Patrick),* The unique characteristics of living organisms can be adequately explained by a new organizing power called *life.*

**The Idealist's view**

Dr. Henry Stephen says, "We can consider life and soul to be the same active self-developing. self-organizing power at different stages of its development into self-sufficiency. In plant and animal, it is only life: in man, it has perfected itself into being self-conscious, self-regulating soul and attained a degree of self-sufficiency which makes it "to be independent of this particular body," (*Problems of Metaphysic.)*

It is one and the same absolute power which manifests

itself first in the organizing activity of life and then in the self-con-scious an self-regulating activity of the soul. So, ultimataly there is no dualism of life and soul, but the monism of the Absolute which manifests itself first in the mechanical forces of the inanimate world, then as the vital power in the world of living beings, and then as the soul in conscious and rational beings.

**Emergence Theory: The Theory of Levels**

Lloyd Morgan holds that life emerges from matter, and mind emerges from life. Matter, life, and mind are three levels of the reality. Life is higher than matter. Mind is higher than life. Evolution proceeds by *creative synthesis*. It means a synthesis of elements, by which new processes, powers, or activities appear, or new entities are created.

Electrons and protons are organised' into atoms, atoms into molecules, molecules into cells, and cells into living organisms, and at each new level of organization new qualities appear, which are new creations. These new qualities are not due to the addition of the qualities of the elements organised. "At each new level of reality we have new powers and new capacities and new qualities. It is a flowering-out process, wholly different from the mechanical sequences which we see in the world of physics. New realities are born at each new level. Life is one of these realities. Thus life is not due to the, presence in the living organism of any mystic 'vital principle', or 'life force'. It is the evolutionary product of organization." *(Patrick)*. Matter, life, and mind are the different stages in evolution. Nature climbs up to life and mind through the organization of matter. Life is the fruition of matter. Mind is the perfection of life. Nature *achieves* life and mind in course of evolution. Lloyd Morgan posits an original *Activity* which is the *nisus* or urge directing the evolutionary process. He calls it God.

**11. The Origin of Life**

**The Theory of special creation**

God created a certain number of germ-cells in the

beginning and "brethed the breath of life" into them; thus life was created by God by an act of divine will.

The theory of special creation is an antiquated doctrine which cannot be maintained.

**The doctrine of Abiogenesis or Spontaneous Generation**

According to this view, life comes spontaneously from the non-living or the lifeless—from inanimate matter—by the working of the forces—molar, chemical and electrioal attached to atoms. The atoms of carbon, hydrogen, oxygen and nitrogen (C, H, O, N) fortuitously collided and struck against one another and working through infinite time produced the proto-plasmic globule, which attained the power of co-ordinating the forces inherent in the constituent atoms and integrating the atoms into a living cell, and multiplying and subdividing the primordial cell, into an infininite number of other cells and differentiating them into the organ of an organism which preserves and develops itself in interaction with the environment. Life, thus, is a mechanical resultant of the physical and chemical forces in the constituent atoms of a protoplasmic cell.

This view is supported by the general belief that we see spontaneous generation of life all around us, in the atmosphere, in the water and the soil, where myriads of living germs (bacteria and infusoria) are found with the help of a microscope, if decaying vegetable or animal substance is exposed to the air.

**The doctrine of Biogenesis or Antecedent life**

According to this view, life comes out of antecedent life and never out of the non-living or lifeless matter. Bergson holds that life is creative and free. It is not mechanically determined. "Everything that has life in it is free, in the sense that what it does from moment to moment is determined from within, by its own spontaneous and novel activity, and not from outside, by the necessity expressed in physical laws." *(Rocking).*

**Criticism of the doctrine of Abiogenesis**

With the further improvement of the microscope and the

more skilful use of the instrument, the theory of abiogenesis or spontaneous generation of life out of lifeless matter gradually lost its hold on the scientific mind. If a liquid containing an infusion of decaying organic matter is boiled and hermetically sealed up so as to entirely shut out the air and the germs which float in it, no new life can appear in it, however long it may be kept. This experiment proves beyond doubt that the living germs which appear so rapidly in rotten substances, are all derived from the atmosphere which is full of germs and bacteria. Thus, life does not arise from lifeless matter, but all life comes out of omni *vivum ex evo est.* This is the theory of biogenesis or the origin of living beings from antecedent life.

## UNIVERSITY QUESTIONS

1. Clearly expound the Atomic theory of matter. Would you accept this theory as an ultimate explanation of matter and the world ? (1911).
2. Explain fully the apparent difference between a machine and a living plant or an animal. Do you think that it involves something essentially new and different ?
3. Explain the nature of mechanism, giving illustrations; and explain fully the difference between a machine and a living organism. (1916).
4. Explain the difference between a living Organism and a piece of Mechanism, and give your own opinion as to whether Life can be derived from Mechanism, with your reasons. (1918).
5. What do you understand by the principle of conservation of energy ? Is it an a *priori* or an *a posteriori* principle, and why ? (1912).
6. Explain fully the nature of Mechanism, and the difference between a Machine and a living Organism; and discuss the question whether Life can be derived, or is a form of Mechanism. (1916 Hon.),
7. Explain fully the distinguishing characteristics of Life and Growth, with illustrations, and discuss the question

whether they can be accounted for as products of physical laws. (1918 Hon.).

8. Analyse and discuss fully the concept of matter. (1921).

9. Explain the difference between a Mechanism and an Organism illustrating.your meaning by examples. What is meant by saying that Organisms are of different spacies ? Give examples of species. (1922).

10. Explain the principal points of difference between a Living Thing and a Lifeless Thing. (1923).

11. Explain the difference, if any, between *life* and *mechanism* (1924).

12. Explain the difference between a Machine and a Living Body, illustrating by examples. Is it possible that Life is only a form of Mechanism ? (1925).

13. Analyse *(a)* your idea of matter, and *(b)* your idea of Soul, bringing out clearly the difference between them; and explain how you have obtained each of these ideas. (1926).

14. Distinguish between life and mechanism, and examine the mechanical theory of life. (1929),

15. State what appears to you to be the truth of the principle of Conservation of Energy. Is its validity determined *a priori* or *a posteriori* ? Determine the meaning of Correlationin this context. (1931).)

## INTER CHAPTER

In the preceding chapter we have discussed the nature of matter and life which constitute the world of Nature. In the-following three chapters we propose to discuss three other most important problems of the philosophy of the World, *viz.* Cosmogony, Cosmology and Ontology,

(1) "What is the origin, of the world, and how has it come into its present order ? The answer of this problem is called Cosmogony." *(Marvin)*.

(2) The next problem is: What is the constitution of the world ? "By the problem of the constitution of the world, or as it is called, Cosmology we mean to enquire: first, Is the world composed of ultimate parts, or elements, or what is the same question, is there but one substance or is there a plurality of substances,? And secondly, if the latter, what is the order obtaining among them ? And next, what are the fundamental laws in accordance with which the activities or changes that constitute the world of events take place ?" *(Marvin)*. That answer to these questions is called Cosmology.

(3) The next problem that naturally suggests itself to our mind is: What is the ultimate nature of the world ? What is the essence, stuff or substance of which the world is composed ? The answer to this questions is called Ontology. Thus there are the problems of Cosmogony (origin of the world), Cosmology (constitution and organisation of the world—the problem of one and many) and Ontology (essence or substance of the world).

As to the origin of the world, we must discuss the question whether the world is created or evolved, and if it is evolved, is the evolution guided by any purpose or not ? Is the evolution of the world mechanical or teleological ? These are the problems of Cosmogony.

As to the constitution of the world, we must discuss the question whether the world is composed of one substance or a plurality of substances. If the former, what is the nature of that one substance ? And if the latter, what is the nature of the many substances that constitute the world ? Are they material or spiritual ? These are the problems of Cosmology.

As to the essence of the world, we must discuss the ques-tion whether the world is completely material, or completely spiritual, or both, and if the world is made up of two substances, viz., matter and spirit, what is the relation between the two ? These are the problems of Ontology.

## CHAPTER VI

# COSMOGONY OR THE ORIGIN OF THE WORLD

### The different theories of the origin of the world

Was the world created on a sudden at a particular point of time and remains the same as it was when it was created ? Or has it come into the present order through a gradual process of evolution from a simple to a complex form ? Thus there are two theories as to the origin of the world – the theory of Creation and that of Evolution. Evolution, again, may be mechanical or teleological; it may proceed according to the inexorable law of causality, being rigidly determined by necessity, or it may be a means to the realization of an end or purpose. Thus there are two cosmogonical theories of Creation and Evolution; and Evolution may be either mechanical or teleological; and teleology, again, may be either transcendent (external) or immanent (internal). The following chart will give a cursory view of the different theories of the origin of the world (Chart on next page):

### The Theory of Creation

According to the theory of special creation, the world was created by God all on a sudden by a single act of volition, with all its contents *(e. g.,* stars, planets, species of plants and animals) in the same forms in which they now exist. The theory of creation may take two forms,

(1) absolute creation (or creation out of nothing), or

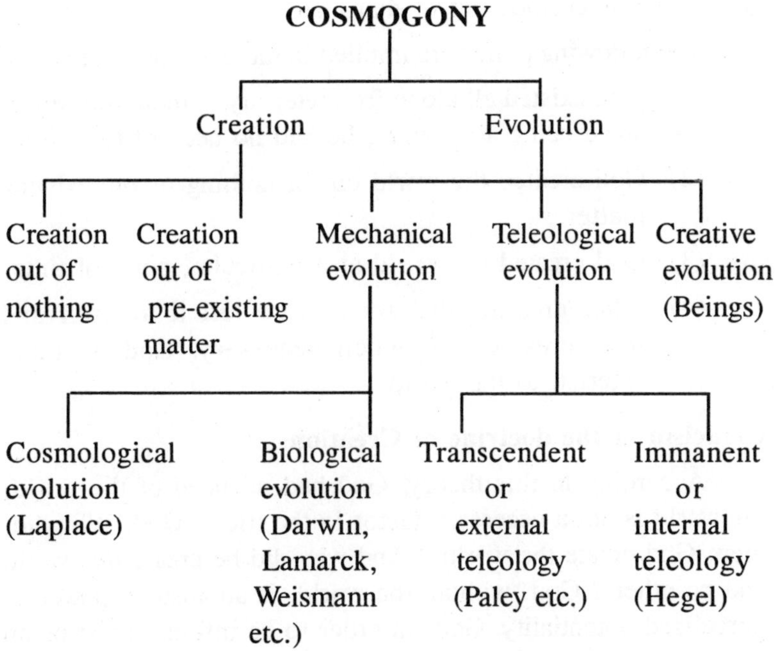


(2) conditional creation (or creation out of pre-existing matter).

**(a) Absolute Creation**

According to this view, God created the world out of nothing by an act of divine fiat. "Let there be world and there was world." There was a time when there was nothing except God. God is an all-perfect being and as such had no need of the world. But he thought of creating the world to communicate his blessedness to the finite beings, and the world came into being.

**(b) Conditional Creation**

According to this view, God created the world out of pre-existing matter. He is like an architect who manufactured the world from the primitive matter. Matter and God are co-eternal; the primordial matter was in a chaotic state; God produced this cosmos out of that chaos.

The following points are implied in the doctrine of creation:

(1) God existed all alone from eternity without the world. since being all-perfect, he had no need of the world.

(2) God created the world out of nothing or pre-existing matter.

(3) God created the world at a particular, point of time,

(4) After creating the world, God left it to itself and interferes with it when necessary. God is, thus, external to the world.

**Criticism of the doctrine of Creation**

According to this theory, God had no need of the world; the world is not a necessary factor in the life of God. Why did, then, God create the world ? And why did he create *this* world and no other ? God. without the world, is an abstract power or unrealized potentiality. God, in order to be infinite, must be an inexhaustible power which manifests itself in the world; God and the world are thus co-eternal.

Farther, nothing can come out of nothing *(ex nihilo nihil fit)*. Even God cannot make it possible. If the world were created out of nothing, then *nothing* would be the cause of the world; and as the cause must communicate its nature to its effect, 'nothing' would impart its nature to the world, and consequently the world would be a non-entity.

If it be held that God created the world out of pre-existing matter, then God would be limited by it and would thus become finite.

Moreover, if God withdraws himself from the world after creating it, the world would limit him and make him finite.

Then, why did God create the world at a particular point of time ? Why not before it or after it ? These questions can be answered, only if we can have knowledge of the life of God before creation. But this is absurd.

Moreoyer, if the world was created at a certain point of time, there *was* a time when there was nothing; but time without content or blank time is inconceivable and hence a non-entity.

We can never conceive the powers and forces of God divorced from his nature and working the world by themselves. If God creates the world with his power, he must sustain it with his forces.

The doctrine of Divine Intervention makes God like a finite and imperfect architect who cannot make his machine perfect. If God is perfect, why should his workmanship become imperfect, so that it would require divine intervention at times and why should there be any seeds of decay in the universe ?

The theory of creation makes God an arbitrary and capricious power. There is overwhelming scientific evidence that the world was not created but gradually evolved in course of time.

God is organically related to the world. God is cause only in the sense of ground, that is to say, the being whose nature is expressed in the system as a whole. God is cause in the sense of reason or ultimate explanation of the whole system of the universe. (Pringle-Pattison: *The Idea of God,* p. 302). "If the universe is to be understood through God the nature of God must no less be expressed in the universe and understood through it." *(Ibid,* p. 304.)

**Scientific Evidences of Evolution**

The evidences of Astronomy, Geology and Biology support the theory of evolution. Astronomy shows that vast periods of time must have been required not only for the condensation of suns and planets, and for the cooling and hardening of the earth into a solid globe, but also for the formation of mountains and valleys, river-beds and seas, on the surface of the earth. Geology shows that the different layers of the earth have been formed by the consolidation of an originally liquid substance and of the sediments of mud and sand in course of countless ages, and when the different layers are explored, the middle layers are found to contain that fossils of species which are now extinct being supplanted by other more highly developed species, while in the uppermost layers species are found approaching more closely to those still extant. These evidences of Astronomy and Geology are corroborated by the testimony of Biology, which shows that the existing species have been evolved from earlier species by differentiation and co-ordination. Thus the world has reached its present stage by a gradual evolution from lower to higher forms, from simpler to more complex ones.

**The doctrine of Evolution.**

**(a) What is Evolution ?**

The evidences cited above are sufficient to prove that the world was not created all at once in the form in which it now exists, but it has come to its present stage by a slow, gradual and orderly process of evolution through a long period of time from a simpler form of primeval existence. Herbert Spencer holds that the process of evolution is always from a simpler to a more complex form, from an undifferentiated and homogeneous to a differentiated and heterogeneous state, from an indefinite and incoherent to a definite and coherent condition. Evolution is a gradual orderly change. All the processes of evolution exhibit certain characteristics which are essential to it. What are these characteristics ?

***(b) The characteristics or Principles of Evolution* (Herbert Spencer)**

**(I) Concentration or Integration**

The primitive elements were, in a state of chaos, scattered here and there. In the process of evolution these widely diffused elements were combined and collected together in order to form a system. Concentration or integration is the first characteristic of evolution. For example, in the evolution of the cosmos or cosmological evolution, the primitive nebulae or cloud-dusts, which were in an extremely diffused condition and in a state of agitation, came together and combined and thus were integrated into the solar system. All organic growth or biological evolution takes place by means of assimilation of meterials from without and absorption of them into the organic tissue, *i.e.,* by concentration or integration of materials scattered in the environment. This feature is also found in psychical and social evolution.

**(2) Differentiation**

But concentration or integration is not the only characteristic of evolution. Only in the simplest cases of development, evolution takes place only as a process of integration. But further development involves the process of differentiation within an integrated system. For example, the primitive germ-cell was evolved by the concentration of the atoms of carbon, hydrogen, nitrogen and oxygen which were formerly diffused in the atmosphere. But the further development of the germ-cell involved the process of differentiation. The germ-cell by the process of differentiation, divided and subdivided itself into many cells, and differentiated these innumerable cells into the organs of an organism. This process of self-division and self-multiplication is nothing but a process of differentiation. Similarly, the primitive nebulae were concentrated into one system by integration; and within this system, many systems (stars, planets etc.) were evolved by differentiation. Thus integration and differentiation are the most essential features of evolution.

**Determination**

But if evolution is characterized by differentiation of an integrated system, devolution or dissolution, too, is characterized by the same process. An organism is dissolved, when the organ are disintegrated or differentiated into their constituent inorganic element (C, H, N, O). What, then, is the differentiating mark of evolution as distinguished from dissolution ? We must add the further characteristic of determination which distinguishes evolution from dissolution. Evolution is an advance from confusion to order—from an indefinite and indeterminate arrangement to a definite and determinate arrangement, from an incoherent to a coherent condition. Evolution is a transition from a chaos to a cosmos, while dissolution, from a cosmos to a chaos; evolution is an upward movement of progress, while dissolution is a downward movement of regress.

Conger holds that evolution implies four fundamental notions:

(1) change in time;
(2) serial order;
(3) inherent causes;
(4) creative synthesis.

**The Mechanical theory of Evolution**

Science advocates the mechanical theory of evolution and holds that the world with all its contents, matter, life and mind, stars and planets, different species of plants and animals including rational beings like men, has been evolved from a primitive state of self-existent matter in the form of atoms, moving about with self-existent motion, in self-existent space. Matter, Motion, and Force are the primordial elements, and everything in the world has been derived from them by a slow process of evolution. The world is the product of the fortuitous combination of material atoms by the random play of mechanical forces. Hence Herbert Spencer has defined evolution as an integration of matter and concomitant dissipation of motion during which matter passes from an indefinite incoherent homogeneity to a definite coherent heterogeneity, and during which the retained motion undergoes a parallel transformation." But what is this primitive homogeneous state of matter ? Spencer does not go further back than the nebulous state of matter as supposed by Kant and Laplace. Thus the "nebular hypothesis" of Laplace is the mechanical theory of cosmological evolution. As to the origin of life, the mechanical theory is the doctrine of abiogenesis or spontaneous generation of life from lifeless matter and as to the origin and development of species, the mechanical theories are the Darwinian hypothesis of "fortuitous variations and natural selection" and the Lamarckian theory of "modification by the influence of the environment." We shall discuss these mechanical theories of cosmological and biological evolution in brief.

**The Mechanical theory of Cosmological Evolution (Herbert Spencer)**

Spencer holds that the whole world is a great evolutionary process. Matter, Motion, and Force are the materials of this process of evolution. They are not the ultimate realities. They are *modes* of the *Unknowable.* The world is the result of the redistribution of Matter, Motion, and Force which are the only modes knowable to us. He defines evolution as "an integration of matter and concomitant dissipation of motion; during which the matter passes from an indefinite, incoherent, homogeneity to a definite, coherent, heterogeneity; and during which the retained motion undergoes a parallel transformation". Evolution is integration and differentiation.

The matter now composing the solar system was extremely diffused in the form of a nebula or cloud of gas, vapour of star-dust which gradually condensed into globular bodies (the sun, planets, satellites) by the physical forces inherent in them, operating according to known physical laws. The atoms composing the primitive nebular mass were in a state of extreme diffusion and agitation; but owing to the gradual dissipation of motion which kept them diffused, they began to condense by gravitation towards their centre of greatest density, and in so doing began to revolve about the centre. As the cloud thus condensed more and more, the revolution became more rapid, and smaller masses of condensing cloud were thrown off, which went on revolving about the central mass, and revolving about their own centres, became planets; some of these, in their own contraction threw off still smaller clouds, which condensed into secondary planets or satellites; the central mass condensing towards the centre of gravity of the whole, became the sun.

In the beginning the world was a fiery mass of homogeneous matter, highly diffused. It was in the nature of nebulae or cloud-dusts. They were all alike or homogeneous. They were scattered about. They were gradually solidified or integrated, and differentiated. Planets were separated from the sun; satellites were separated from the planets. Land, water, and air were futher differentiated on earth. Thus integration and differentiation went on in the process of evolution.

In biological evolution also there was the two-fold process of differentiation and integration. At first, there was the homogeneous mass of protoplasm. Gradually different organs were differentiated from it to perform different functions. The eyes were set apart for vision; the ears, for hearing; the hands, far grasping; the legs, for locomotion; and the like. These different organs resulted from the integration of their-constituent parts.

In social evolution the same two-fold process of differentiation and integration is found. Different families are integrated or combined into a society. Different classes are differentiated from it by division of labour, and adopt different professins, and perform different functions. Labour is becoming more and more specialized at the present time. These different classes are closely knit units. They are highly" integrated corporate bodies.

### Criticism of the Spencerian doctrine of Evolution as taken from Laplace

Herbert Spencer assumes the exis-tence of nebulous matter and motion, the laws governing them e. *g*. conservation of mass and motion, the law of gravitation etc.) and the primitive collocation of the constituents of the nebula. He cannot go further back than the nebula. But what is the cause of the original state of matter ? Why should the nebulous state be ultimate ? How did the original collocation take place ? All these questions are left unanswered.

The primitive matter was in a state of perfect homogeneity. But why did the homogeneous matter become heterogenpas ?

Herbert Spencer supposed that the primitive homogencous matter was in a state of unstable equilibrium and consequently in eonstant agitation. But simple and homogenous things (*e. g.*, rocks. and hills) are comparatively more stable and permanent than complex and heterogeneous things *(e. g.*, plants and animals).

Spencer's doctrine of evolution cannot apply to the whole of the universe, but only to the phenomena within the universe. For, if evolution is an integration of matter and dissipation of motion, how can there be dissipation of motion from the whole universe ?

Spencer's theory of evolution is based on the doctrine of conservation of energy or persistence of force which cannot be taken as absolutely true.

Spencer's attempt to derive even life and mind from lifeless matter and motion—from the integration of matter and dissipation of motion, is absurd. Life cannot spring from lifeless matter. Mind cannot spring from unconscious matter or life.

Spencer's mechanical theory of evolution cannot account for the order and unity of the world without the guidance of an intelligent principle and without reference to an end or purpose.

Evolution is purposive or teleological. It is not mechanical. It is gradual and orderly progress towards an end. It is gradual realization of a purpose. The world cannot be the result of a random combination and separation of matter, motion, and force.

Lastly, Spencer regards matter, motion, and force as *modes* of the *Unknowable*. The ultimate reality, according to him, is unknowable, with capital *U*. If it is unknowable, it cannot account for matter, motion, and force, or, for the matter of that, any phenomena of the universe. It is not an explanatory principle. It is a refuge of ignorance. And yet Spencer sometimes calls it inscrutable power.

**(1) The Idea of Species (or the Nature and Origin of Species)**

A species consists of an indefinite number of individuals which are essentially similar in structure and life, and different species are essentially different from one another. There are two theories as to the nature and origin of species,

**(a) The theory of Immutability of Species**

According to this theory, species are fixed and immutable; there is a sharp line of demarkation between different species. This theory may take two forms as shown below:

(i) *The Deistic theory of Special Creation* which holds that God created all the existing species in their present forms and told them to multiply, so that one species cannot be derived from another, the later species from the earlier ones.

(ii) *The Platonic theory of the Immutability of Species,* Plato holds that every species has a special reason or ground for existence in the eternal nature of things – in the eternal Idea and plan of the world, which is always realizing itself in individuals, but is never exhausted in them. Hence individuals are born and perish, but the species abides and lives through them all. Species, thus, are the universal essences of things or eternal and immutable types or Ideas in the ultimate nature of reality, of which the individuals are mere shadows or adumbra- tions. This theory was slightly modified by Aristotle, according to whom, the universal essences or eternal and immutable types are not above and beyond the individuals, but are immanent in them.

**(b) The theory of Mutability of Species**

The modern theory of biological evolution introduced by Darwin and Lamarck explodes the theory of immutability of species and the eternity of type. Species are not fixed and immutable, but tend to vary from age to age fortuitously (Darwin) and with changing circumstances (Lamarck). The higher species have been evolved from the lower species by continuous modifications, without any end or purpose. There is no 'eternal reason", for any particular species. "No two members of a species are really alike, and no type is really fixed for

(1) There is no absolute line of demarcation between one species and another, as the Platonic theory assumed. They shade gradually into one another; and between one type and another there are always *varieties,* which cannot be assigned with certainty to either the one species or the other.

(2) Species are not immutable; organisms are constantly changing in structure—to some extent fortuitously, and to some extent, in response to the forces constantly acting on them from the outside. Such differences, at first small, gradually deepen, and constitute new *varieties.* And varieties go on deepening until they become distinct species."

(Stephen: *Problems of Metaphysic,* 1918, p. 176.)

But though species are not fixed and immutable, but are mutable or variable, they must have a reason for their existence in the divine plan and purpose; without which the process of evolution cannot be adequately explained.

**The Individual and the Universal in Species: Nominalism and Realism**

The biological question of the relation of a species to its individual members closely corresponds to the logical question of the relation of particular to general ideas, and the metaphysical question of the ultimate relation of the individual to the universal in nature. As to the metaphysical question of the relation of the universal to the individual, there are two doctrines, *viz.,* Realism and Nominalism.

**(a) The doctrine of Metaphysical Realism or the theory of universal essences**

According to this doctrine, the universal, being the essence, is more real than the individuals. But it has two forms:

(i) The theory of **Universalia ante res** held by Plato maintains that the universal or the eternal types and essences of things exist before and independently of the individual thing which they evolve and sustain. Thus there is an 'Idea' or universal and eternal archetype of man in the mind of God, of which the individual men are mere copies or imitations-Universals, thus, are not only anterior to and independent of individuals, transcending them in an ideal world, but are more real than the individuals, since they cannot be completely embodied and exhausted in individuals. This was the doctrine of Plato.

*(ii)* The theory of **Universalia in rebus** held by Aristotle maintains that if universals are the formative essences of things, they must not be external to, and independent of things, but immanent in them. Universals apart from their concrete embodiments in individuals or particulars are meaningless abstractions. Hegel also is an exponent of this view.

**(b) The theory of Metaphysical Individualism or Nominalism:**

According to this theory, only individuals or particular things are real; universals have no existence of any kind anywhere (which leads to logical nominalism), or exist only in thought as artificial products of thinking mind (logical conceptualism). The universal is merely a mechanical aggregate or an arithmetical sum-total of particulars.

This doctrine of metaphysical individualism leads to the logical doctrines of nominalism and conceptualism. According to nominalism, only individuals are real; there are no universal objective class-essences in nature; there is nothing really universal or common to things except the *name.* According to conceptualism, though there are no universals or objective class-essences in individuals, we can abstract from them their common. attributes, and construct in our minds abstract concepts or class-ideas. Thus, universals are neither anterior to, and independent of particulars or individuals (universalia ante res) nor co-existent with, and immanent in individuals (universalia in rebus), but exist posterior to individuals in the form of abstract concepts (universalia post res).

## Biological Evolution

As to the development of species, there are two rival hypotheses – Darwin's theory of 'fortuitous or accidental variations and natural selection' and Lamarck's theory of modifications by the influence of the environment.

### (1) Darwin's theory of fortuitous variations and natural selection

Darwin has propounded his theory of biological evolution in his two works, "Origin of Species" and "Descent of Man." According to him, new species arise from the fortuitous variations within the germ-cells by means of natural selection or survival of the fittest in the struggle for existence. Thus

Darwin's theory of evolution involves the following principles:

***Fortuitous or spontaneous variations***

According to Darwin, protoplasmic cells, though apparently simple, are really extremely complex, and therefore liable to variations; spontaneous, fortuitous or accidental variations are constantly going on within the germ-cells which cause variations in the mature organisms. Some variations are favourable, while others are unfavourable. If unfavourable variations accumulate, the species gradually die out. If favourable variations accumulate, the species survive in the struggle for existence.

***Transmission of these fortuitous variations by heredity***

These spontaneous variations in the germ-cells are transmitted to posterity by heredity, which essentially affect and modify the structure of their organisms. "If those variations which happen to appear in the individual organism and prove advantageous to it in its straggles to exist are to prove advantageous to the species as well, they must obviously be transmitted from generation to generation of organisms. This transmission of characteristics from an individual organism to its offspring has been shown to be an actual fact, and to it is given the name of heredity." (Cunningham, *Problems of Philosophy,* p. 219.)

### *Natural Selection or Survival of the Fittest*

These variations, accumulated and deepened by inheritenee, are either beneficial to the creatures or detrimental to them in the struggle for existence. The natural resources are not sufficient for all the creatures existing on the face of the earth; so there is a scramble, as it were, for food; this is the struggle for existence. In this struggle, Nature selects, as it were, the fittest, *i. e.,* the strongest creatures which abound in favourable variations; the weakest or those which abound in unfavourable variations die out. The survival of the fittest or the strongest in the struggle for life is figuratively called Natural Selection.

Every animal species is enormously prolific, and tends to increase in geometrical ratio. But there is a limited amount of food in the wdrld. Hence follows a *struggle for existence,* in which there will be a *survival of the fittest.* Who are the fittest? Those individuals who are best adapted to the environment. Who are best adapted to the environment ? Those individuals, which abound in favourable variations, are best adapted to the environment. Like begets like, but not just like. Slight variations occur in the structure or function between individuals of the same specis, even those who are born of the same parents. Those individuals which abound in favourable variations are selected and preserved. They will survive in the struggle for existence, thrive, and propagate, and transmit their favourable variations to their offspring. Those individuals, which have a large stock of unfavourable variations, will perish. This is called *natural selection. (Patrick).*

Darwin holds that organs precede their functions. First, organs are evolved accidentally, and then they perform their functions. They are not due to the influence of the environ-ment. They are not due to the effort and activity of the organism to satisfy its organic needs. and desires. Eyes are accidentally evolved owing to spontaneous variations in the cells. Then they perform the function of seeing. Bars are accidentally evolved, and then they hear.

### (2) Lamarck's theory of modifications by the influence of the environment and inheritance of acquired characters (adopted by Herbert Spencer).

#### Modification by the influence of the environment

Lamarck holds, on the contrary, that variations cannot go on spontaneously or fortuitously, in the germ-cells as fortuitous variations can never lead to any definite result. So Lamarck holds that variations or modifications are not spontaneous, but caused by external forces of the environment. Thus, when the external forces act upon the organism, it is forced to react upon them; and in its reaction upon the environment, to satisfy a need or want, different sense-organs, *e. g.*, eye, ear, skin, etc., are evolved in response to the different kinds of external forces, *e. g.*, light, sound, heat, pressure and so on. "Lamarck seems to think that there are deep desires or 'needs' in the organism resulting from internal forces tending toward development." *(Patrick)*. Darwin holds that organs precede the functions. But Lamarck holds that functions precede the organs. First, there are some needs or wants of the organism, which are turned into desires. Then there is an effort, on the part of the organism, to develop the necessary organs to perform specific functions. First, there is the desire to see, hear, smell, taste, and touch. Then, the sense-organs, eyes, ears, nose, tongue, and skin are evolved. The more they are used, the more they are strengthened. The more they are not used, the more they are weakened. Thus, organs are developed by the organism under the pressure of the environment to satisfy deep organic needs, and they are strengthened by use.

#### Inheritance of acquired modifications

The modifications of structure, thus, acquired by effort and practice, are transmitted by inheritance, and go on accumulating from generation to generation.

"Lamarck supposed that the environment modifies individual organisms and that the modifications thus produced are transmitted by the organisms to their offspring. In the case of animals he recognized also the modifying effect of use and disuse of bodily organs and the influence of effort and desire on the part of the animal. Since, now, the modifications which result from the action of the environment and from use and disuse are said to be passed on by inheritance, his theory involves the *inheritance of acquired characters.*" (Patrick: *Introduction to Philosophy,* pp. 127-28).

For instance, giraffes did not have long necks. They constantly stretched their necks to eat the tender leaves at the tops of the trees. This act of stretching the necks constantly elongated them. This elongation of the necks was inherited by the next generation. In this way, modifications were made in tha structure of the animal bodies, and, in course of generations, so many modifications were made that new species were formed.

**Comparison of Darwin and Lamarck's theories of Evolution**

According to both, species are not fixed and immutable, but are the products of evolution. (l) But according to Darwin, there go on spontaneous or fortuitous variations in the germ-cells, which cause variations in the mature organism. According to Lamarck, variations or modifications are imposed on organisms by the force of the environment from without and hence they are not spontaneous, but acquired by creatures through interaction with the environment. (2) According to the former, only spontaneous variations are transmitted by inheritance; according to the latter, acquired modifications' are transmitted by inheritance. (3) According to the former the organ comes first, and then we use it; nature provides us with legs and we walk. According to the latter, the function makes the organ; nature compels us to move, and the need and effort develop the organ of locomotion.

Darwin's theory does not depend upon the modifying action of the environment, nor upon the modifying effect of use and disuse, nor does it involve the inheritance of acquired characters. It assumes only the occurrence of small variations which might be accidental, and the preservation of the favourable ones by natural selection," *(Patrick).*

**(3) Weismann's theory of germinal variations and continuity of the germplasm**

**(i) *Transmission of germinal variations***

Closer investigation led Weismann and others to the conclusion that 'acquired' modifications, *i. e.,* modifications acquired by the efforts of the individual cannot modify in any way the germ-cell, and are not, therefore, transmitted by inheritance. Only the spontaneous variations within the germ-cell itself *(i.e.* germinal variations) can pass over into other germs derived from it, and be transmitted by inheritance.

**(ii) Continuity of the germ-plasm or germinal continuity : Immortality of the germ-cells.**

"According to it, the whole of the germ-plasm contained in 'a parent germ-cell or egg' is not used up in the construction of the *body* of the offspring; a portion is reserved unchanged for the formation of germ-cells of the offspring. Thus the germ-cell of an individual of one generation gives rise not only to the body of an individual of the next, but also directly to its germ-cells, so that the body does not produce germ-cells, but only contains them. The line of descent is from germ-cell to germ-cell," so that there is germinal continuity or continuity of the germ-plasm from generation to generation.

Weismann holds that heredity depends entirely upon the transmission of the *germ-cells.* They are not affected by changes in the body-cells. The body-cells are not transmitted to the offspring. The *germ-cells* are transmitted from generation to generation, though variations or mutations may occur in them. Darwin susposed evolutionary changes to originate in modifications of the *body-cells* whereas Weismann showed that the *germ-cells* were not affected by modifications of the body-cells. The *germ-cells* are "immortal," They pass from the parent to the offspring. They are transmitted from generation to generation.

**Criticism of Darwin and Lamarck's theories of evolution**

**(a) Criticism of Darwin's theory**

The range given to chance is quite inadmissible. Fortuitous or accidental variations cannot account for the origin of new species, since accidental variations, which are advantageous and beneficial to creatures, are very rare. They cannot account for the evolution of complex species from simple species.

Natural selection cannot account for the conservation of the stable forms (or survival of the fittest) and total elimination of the unstable or unfit. Rational or Subjective Selection must take the place of Natural Selection to account for the survival of the fittest. *(Ward)*. An organic modification, according to Darwin, is accidental and therefore very rare. Consequently, it can seldom occur simultaneously in individuals of different sexes. Even if it does occur, two individuals having such characteristics will seldom meet and unite. Hence there can be no hereditary transmission of accidental variations on which the Darwinian hypothesis depends.

Darwin's theory is based upon three postulates. They are the struggle for, existence, Heredity, and spontaneous variations Darwin does not explain these fundamental assumptions. The struggle for existence presupposes the activity, insurgency, and spontaneity of life. The development of complex species from simple species may be due to the insurgency of life, rather than to the action of a negative principle like natural selection. Biological evolution is due to the very nature of life, the will to live, the insurgency of life, the inner urge and impulse to create, thrive, and prosper. Darwin missed this premordial impulse to live.

Heredity is not due to the transmission of *body-cells* with their spontaneous variations from the parent to the offspring. It is due to the transmission of the *immortal genn-cells* from the parent to the offspring. There is germinal continuity or continuity of the same germ-cells.

'Natural Selection' is a metaphor. Nature is personified and supposed to select the fittest or the individuals with many favourable variations. Nature is supposed to be some kind of *force* or *agency* which intelligently directs the affairs in the animal kingdom. This is an anthropomorphic view of Nature. In fact, Darwin uses the term to represent a sifting process in nature. Nature does not select or reject. Selection is an intelligent action. It implies intelligent *inspection, appraisement,* and final *decision.* In this sense, there is no selection in nature. Natural selection is a mechanical, unintelligent process of survival of the fittest individuals abounding in favourable variations, and elimination of the weakest individuals abounding in unfavourable variations.

**(b) Criticism of Lamarck's theory**

The Lamarckian doctrine of hereditary transmission of acquired modifications (adopted by Herbert Spencer) is rejected by Weismann and other distinguished biologists, who hold that only the internal germinal variations can be transmitted by heredity.

According to Lamarck, modifications are imposed on organisms by the force of the environment. But the environment has a *"perturbing or exciting* rather than a *plastic* or *moulding* action. The true formative principle is an *inner* power—the power of *life* It is this power which brings about the progressive complication of organisms." This is admitted even by Lamarck himself and his followers.

According to Lamarck, the function or need produces the organ, and exercise and habit develop and strengthen it. "But how can a mere need create an organ ? The need must be either a felt or an unfelt one. If it is a felt need, it gives rise to an effort. The need, even when felt, is generally vague; the effort is uncertain." (P. *B'. Chatterjee.)* How, then, can a vague need and uncerbain effort produce a necessary organ ? So long we are considering the highest forms of organism in which the need is felt. But in the lowest forms of organism, the need is not felt. And how can an unfelt need create a new organ there? Moreover, exercise and habit can increase the strength and size of an existing organ, but they cannot bring about increase of complexity in the internal structure of an organ.

**General Criticism of the Mechanical theory of Evolution**

This theory leaves too much to chance. The random play of mechanical forces can no more produce the wonderful unity, order and harmony of the world-system, than the blind combination of the alphabet can produce Shakespeare's *Macbeth.*

This theory cannot bridge over the gaps between matter and life, and life and mind. The phenomena of organic life abound in complex adaptations of means to ends which cannot be explained by fortuitious combination of material atoms. The physical forces and organic forces are in their nature opposed to each other the, former having a katabolic tendency, tending to dissipate and bring about stagnation, and the latter having an anabolic tendency, tending to concentrate. and Droduce activity, And also the human mind with its powers of intelligent activity and freedom of will cannot be the result of a blind conglomeration of atoms.

Evolution is a process of development; and the process means the *modus operandi* or mode of operation; but the process or the mode of operation must be towards a definite end or purpose; so there must be a directive principle to guide the movement. Thus the theory of evolution is not inconsistent with teleology or finality.

The mechanical theory of evolution seeks to explain everything of the universe by physical and mechanical forces and thus reduces everything to a mechanism. But physical or mechanical forces cannot act, unless they are guided and controlled by the superior forces of an intelligent principle; a mechanism is only a system of means adapted to one another for the realization of an end; hence mechanism is not inconsistent with finality or teleology.

The theory of evolution cannot apply to the universe as whole, but within the universe to its particular parts.

## The theory of Teleological Evolution – the Evidence of Teleology

### (a) Evidence from the adaptation of means to ends in nature

The world abounds in infinitely complex adaptations of means to ends, and the lower ends to higher ones (*e.g.*, in instincts and in organs and their functions) which cannot be explained as accidental products of blind mechanical forces; they exhibit clear marks of design which require the guidance of an intelligent designing principle in nature. Selection, combination and gradation are marks of intelligent design; these signs of intelligence are abundantly found in nature, especially in organic nature. *(Martineau.)* For example, the different limbs of animals have been so selected as to fit them with one another and adapt them to the different media in which they live, on the land, under water, in the air. Combination is strikingly found in what is called the 'correlation of organs' *(Cuvier)*, 'correlation of growth', *(Darwin)* which means that the whole organism is so tied together during its growth and development, that none of the organs can change in form without the others also changing. There is also a wonderful gradation of arrangement, "by which a given end is attained through a train of independent means, each making provision for the next, till the series is.consummated and crowned by the fulfilment." *(Martineau.)* For example, life depends upon lifeless matter for its existence, and conscious existence depends upon life for its support. Thus there is an all-pervading, continuous gradation of arrangement in the causality of nature which is a distinguishing mark of intention. Thus the complex adaptations as revealed in selection, combination and gradation are regulated by an end or purpose, being designed by an intelligent Being,

It is evident that human beings work towards ends. Their actions are purposive. Their behaviour is intelligent, and directed to the fulfilment of ends. There is teleology or purpose in human affairs. In the human organism the parts are related to the whole, and the whole is related to the parts. The organs are adapted to their ends, and they are correlated to one another. There is adaptation in the human organism.

In the plant organism also the organs are adapted to their ends, and they are correlated to one another. "In organic bodies *the part is for the sake of the whole and the integrity of the whole is a value;* and this is all that is necessary to give us the teleological or purposive character of nature". (Patrick: *Introduction to Philosophy,* p. 170). There is adaptation, organisation, structural harmony in organisms. They are governed by the law of *causality* subordinate to teleology. Mere *cause* and *effect* cannot account for their behaviour. *Means* and *end* only can adequately explain their wonderful adaptation and harmony which can never be accidental. "The cause-and-effect relation, so fundamental in the mechanical sciences, no longer furnishes the key to the world of living organisms; a new relation appears, namely, that of *means* and *end*. It does not, of course, replace the relation of cause and effect; it supplements it. With the coming of life, something appears which we must designate as *value*. Life is a good; and whatever contributes to it is an instrumental good; for instance, food, air, water, sex, exercise." *(Ibid,* p. 168). There is organization, adaptation, structural harmony in living organisms, which cannot be explained by mechanical causation, but by teleology only. There is immanent teleology or purposiveness in living organisms. "Even the simplest organism *selects* certain things for food and *avoids* other things because they do or do not serve its purpose." *(Ibid,* p. 170). Concepts such *as* matter, motion, cause and effect are not sufficient to account for the purposive behaviour of organisms. Means, ends, purpose, value, can adequately account for them. But teleology or purpose does not annual mechanism. The cause-effect relation is subordinated to the means-and-end relation. Mechanism is subordinated to teleology. Mechanism and teleology are reconciled with each other in immanent finality. Mental energy selects a particular cause or means to produce a particular effect or fulfil a particular end or purpose. Causality is not mechanical but purposive or teleological. Thus, mechanism and teleology are not opposed to each other.

There is teleology not only in organisms but also in inanimate matter. "When we contemplate the order in Nature, the system of the spheres, the universality of law, we seem to see a great design—a pattern in the whole. The world exhibits evidence of an Infinite Intelligence that holds the worlds in order." *(Ibid,* p. 165). The whole world is governed by Law. There is order, unity, harmony in the whole universe. The parts of the world are inter-related to one another. This inter-relation cannot be accidental. It must be due to an Intelligence which inter-relates them to one another. Order is the expression of a *reason*. It is irrational and blind. It cannot be due to random play of mechanical forces. It cannot be explained by blind matter, motion, and force.

Henderson points out that there is purposiveness in inorganic nature. He finds that before life appeared on earth there was a peculiar *fitness* of the environment for it, which appears to be in the nature of a preparation. Before life appeared, the surface of the earth cooled, carbon, oxygen, and hydrogen appeared in the necessary proportions and were combined into their chemical' compounds; great quantities of water and carbonic acid appeared; the ample rainfall, the temperate atmosphere, rivers, lakes, and oceans, the cycles of summer, rainy season, and winter appeared. "All these and many other peculiarities of the environment illustrate its unique and remarkable fitness for life. It is almost infinitelly improbable that the unique totality of properties of the physical elements which provide the maximal fitness for organic life should be the result of accident. Mechanism rules throughout the world, but does not rule supreme. There is an organisation and order independent of mechanism. Not only is life itself something transcending mechanism, but the tendency towards life is also something transcending it." *(Ibid,* p. 167).

Henderson does not conclude that there is purpose or design in the inorganic world.' But. he concludes that the universe is *biocentric.* "The world in its inorganic stage looks forward to the coming of life, is adjusted to it, is in some sense a preparation for it." *(Ibid,* p. 168). But this is a halting conclusion. If the properties of matter are adjusted to the structure and functions of the living organisms, there must be immanent teleology in the inorganic world. There is purposiveness throughout nature—inorganic, organic, and conscious, and it is due to the cosmic mental energy striving to realize its goal through cosmic evolution. Thus, the universe is not mechanical but teleological. There is *mind* immanent in the world, which is the driving force in all evolutionary change.

**(b) Evidence from the nature of Causality**

A cause is a force or energy which produces an effect. But what is the nature of energy ? We know only one kind of energy *(vis.,* mental energy) in our effort of attention and volition. In attention we concentrate our mental energy upon a thing or an idea; in volition, we create energy by the free energising of our minds; so in natnre, too, force or energy must originate in mind; there can be no brute physical energy – all energy must be mental energy. For "all energy and activity is striving to do and attain something, without a result or end to be attained there could be no change. Therefore it is the end that both produces the energy, and guides the movement. But how is this possible ? Only in this way: the end must be present from the very beginning in the form of 'tendency' or 'idea ' and must work out its own realization." *(Stephen.)* Thus energy is the effort of mental power to overcome a defect and realize an end or purpose.

Besides, a particular cause produces a particular effect. A produces B and not C or D. But why does A produce B and not C or D ? What accounts for the rejection of alternate possibilities ? A blind mechanical force cannot account for it; the selection of a particular effect and the rejection of alternate possibilities are only possible in the choice or volition of mind for the realization of an end. Thus all causaliby is will-causality, and hence subservient to finality. Thus the evolution of the world is determined by an end or good and consists in co-ordination of means for the realization of ends. This is the theory of teleological evolution.

**Transcendent or External Teleology and Internal Teleology or Immanent Finality**

Teleology seems to be opposed to mechanism. Purpose and causality work in different ways. "Causality we might roughly describe as the determining of events from behind in time. Purpose on the contrary is the determining of events from ahead in time Causality works from the past into the present and purpose from the future into the present." (Hocking: *Types of Philosophy,* p. 106).

Ends may be realized in the world in two ways. First, they may be imposed on the world from without by an intelligent Being, *i. e.,* God (external or transcendent teleology). Secondly, the world may be evolved by the self-realizing power of the Absolute Idea which is immanent in the world-system (internal or immanent teleology). According to Transcendent Teleology, God is transcendent or external to the world. He forms plans or designs in his mind, like a human artificer, and imposes these designs upon the world from without after creating all materials out of nothing. But if God is external to the world, he is limited by it and becomes finite. (See above the criticism of the theory of creation 3). So we must fall back upon the theory of Internal or Immanent Teleology, which holds that God is immanent in the world, expresses himself in it, and realizes his end in it. God is the indwelling principle in the world, and the world is the self-expression or self-manifestation of God.

**Criticism of External Teleology**

The notion of external teleology is defective. If God is conceived as existing outside the world and imposing his plan on the world from the outside, he cannot be free from the defects of a human contriver. A human architect constructs a machine out of pre-existing materials by imposing his own plan on them, and then leaves it to itself to work out its own destiny with the help of the forces of nature. The relation between him and the machine is external, and arbitrary. So, if God is conceived as an external designer of the world, the relation between him and the world would be external and arbitrary.

God is external to the world. He created the world out of nothing and imposed his own plan on it. Thus he is limited by the world created by him.

The world is not necessary for the life of God and God is not necessary for the world. There is only an arbitrary relation between God and the world. God is the arbitrary Creator. Contriver and Sustainer of the world. And there is no inner connection or unity among the three functions of God, *viz.*, creation, contrivance and sustenance of the world. Thus the doctrine of external teleology cannot be maintained.

**Internal Teleology or Immanent Finality**

There is another kind of teleology which is called Internal

or Immanent Teleology. In immanent finality the contradiction between mechanism and teleology is solved. Mechanism or causality is a means through which an end or purpose is realized. Every event has both a cause and a purpose. It is determined by a. cause and realizes a purpose which is not imposed on it from without. In the animal organism we have an example of this kind of teleology. "The thought or design which is at work in the growth and development of organised structure is not a. mere mechanical power or cunning acting from without—shaping, adjusting, putting together materials prepared to its hand, constructing them according to an ingenious plan, after the manner of a maker of machines. Here, on the contrary, the idea or formative power goes with the matter, and constitutes the very indwelling essence of the thing From first to last it is self-formative, self-developing; the life within resists all merely outward interference, and subordinates all outward condition to its own development."

"Now, if it were possible to extend this teleological idea to the whole finite world we should then have one vast, self-consistent system, one organic whole, one self-evolving, self-realizing idea, infusing the lucidity of reason into all things potentially present in the lowest order of existences, slowly advancing itself, without cleft or arbitrary leap, from lower to higher; so that the lower, though not the cause, would be the presupposition and the unconscious prophecy of the higher, the higher the explanation of the lower, and the highest of all that in which the meaning, end, or aim of the whole would be clearly seen. Such a teleologieal view of the world would not involve a representation of Divine Intelligence as an arbitrary agency brought in from without to fill up gaps or improve on its original products, nor as a power acting in different isolated capacities—now as creator, now as contriver, now as sustainer—but as the inward life and reason of all things anticipating and fore-shadowing the end from the beginning and moving onwards in its own continuous, self-conditioned process to an end which itself determines." *(Introduction to the Philosophy of Religion,* pp. 137-139.)

Thus, according to this view, God is the immanent essence

of the world, and the world is the expression or manifestation of God. There is an intimate connection between the two. There can be no God without the world and there can be no world without God. God evolves the world from within his own nature, and realizes his own end in it.

**Creative Evolution**

The great French philosopher, Bergson, holds that teleology is as much mechanical as mechanism itself. Mechanism derives the present order of the world from its past condition, while teleology derives the present state of the world from the future end, plan or purpose of the world. According to mechanism, the present is determined by the past while according to finalism (or teleology), the present is determined by the future. Thus, according to both, the world is determined or caused; determination by the future is as much determination as determination by the past. Teleology is inverted mechanism. Mechanism and finalism both are fatalistic; they do not leave any scope for freedom or indetermination. According to Bergson, the world is absolutely undetermined and free; the evolution of the world is neither mechanical nor teleological, but creative. Bergson's conception of the creative evolution of the world is romantic; the world, according to him, is a continuous flow and flux; cosmic evolution is a ceaseless advance towards absolutely new creations-undetermined by the past or the future.

**Criticism of Creative Evolution**

Bergson's artistic conception of Creative Evolution strikes our fancy and fascinates our heart, no doubt; but it is nothing but poetry and its dream. It cannot stand the severe test of philosophical speculation which has been much discredited by the romantic philosopher. If cosmic evolution is neither determined by the past nor by the future, if there is no stable or permanent element in the world, if it is a ceaseless flux of absolutely new creations, then it is, indeed, a miracle; a continuous flow of entirely new and absolutely free creations can neither be conceived nor explained by the human mind;

and life becomes impossible, if the world is a heterogeneous medley of surprising novelties.

The present must be determined by the past, but not without a purpose. The present order of the world must be determined by the past in order to realize an end or purpose which is not imposed on it from without, but immanent in it. Mechanism is not inconsistent with finality. The doctrine of Immanent Finality offers the most satisfactory solution of the problem of cosmogony.

**Emergent Evolution**

There are two different views of the process of evolution when it is applied to the world as a whole. One may be called emergent evolution, and the other, repetitive evolution. According to the first view, in the evolution of the world, something new is being continuously evolved; life is quite a 'new' thing, which is different from matter; and mind is quite a 'new' thing, which is different from life. Cunningham says, "This view of evolution holds that in the ongoings of the world-order something 'new' is being continuously created as the process goes from level to level of existence – from the inorganic to the organic, and from the biological or vital to the psychological or mental—It holds that the novelty of life grows out of inorganic forms, and that the novelty of mind grows out of organic forms, the higher levels being real additions, to the lower; when life appears in the process something 'new' is created, and with the appearance of the mind another 'new' element is added which before was not explicitly present within the process. This is the conception of evolution as *emergent.*" *(Problems of Philosophy*, p. 244.)

This doctrine of emergent evolution is advocated by Prof. Alexander and Lloyd Morgan.

This theory, like the doctrine of Creative Evolution, is opposed to the theory of repetitive evolution, according to which, "nothing 'new' appears in the process of the world's development, but that very level is a bare repetition of the.preceding level. Mind is merely a different and more complex expression of life, life is merely a different and more complex expression or product of matter, and matter is the ultimate form of existence or reality." *(Ibid,* pp. 244-45.)

"There are two kinds of effect in nature, which George Henry Lewis distinguished as 'resultants' and 'emergents'. The resultants are the effects which we are able to deduce from the causes. The emergents are the unpredictable effects which, so to speak, supervene together with the resultants. Now may it be that life and mind 'emerge' in this abrupt way when ever in the rearrangements of physical elements the right kind of order or form happens to be struck out ? This is the suggestion of Lloyd Morgan." (Hocking: *Types of Philosophy,*,p. 58.)

"Evolution is a series of stages, in which there supervenes at each new level a new form of 'relatedness', a new structure or organisation and from this new form of relatedness something new 'emerges'. Thus, from matter emerges life—and from life, mind.

But what causes the ·emergents to emerge ? What is the *agency* which lifts the world, so to speak, from one level to the next ? Here Lloyd Morgan definitely takes his stand on the necessity of affirming a power which he calls Activity, or Mind, or God. (Patrick: *Introduction to Philosophy,* p. 150).

Lloyd Morgan says, "I acknowledge God is the Nisus through whose Activity emergents emerge, and the whole course of emergent evolution is directed" *(Emergent Evolution,* p. 36).

Lloyd Morgan's doctrine of *Emergent Evolution* is similar to Bergson's doctrine of *Creative Evolution.* Both hold that something new emerges out of the old. Protons and electrons are combined into atoms; atoms are combined into molecules molecules are combined into cells; cells are combined into organisms simple acts of organisms are combined into complex Intelligent behaviour of men. Thus, life emerges from matter, mind emerges from life. In the course of evolution something appears as a novelty, a new creation, possessing new characteristics, and governed by new laws. Evolution is creative not repetitive. It is forward-looking not backward-looking.

Lloyd Morgan assumes the existence of God as the Nisus through whose activity emergents emerge, whereas Bergson assumes Elan Vital, Stream of life as the evolutionary urge which creates new things perpetually.

The theory of emergent evolution has the merit of recognizing the novelty and uniqueness of life and mind. It is forward-looking, like the doctrine of creative evolution. And as forward-looking, it is inexplicable without teleological causation. A forward-looking process or progress is always directed towards a future end, or good and is determined by it. Emergent evolution without teleology is as miraculous as creative evolution.

## Matter, Life and Mind

Lloyd Morgan is the propounder of the doctrine of emergent evolution. It is based on the fact that *organization* takes place, and as the outcome of such organisation new things appear with new properties and powers—making new laws necessary, not abrogating others. Protons and electrons get into new relations and combinations and produce atoms; atoms are organised into molecules; molecules are organised into compounds; cells emerge out of the organization of protoplasmic matter; organisms emerge out of the organisation of cells; mind or consciousness emerges out of the complex organisation of the nervous system. Thus matter, life and mind emerge out of the organisation of the previous elements. They are the different stages in the evolution of the cosmos. Life is a higher stage than matter. Mind is a higher stage than life. Matter, life and mind are the different *levels* of existence. Life cannot be reduced to matter or chemico-meehanical force. Mind cannot be reduced to life. Nor can be an epiphenomenon of the brain.

But what causes these emergents to emerge ? What is the *agency* which lifts the world from one level to the next ? Lloyd Morgan feels the necessity of God as ths nisus or urge through whose Activity emergents emerge, and the whole course of emergent evolution is directed. Emergent evolution is forward-looking. New things emerge out of old things, with new properties and powers. These things effectively determine the course of future events. The doctrine of emergent evolution combines the advantages of mechanism and vitalism, though missing the defects of both. (Patrick: *Introduction to Philosophy,* pp. 151-52).

**Emergence Theory–Mind and Body**

"Mind and body do not interact, as Interactionism and Dualism teach; The mind is not a form of the mechanical interplay of atoms, as materialism teaches. The body is not a phenomenon, or appearance, or externalization of mind, as Idealism teaches. Mind and body are not parallel, as Psychophysical Parallelism teaches. Neither are they two aspects of the same reality, as the Double-aspect theory teaches Mind is something which; the body achieves, or which nature achieves by means of the body. When nature achieves the molecule, the atom ceases to be of primary importance, worth, or reality. When nature achieves the cell, the molecule is eclipsed. When the organism. is achieved, the cell is eclipsed. When mind is achieved, the body is eclipsed. Mind is a new reality, gained, achieved; won." (*Ibid,* pp. 298-99).

Body and mind are different levels of reality. There is no correlation, there is no parallelism, there is no double-aspect. It is rather a case of differt levels of reality. There is a series of *vital* processes, which, when *integrated* or *organised,* exhibit capacities that we call *mental* or *psychical.* When they are so organised as to yield *intelligent control,* we *no* longer call them vital or neural processes, but *psychical.* "We are upon a new level, among new realities, in a new atmosphere, dealing with new things having their own laws and peculiarities. Mind has emerged from matter; the spiritual has) emerged from the physical." (*Ibid,* p. 300). This is the relation between body and mind according to Emergent Evolution.

## UNIVERSITY QUESTIONS

1. What is your idea about creation ? What place do you give in it to Spencerian doctrine of Evolution ? (1910).
2. Distinguish carefully between the conceptions of

mechanism and teleology, with special reference to the phenomena of life. (1910 Hon.)

3. In what sense, if any, is a 'teleological' view of the universe incompatible with a 'mechanical' view of it ? (1913 Hon.)
4. Is the modern theory of evolution anything more than the ancient theory of change ? Does it really help us to explain any philosophical problem ? (1914 Hon.)
5. Can you reconcile the modern theories of Evolution with Teleology ? Examine, in this connection, the proposition: Evolution is not a Cause, or even a Force, but a *Method.* (1915 Hon.)
6. Nominalism, Conceptualism, and Realism: explain and illustrate the meanings of these terms in Logic, and the corresponding theories in Philosophy, giving the meaning and different views of Universal. (1918 Hon.)
7. Explain fully the meaning and significance of Nominalism and Realism (a) in their logical, and (b) intheir metaphysical meaning:

   and exhibit the bearing of this question on the question of Species in the organic world. (1916 Hon.)
8. Explain the meaning of Evolution in nature, and give seasons why many think that Nature must be explained by some theory of Evolution. Which of these theories do you consider to be the more adequate, and why ? (1913).
9. Explain what is meant by the theory of evolution. Within what limits is the law of evolution applicable ? (1914).
10. Write short notes on the meaning of the mechanical theory of the universe. (1914).
11. State and examine the arguments for and against the doctrine that the world has an end. (1915).
12. What is meant (in natural science and philosophy) by a Species ? What different opinions have been held with regard to the nature and origin of Species ? On what reasonings are these opinions founded ? (1916).

13. Discuss in detail the Mechanical and Teleological views of the Universe. (1917).
14. What do you understand by Evolution ? Distinguish between its mechanical and teleological forms. Which of them do you consider to be a satisfactory account of natural phenomena ? (1920).
15. State and examine the conception of evolution. (1924).
16. Explain fully what is meant by Evolution in Nature, with illustrations. Sketch briefly the main reasons for believing in Evolution. Is there any other theory of the origin of nature? (1926).
17. Explain the meaning of Realism and Nominalism in Metaphysics and show the bearing of this question on the meaning of Species in nature. (1926).
18. Write a short note on the nature of evolution, with special reference to the problem of creative *versus* emergent evolution. (1928). [See 18, 19 & 20.]
19. What is meant by saying that 'the world is only a vast machine' ? Point out evidences which suggest a different interpretation. (1923).
20. 'Evolution unfolds what is enfolded, and so the tree pre-exists in a seed'. (Mechanical Evolution.) 'Evolution brings about a new product and so the tree is in no sense present in its seed'. (Teleological Evolution.)

    Explain the above concepts of evolution and show how they are related to mechanical and teleological evolution. (1929).
21. Show how far the species-idea is modified by the concept of Evolution. What are the main points at issue between mechanical and teleological evolution ? (1931).
22. Discuss briefly the different forms of the doctrine of Biological Evolution, and state which of them appeals to you and why ? (1932).
23. Discuss fully the different theories as to the nature and origin of Species. (1933).

24. Explain the principle of evolution in nature. What is meant by teleological evolution ? (1934).

25. Give a critical estimate of the doctrine of evolution as an explanation of the origin of species. (19S5).

26. Explain the meaning of final cause. What do you understand by the teleological view of the universe ? How is it distinguished from a mechanical view ? (1936).

27. Contrast the teleological with the mechanical explanation of the world. (1937).

28. What is Evolution in Nature ? Explain your reasons for believing in Evolution. Can the theory of Evolution be applied to the human soul ? (1946).

29. What is a 'Final Cause' ? State clearly the distinction between a teleological and a mechanical view of the universe. (1947).

30. What do you mean by Evolution ? How does Herbert Spencer explain the universe by the theory of Evolution ? Is it a satisfactory theory ? (A. U. 1948).

31. Show how the Emergence Theory explains the relation of Body and Mind, and compare it with Interactionism and Parallelism. What are its limitations ? (A. U. 1948).

32. Give a critical estimate of Darwin and Lamarck's Theories of evolution. (A. U.)

33. Is the world mechanical or teleological. Discuss the question and give reasons for your own view. (A. U. 1947).

84. What do you understand by the process of evolution ? Can Matter, Life and Mind be regarded as stages in the natural process of evolution ? (1947).

## CHAPTER VII

# COSMOLOGY

### The problem of Cosmology or the problem of One and Many

We have discussed the question of cosmogony or the origin of the world. Now let us turn to the second problem about the world, the problem of cosmology or the problem of the *constitution* and *organisation* of the world. The world at first appears to our common experience as a plurality of self-existent and independent objects unconnected with one another. But an deeper reflection it appears as a unitary system of a plurality of substances acting and reacting on one another and organised throughout. The world is a system of reals all inter-related with one another in time and space forming on organised whole?) Thus not only does it exhibit the characteristic of unity and organisation but also that of individuality and relative independence of things. It is not merely an aggregate of a plurality of self-existent and independent objects, but a concrete whole or unity consisting of a plurality of interdependent and inter-related objects. Unity and *plurality thus* are *correlative to each other. Neither* can be resolved into the other without rendering it meaningless. Unity must not be sacrificed to a plurality, nor plurality to unity.

But this correlation of unity and plurality is often disregarded and unusual stress is laid either on one or on many, which 'leads to two different types of thinking, *viz.*, monism and pluralism, But, as a matter of fact, unity and plurality both are empirically real; hence both must be explained. Pluralism, therefore, will have to explain the unity of the world, while monism will have to account for the empirical reality of individuality and diversity of things, the plurality of finite minds and objects. Indeed, unity and plurality must be reconciled in a higher unity which is not an abstract unity, but a rich concrete unity containing plurality within itself or a unity in plurality. This doctrine is called concrete monism. Pluralism, again, may take two forms, materialistic pluralism (or atomism) and spiritualistic pluralism (or monadism), the former regarding the ultimate constituents of the reality as material and the latter regarding them as spiritual. Thus the problem of cosmology is the problem of one and many. The cosmological theories may be classified as follows;

**COSMOLOGY**

- Pluralism
  - Materialistic pluralism or atomism (Demmocritus and others)
  - Spiritualistic pluralism or atonadism (Leibnitz)
  - Pragmatist pluralism
  - New realist pluralism
- Monism
  - Abstract monism (or Pantheism (Eleatics and Spinoza)
  - Conditional monism or conditional dualism (or Deism)
  - Concrete monism or Panentheism (Hegel)

**Pluralism**

"Pluralism emphasizes the individual and the part played by the individual in the constitution of the world. Though not denying the unity of the universe, pluralists explain it as a unity made up of the individual parts." *(Marvin)*. They explain the world as a mechanical aggregate of a plurality of self-existent and independent entities. Pluralism stresses the manifoldness and variety of the world, its infinite diversities and novelties, whereas monism stresses the unity and order of the world. Pluralism emphasizes the system in thins, while monism emphasises their discords and dissonances.

We may ask two questions concerning these individuals: first, their ontology secondly, their cosmology proper, or the relation among them that makes up the order or constitution of the world. The individuals may be thought of as material or as spiritual; in the former case, we call them atoms in the latter, spirits, souls or monads. Thus pluralism is divided. into materialistic pluralism or atomism and spiritualistic pluralism or monadism. As to the order and relation among the constituent elements atomism believes in the theory of Interaction, and monadism, in the theory of Pre-established Harmony.

### (I) Materialistic Pluralism (or Atomism)

Atomism makes a number of assumptions. It assumes the self-existence of empty space as a thing by itself. It assumes an infinite number of self-existent material atoms, distributed at random through space. It assumes that these atoms are endowed with self-existent motion of attraction and repulsion. By the fortuitous combinations and recombinations of these in infinite time and space, the world is made with all its things and qualities, including even life and mind.

Thus atomism dispenses with the idea of God, since it derives the world from a chance combination of atoms. Hence atomism may be called Atheistic Pluralism. Or it may be assumed that self-existent and independent atoms by their chance combination cannot produce the beauty, complexity, order and harmony of the world; it is God who created the atoms and endowed them with motion to react upon one another and work out the world-system, or God manufactured the world out of the original chaos by organising and directing the movement of atoms according to his own plan or design. This form of. atomism is called Theistic Pluralism.

### Criticism of Atomism

Atomism assumes many things. *It* assumes *the self-*

*existence of* space *and time and* the self-existence of matter and motion.

(1) Atomism cannot explain the unity and order of the world. Atoms are self-existent, independent entities; they are different worlds by themselves. How then can they come into contact with one another to form the unity of the world ? What is the principle of unity among them ?

(2) Atomism believes in blind chance to bring the atoms into contact with one another. chance combinations of atoms cannot account for the order and harmony of the world.

(3) Atomism believes in the theory of Interaction. It tries to explain interaction among bodies by assuming the transference of motion or an influence. But the transference of motion involves a great metaphysical difficulty.

Atomism indulges in abstractions. Atoms are only abstractions. There are no atoms in the world, but there are atomic things, just as there are no triangles or circles in the world, but there are triangular or circular things. Thus atomism hypostatizes abstractions when it holds that the world comes out of the chance combination of atoms.

Atomism is a form of materialism and as such involves all the difficulties of materialism. It cannot bridge over the gulf between matter and life, and between life and mind. It believes in the doctrine of abiogenesis or spontaneous generation of life out of lifeless matter, and in the doctrine of epiphenomenalism which regards mind as an epiphenomenon of the brain. Hence it involves all the difficulties of these hypotheses.

**(1) Spiritualistic Pluralism (or Monadism)**

Leibnitz. is the father of spiritualistic pluralism which assumes the form of monadism in his doctrine. According to him, the ultimate units of the reality are spiritual atoms or monads. Monads are unextended, immaterial substances or spiritual atoms which are essentially self-active in nature; they are metaphysical points, as opposed to physical points and mathematical points. They differ from the former since they have no extension, and from the latter, since they are objective realities. Monads are spiritual atoms or forces.

"Further since their essence consists in self-activity, they cannot receive any impression, nothing can penetrate them and the apparent interaction of processes in the visible world depends solely upon a wise fore-ordination, the 'pre-established harmony in virtue of which the states of all substances correspond to one another without exerting any mutual influence." (Kulpe: *Introduction to Philosophy,* p. 127.)

Thus every monad ideates or represents the whole universe and is, in this sense, a microcosm, a mirror of the whole universe. There is a hierarchy of monads, self-conscious, conscious, subconscious, and unconscious. Human souls are self-conscious monads. Animal souls are conscious monads. Plant souls are subconscious monads. Material things are unconscious monads. In fact, there is no matter. The universe. is composed of monads. They were created by God, the Monad of monads, who pre-adjusted them to one another. The mind is the queen monad, the dominant monad. The body is a cluster of subordinate monads. Though mind does not act upon the body, it dominates it. There is a pre-established harmony between them.

**Criticism of Spiritualistic Pluralism or Monadism**

As regards the ontology of the ultimate reals, they are spiritual in nature; hence monadism involves all the difficulties

And monadism is a form of pluralism and as such involves all the difficulties of pluralism. How can self-existent and independent monads come into, connection with one another to form this world-system ? Atomism believes in blind chance and in the theory of interaction among the atoms. Monadism brings in the conception of God or the "Monad of monads" who pre-adjusted the monades to one another at the time of creation. But the theory of Pre-established Harmony fares no better than the theory of Interaction. By the former theory, "you take change out of the world, put it in God and then bring it back again. But how does God act on the world is the question, and you have left it unanswered; and it is the same question, twist as you will: 'How does an entity act upon another entity?" *(Marvin)*.

Atomism does not believe in God and is therefore Atheistic

Pluralism. Monadism believes in God, and is therefore called Theistic Pluralism.

### (III) Pragmatic Pluralism

There is a strong pluralistic-tendency at the present time. Pragmatism is a revolt against Absolutism. Hegel and his followers made too much of the Absolute. He holds that the world is a systematic unity of inter-related reals. It.is the outward expression of the Absolute Idea. It is the externalization of the idea of God. The finite spirits are the finite reproductions of the Absolute Spirit. Society, state, morality are the outward expressions of the Divine Mind. The world is Absolute Experience. Everything is determined by God or the Absolute. There is no scope for freedom, novelty, new creation. Hegel was a typical exponent of monism.

William James, the founder of Pragmatism, revolted against this monistic Absolutism of Hegel and his followers. He propounded the doctrine of *'Pluralastic Universe'.* He holds that the world is an aggregate of many things. They are not inter-related to one another. They do not form a system. The world is manifold and varied, discrete and chaotic. It is not a universe, but a multiverse.. It is not a cosmos but a chaos. It is a pluralistic universe. It is not an expression of God. It exists in its own right, independent of God and finite minds. The world is not a *block universe,* in which everything is pre-determined by God. It is undetermined, free, contingent, full of novelty, variety, new creations. There is chance in it. There is freedom in it. Human beings have freedom. They create new values. Evil is real and positive. We freely fight out evil and bring about a better order. God is finite. He is not infinite and Absolute. He works in an environment like us. He inspires and guides us in fighting out evil. There is chance, freedom, progress in the world.

"James was not interested in the One, but in the Many. It is the 'each-form', rather than the "all-form' of things that impressed him—their discreteness, their separateness, their independence, their novelty, their freedom, their contingency, their spontaneity, their manifold, even their chaotic character. He did not find any 'block universe' with 'a through-and-through unity'. Reality is of 'the strung-along type'. The word 'and' trails along after every sentence. Reality is distributive rather than collective. Freedom exists, and chance and novelty and progress." (Patrick: *Introduction to Philosophy,* I). 231).

James' pluralism gives us a real freedom, power of free creations. It gives a real progress. It solves the problem of evil. Evil is real and can be exterminated by free human efforts. It gives us a God who is not a mere all-embracing omnipotent world-unity. It does not believe in fatalism.

"The universe is tychistic. Chance is real in it Evil is as actual as good. There is no eternal law; there is no over-arching destiny, no all-compelling Providence." *(James).*

Hegelian Absolutism made too much of the One the Absolute, God, and belittled the freedom of man. James made too much of the Many, human freedom, chance. novelty "discreteness, manifoldness.

But James cannot account for the relation of the world to the finite minds and God. He cannot explain the relation of different things to one another and finite minds to one another. His conception of finite God is not satisfactory. Human freedom is not absolute. There is no chance in the world. Chance is our ignorance of law. Law pervades the universe. It is an expression of mind, the Divine Mind. Human freedom is not; swamped in Divine Freedom. Man is free and can-make new creations within the plan of God, His freedom is limited. The world is not a block universe. It is dynamic progressive, free flowering out of the infinite wealth' of the Divine Mind.

**(IV) Pluralism of the New Realists**

James emphasizes the richness and variety of the world of perception. The New Realists emphasize the richness and variety of the world of reason, of thought, and of values.

The New Realists hold that the manifold world of discrete and unconnected things is real. They are not inter-related to one another into a system. The relations among them are external. There are no internal relations among them. Mental events and processes also are real. Physical events and mental events are the same stuff in different relations and contexts. A book is a physical thing in relation to other things. It is an idea or a mental process in relation to the nervous system. The physical events and the mental events are composed of a neutral stuff which is neither physical or mental. This theory is called neutral monism.

The physical things in time and space are called *existents*. The non-physical and non-mental entities are called *subsistents*. They are principles of reason, logical principles, relations, numbers, space, time, truth, good, and beauty. The ideal values are not conditioned by space and time. They are subsistents.

Matter, life, and mind are the different levels of reality. Life is a higher reality which emerges from highly organised matter. Mind is a higher reality which emerges from the highly organised nervous system. There is emergent evolution. "At each new level, as the result of organization, new realities emerge not found in the elements which make up the lower level. Life and mind are such new realities emerging from the synthesis of simpler elements. No higher level *violates* the laws of those lower levels, but also no *lower* level, *causally* determines any higher level. Freedom subsists, therefore, at each level as we ascend from the inorganic to the chemical, and then to the living and then to the mental and then to the ethical". (Patrick: *Introduction to Philosophy,* p. 233).

Evolution does not apply to God, nor to logical principles, nor to truth, good and beauty, the eternal values. Justice and beauty and goodness are models which we are ever approaching, but never completely realizing. They are eternal archetypes, in the language of Plato. They are subsistents, not existents conditioned by space and time.

The world is manifold, dynamic, purposive, and creative of values. It is not a dead mechanism, static and material. It is teleological. it is not dead to all values.

The New Realist regards God as "the totality of values, both existent and subsistent." "God is Value, the active, living principle of the conservation of values and of their efficiency".

Pluralism of the New Realists is a healthy check to the over-hasty monistic impulse which sacrifices manifoldness and individuality to unity. But it is an ill-assorted jumble of many inconsistent ideas. It cannot account for the relation among the things of the world. It reduces mind to physical things as related to the nervous system. It identifies mind with body and physical things. It posits a neutral stuff which becomes physical and mental in different relations and contexts. This is pan-objectivism. It ignores the subjectivity of mind and consciousness. It is absurd to hold that a physical event itself becomes a mental content in relation to the nervous system. This is over-simplification of a complex problem.

The New Realists make too much of Emergent Evolution. New entities emerge as a result of creative synthesis of elements in the lower level. But the New Realists do not explain the reason of creative synthesis. The world is purposive and creative of values. But the New Realists do not believe in a Mind or *Elan vital,* which directs the evolutionary process. They look upon God as ' the totality of values, both existent and subsistent." This conception of God is novel but hazy. God is the eternal embodiment of the ideal values, truth, good, and beauty. The ideal values find their eternal fulfilment in God, which we realize in time and space imperfectly.

The pluralistic world-view of the New Realists contains many truths which, if reconciled with one another, can logically lead to an idealistic view of the world. They do not bring out the full implications of their position.

### Monism—its three types

Pluralism emphasizes the individuality and multiplicity of things, either denying the unity of the world or explaining it as a mechanical aggregate of a plurality of independent reals. Monism, on the contrary, affirms that the self-subsistent Absolute is one, and that finite things possess no independent reality of their own, but derive whatever reality they have from the absolute one. But the relation between *one* and *many,* between the self-subsistent one or the Absolute and the world of finite things may be understood in three different ways, giving rise to three different types of monism. Thus, it may be supposed that the world of finite things has no *real* existence at all, that it is only an appearance, nothing being truly real except the absolute one (abstract monism); that the world of things has real existence outside and independent of the absolute one, but that it has received its independent existence from the one, and is not essentially necessary to the one, so that its existence is temporary and conditional (conditional monism); or that the absolute one evolves the world of finite things from within itself as the material of its own life, so that the absolute and the relative are each necessary to the other as factors of one concrete and living reality (concrete monism).

**Abstract Monism (Pantheism)**

Abstract monism carries the principle of unity to the utmost extreme, and assumes that reality is an indivisible unity, excluding all contradiction and thereby all ground of plurality. The world of finite things and minds can have no substantial and independent existence, apart from the existence of the absolute one; the plurality of finite things and minds can be only illusory appearance of the Absolute to our finite consciousness. Abstract monism, thus, merges the many in the one.

"Spinoza is its first typical exponent. Spinoza's one infinite substance, God or *causa sui,* is possessed of innumerable attributes. Only two of them are accessible to human knowledge, extension and thought. Each of these finds expression in particular 'modes'. Thus the various physical bodies are modes ot the attribute of extension, and the different individual minds-modes of the attribute of thought" *(Kulpe.)* Thus finite things and minds have only a phenomenal existence being immanent modifications of the one substance *viz.* God. Thus Spinoza merges the world in God. (Pantheism: *pan* = all; *theos* = God).

**Criticism of Abstract Monism (Pantheism)**

Abstract monism goes to the extreme of abstracting the one from the many, and giving real existence to the one by itself, while denying all reality to the many. Hence if it regard the one as God it will be pantheism, making God to be one and all, and leaving no room for any independent reality, other than apparent or finite beings." *(Stephen).*

It denies the reality of the world, merging it in that of God, and thus leads to acosmism (the doctrine of the unreality of the world).

Without altogether denying the existence of the world, pantheism ascribes to the world of plurality an illusory or phenomenal existence, and thus leads to illusionism. But illusions, too, must be explained as such. You cannot explain a thing away simply by calling it an illusion.

It denies the reality and independence of finite minds, and, thus contradicts the direct testimony of our general self-consciousness and moral consciousness. We are clearly conscious of ourselves as distinct, individual personal beings, having the power of free initiation and self-determination. But abstract monism, denying the independence and personality of finite beings, and explaining away the distinction between right and wrong as illusory, destroys the foundation of morality. Thus abstract monism (or pantheism) is anti-ethical or non-moral.

It makes *religion* impossible. Religion consists in the communion of the finite mind with God. But, according to abstract monism, the finite mind has no reality at all; it is only a mode of God. Thus religion becomes impossible.

**Conditional Monism (or Conditional Dualism of Deism)**

This doctrine combines some characteristics of abstract or pantheistic monism with some of dualism. Like pantheism, it affirms that there is one absolute self-existent reality (*viz*.. God), and that this absolute reality existed from eternity, without needing any world of finite things and minds, an absolute without any relative, God without any world. This is evidently the abstract unity of pantheism, considered as a personal and self-conscious being. But this personal absolute, at a certain point of time, in its eternal self-sufficient being, willed into existence, out of nothing, a world of finite things and minds, gave them plan and co-ordination, and set them working as new independent realities, not evolved out of itself, but created out of nothing, and made independent of itself. Thus God has created the atoms of matter, and invested them with their attributes of resistance and motion, and left them to work according to the mechanical laws imposed on them the has created also finite minds and endowed them with freedom of the will and left them to work out their own destinies independently. Thus according to conditional monism or deism God has an independent and absolute reality; the world of plurality has only a relative and dependent existence, being created by God. out of nothing. Hence this doctrine is called conditional monism or conditional dualism (or Deism).

**Criticism of Conditional Monism**

This doctrine based on the theory of creation, involves all its characteristic difficulties. It makes God to be an abstract power before the creation of the world which is not a necessary factor in the divine life. It reduces God to a finite being after creation as he is limited by the world which is external to him; and it makes him a *Deus ex machina* as it believes in the doctrine of occasional divine intervention to set right the disorders of the world, when necessary. (See the criticism of the theory of creation. Ch. VI.)

Dualism cannot be an ultimate explanation of the world, even though it be in a conditional form. The dualism between God and the world presupposes the existence of another higher principle which makes the relation possible. The world must be a necessary factor of the divine life, being evolved by God to realize his purpose.

**Concrete Monism (Panentheism–Hegel)**

Abstract monism (or pantheism) practically denies the reality of finite things, making them to be only unreal appearances. Conditional monism (or deism) supposes that finite things have their existence outside and alongside of the infinite without limiting it, being created by God out of nothing. Concrete monism, however, conceives the one and the many, infinite and finite, absolute and relative not as mutually exclusive, but as correlative to each other, so that the two together constitute one concrete reality. "Thus we may suppose that the ultimate unity (as abstract infinite) evolves inexhaustibly from within itself the plurality of the world, and at the same time gives relation and co-ordination to this plurality of things and minds, and thereby retains them all within its own all-comprehensive unity, as factors of one unitary system, contributory to one ultimate end (the concrete infinite). In this way, the many will be understood as factors in the life of the absolute one. The absolute one will thus be conceived as making itself real by evolving the many from within itself and at the same time co-ordinating the many as factors of its self-conscious life. The many, therefore, will have relative reality as factors in the concrete life of the one absolute reality." *(Stephen.)* Hegel is the exponent of this view.

**Types of Monism compared**

Concrete monism difers from abstract monism (or pantheism) in this, that it gives relative reality to the world of things, making finite things and minds to be the materials of the conscious life of God; and at the same time makes God transcendent above the world as well as immanent in it. It makes God transcendent because, according to it, the world is the means to which God is the end, and God is not exhausted in and co-extensive with the world, in the sense of being but the sum-total of finite things, because no sum-total of finite things can exhaust the infinite; and God is the subject to which the world is the object, and therefore

God thinks it without being identical with it. It is not pantheism (*pan* = all, *theos* = God; all is God,) but panentheism (*pan*= all, *en* = in, *theos* = God; all are in God). *(Stephens.)*

Concrete monism (or panentheism) differs from conditional monism (or deism) in this, that it supposes a vital connection between God and the world, regarding the world as a necessary factor in the divine life and consciousness, and at the same time exhibits the necessary existence of God as the ultimate ground and explanation of the world, and reconciles the infinitude of God with His absoluteness regarding the infinite as the inexhaustible power or potentiality which realizes itself in the world of finite things and minds.

**Review of the different theories of the world**

We have discussed the different theories of the World in

connection with Ontology and Cosmology. Now we shall review all these theories in brief, as they have a bearing upon the conceptions of God. We may represent the different theories of the world, both from the ontological and cosmological points of view, in the following way:

## A. Monism

Monism asserts the self-existence of the absolute one and denies the independece of the plurality of finite things and beings, and conceives the relation between the one and the many in three differeent ways, thus giving rise to three different types of monism.

### (1) Abstract Monism

Abstract monism goes to the utmost extreme of attracting the one from the *many,* and giving real existence to the one by itself and regarding the many as illusory appearances of the one. Thus the world of finite things and minds is explained away as an illusion; it has no real existence. Spinoza is the typical exponent of this doctrine.

**Criticism**

*(i)* Abstract monism leads to pantheism, as it makes God to be one and all, leaving no room for any independent reality of finite things and beings.

*(it)* Abstract monism, thus, leads to acosmism, as it denies the reality of the cosmos or the world.

*(iii)* Abstract monism leads to illusionism, as it assigns only an illusory existence to the world.

*(iv)* Abstract monism, denying the personality and independence of finite minds, strikes at the root of morality and thus becomes non-moral or anti-ethical.

### (2) Conditional Monism

Conditional monism asserts the self-existence independence dance only of the absolute one, but admits the reality of the world of plurality, which it has received from the absolute one. This doctrine is called conditional monism, as it regards the absolute one as an ultimate and independent reality, and the many as derived from the one being created out of nothing. It is also called conditional dualism, as; it regards both the one and the many, God and the world as real (dualism), but the former as absolutely real and independent, while the latter as created by, and hence dependent upon the former (conditional dualism).

**Critism**

*(i)* God without the world is an abstract power or potentiality without any concrete reality. Hence the world must be a necessary factor in the life of God. God and the world are, in a sense, co-eternal as essence and manifestation. The one without the many is an unreal abstraction.

*(ii)* If God or the absolute one creates the world of plurality out of nothing and then leaves it to itself, and interferes with its operations to save it from decay at times, then God is no better than a human architect he is limited by the world, and thus becomes finite.

**(3) Concrete Monism**

Concrete monism incorporates the truths of both abstract; monism and conditional monism in itself. Abstract monism asserts the reality of the one denying the reality of the many and making them to be only unreal apppearances. Conditional monism (or conditional dualism) asserts the reality, of both the one and the many, but regards the former as the ultimate, eternal, independent and self-existent reality, while the latter as a derivative, temporary, dependent and created reality. Abstract monism dissolves the many in one, while conditional monism puts them side by side, external to each other. Concrete monism neither merges the many is one (abstract monism), nor the one in many (pluralism), but regards them as correlative factors of a higher unity, which is neither an abstract unity nor an abstract plurality, but a rich and concrete unity-in-plurality or identity-in-difference. Nor does it regard the one and the many as separate from, and external to each other (as conditional monism holds), but as correlative and complementary to each other, the one (God) being the essence of the many which are its manifestations. Thus, according to concrete monism, both God and the world are real; they cannot be separated from each other; they are co-eternal; the world is the necessary factor in the divine life; it is in and through the world that God manifests himself and realizes his infinite potentialities the world, too, cannot exist without the sustaining energy of divine will; God is the final explanation, the ultimate ground and reason of the worlds (See above the detailed criticism of the theory of creation. Ch. VI.)

## B. Dualism

According to dualism, there are two ultimate principles of the world, which are self-existent realities independent of each other. Dualism takes two forms—absolute dualism and conditional dualism.

### (i) Absolute Dualism

According to absolute dualism, the, the two ultimate principles are quite independent of each other; one is the principle of good, the other is the principle of evil. This doctrine of absolute dualism has been worked out by Plato and Aristotle According to Plato, the *Idea of the Good* and. the self-existent *hyle* or matter are the two ultimate principles of the world. The Idea of the Good seeks to evolve a world perfectly good and beautiful, but it is resisted by matter which brings about evils and imperfections of the world. According to Aristotle, God is the *actus purus or* pure activity, and matter is entirely passive. The conflict of these two principles is the cause of evil. Absolute dualism also takes the form of *Manicheism,* according to which, God manufactured the world out of the pre-existent primordial matter.

### (ii) Conditional Dualism

According to conditional dualism, matter and spirit, the world and God both are real and independent, but God is absolutely independent, self-existent and external, whereas the world has derived its existence and independence from God, so that it has a created, temporary and conditional existence. Conditional dualism is another name for conditional monism.

**Criticism**

(i) Dualism cannot be the ultimate explanation of the world : the dualism of God and matter—the *Idea of the Good* and hyle—the conflict between the two radically opposed principles, presupposes a higher principle of unity to overcome this conflict and opposition and reconcile the two hostile principles.

*(ii)* Dualism, in both of its forms, makes God to be finite, as he is limited and resisted by matter; it makes God to be like a human architect who cannot create anything new, but constructs something out of pre-existing materials.

## C. Pluralism

While monism assumes God or the Absolute as the only self-existent reality of which the world is either an appearance (abstract monism) or a manifestation or expression (concrete monism), and dualism assumes God (or the idea of the Good) and matter as two absolute self-existent principles, pluralism goes further than this and assumes that there are not merely two, but many self-existent realities. Pluralism takes two forms, materialistic pluralism or atomism and spiritualistic pluralism or monadism.

### (I) Materialistic Pluralism or Atomism

According to atomism, the world is the chance combination of self-existent material atoms endowed with self-existent motion, distributed at random through self-existent space. Life and mind are products of matter. This type of pluralism does not believe in the existence of God; hence it is the *antitheistic* variety of *pluralism.*

**Criticism**

*(i)* Many self-existent and independent principles cannot borne together to form the unity of the world

(ii) Atomism leaves too much to chance. Chance combination cannot account for the unity, order, beauty and harmony of the world, which is evident in the wonderful adaptations of means to ends specially among the living beings.

(iii) Atomism believes in the theory of interaction which involves many metaphysical difficulties,

*(iv)* Atomism assumes everything and explains nothing. It assumes the self-existence of atoms, the self-existence of motion and the self-existence of time and space,

*(v)* Atomism is a form of materialism and as such involves all the difficulties of materialism. For example, it cannot account for the origin of life, as it believes in the doctrine of abiogenesis or spontaneous-generation which has been exploded by recent investigations.

*(vi)* It cannot account for tbe origin of consciousness; consciousness cannot be regarded either as a function, or a secretion, or a by-product, or an epiphenomenon of the brain,

*(vii)* It cannot account for our moral consciousness as it takes away the independence and personality of the human mind and there-by saps the very foundation of morality.

(viii) It involves an epistemological, difficulty and is based on a 'circular argument'.

**(2) Spiritualistic Pluralism**

According to spiritualistic pluralism, the ultimate or elementary units of the world are essentially spiritual in nature and may be described as potential or subconscious souls capable of developing into actual conscious beings under favourable conditions. Though they are self-contained and self-sufficient reals, independent of one another, they produce the cosmos not by interaction with one another but by spontaneous self-development from within, in absolute correspondence or harmony with pre-established by God at the time of creation. Monadism or spiritualism is consistent with Theism, *i. e.,* belief in the existence of God; hence it is called *Theistic Pluralism.*

**Criticism**

*(i)* Pluralism, in any of its forms, materialistic or spiritualistic, cannot explain how a plurality of unconnected and independent units could come to co-operate together and produce an orderly cosmos. Pluralism can, in no way, explain the unity, order, and harmony of the world.

*(ii)* Spiritualistic pluralism or monadism believes in the theory of Pre-established Harmony. But this is simply disguising the difficulty. It explains it away as a miracle.

*(in)* Spiritualistic pluralism involves all the difficulties of spiritualism. By reducing material objects to spirit, it makes knowledge impossible, which presupposes the duality and correlativity of subject and object.

## UNIVERSITY QUESTIONS

1. Clearly expound the Atomic theory of matter. Would you accept this theory as an ultimate explanation of matter and the world ?

2. What is Pluralism ? Distinguish between its Theistic and Antitheistic varieties and discuss the relation to each of Pantheism. (1912).

   [ See 2, antitheistic pluralism – atomism, theistic pluralism = monadism; atomism also may be theistic, if atoms are supposed to be created by God. See 3 and 6. ]

3. What do you consider to be the most adequate meaning of the term 'substance' ? Must we assume that there is but one substance or that there are more than one ? Classify philosophical systems according to the view regarding substance on which they are based. (1913). [Explain the different cosmological theories of monism and pluralism.]

4. What is meant by Pluralism (in Philosophy) and by a pluralistic theory of the world ? Can the theory of a 'Pluralistic Universe' be reconciled with the idea of God ? Explain your meaning fully. (1910).

5. Determine the relative claims of Monism and Pluralism'

as philosophical theories. Which of" them offers the more satisfactory explanation of the facts of our moral and religious life. ? (1920).

6. State clearly the points at issue 'between Monism and Pluralism. Which do you consider to be the more satisfactory position ? Give reasons for your answer. (1914 Hon.)
7. Pluralism and Monism in Philosophy: explain the meaning of each fully, and discuss the question whether the universe is a 'Pluralistic Universe' or a monistic one, exhibiting the consequences of each hypothesis. (1918 Hon.)
8. Is the pluralistic conception of the universe consistent with Theism ? What solution does Concrete Monism offer ? (1919).
9. Determine the relative claims of Monism and Pluralism as philosophical theories. Which of them offers the more satisfactory explanation of the facts of our moral and religious life ? (1920).
10. State and examine the docrine of Pluralism. (1924).
11. Explain the difference between Monism, Dualism and Pluralism in Philosophy, and give your opinion regarding them. (1925).
12. Is the Pluralistic conception of the universe consistent with Theism ? Discuss fully. (1928).
13. Elucidate fully the implications of the conception of the world as a system of reals. Determine the significance of such a conception from the standpoints of Monism and Pluralism. (1932).
14. What arguments are advanced by William James for a 'pluralistic universe' as distinguished from a 'block universe' ? Is James' pluralism convincing ? (A. U. 1947).
15. Explain the Pluralism advocated by the New Realists, and examine its validity. (A. U. 1948).

CHAPTER VIII

# ONTOLOGY

## MATERIALISM AND IDEALISM

### The problem of Ontology

In then preceding two chapters, we have discussed the Cosmogony or the origin of the world and the problem of Cosmology or the constitution and organisation of the world. Now, it remains for us to discuss the problem of Ontology or essence of the world. The popular view of Ontology is dualism, according to which. the world is both material and spiritual; the objects of the world are divisible into two different kinds, *viz.*, material and mental: they cannot be reduced to each other. This popular view of dualism has found its staunchest advocate in Descartes who is the father of modern philosophy. But the difficulties in explaining the relation between the two heterogeneous substances of matter and mind led to the two most rival monistic theories of Ontology, *viz.*, materialism and idealism or spiritualism. Materialism asserts: Corporeal world is the only reality; mind is a by product of matter; whereas idealism asserts: mind is the only reality; matte r is the product of mind. Materialism reduces the whole reality to matter: idealism resolves the whole reality into spirit. The former reduces spirit to matter, while the latter reduces matter to spirit. Materialism materializes spirit, while idealism spiritualizes matter. Thus materialism and idealism are the two different types of monism. Others, again, try to reconcile dualism with monism either by regarding matter and mind not as two independent substances as dualism does, but as parallel attributes or mani-festations of the Absolute Spirit. The former doctrine is called parallelistic monism, and the latter, absolute idealism. The diffenret theories as to the ultimate nature of reality may *be* represented thus:

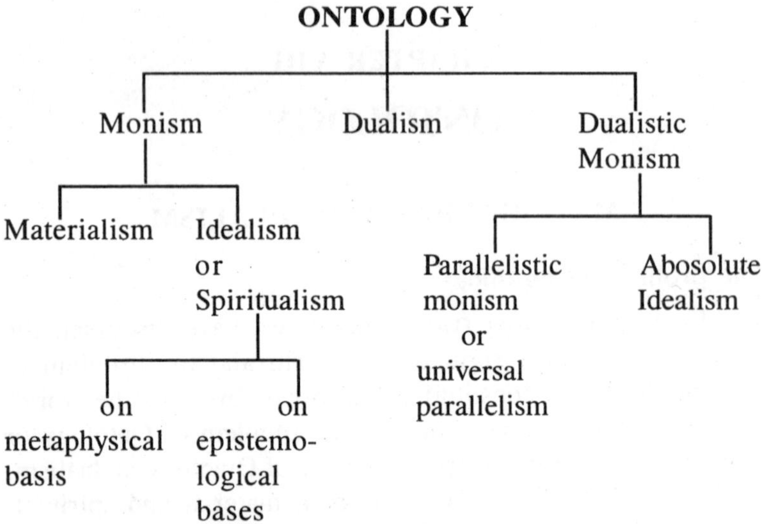


**Materialism: Its three forms**

According to materialism, matter is the only reality; life and mind are the products of matter. It answers the question of ontology as follows: "Reality as such is body; its attributes are extension and impenetrability, its primary and essential form of activity is motion." *(Paulsen.)* Matter and motion can explain all processes in reality, the vital processes of organisms as well as the state of consciousness. There is nothing but matter and motion. Matter and motion: these principles explain the whole of cosmic reality—mechanism, life and mind. Matter is the primary substance. The universe is a meterial world. All objects known are composed of matter. Life is a complex physicochemical force. Mind is a form or function of matter.

The most distinctive feature of materialism is that, it resolves all *qualitative* distinctions of things into *quantitative* distinctions. This truth has been fully confirmed by the discovery of the correlation of forces. Light, heat, electricity, magnetism, chemical affinity, and mechanical motion are convertibel into one another. Any one of them may be transformed into any other without any diminution of quantity. They are but different modes or manifestations of a common force, which is unchangeable in quantity, though variable in quality.

But materialism does not stop here. It carries us much further. It proves not only the convertibility of physical forces,—light, heat, electricity, magnetism, chemical affinity, and mechanical motion, but also the convertibility of the physical forces into vital force, regarding it as nothing but transformed mechanical or chemical force. Thus life or vital force is resolved into the mechanical properties and chemical process of matter. Hence materialism tries to explain life as a product of matter by the theory of "*abiogenesis*" or spontaneous generation that is, the view that life originates in lifeless matter as a product of the interaction and combination of physical forces. Thus life or vital force is nothing but a form of physical force.

But materialism does not step here. Trying to explain lfie by the theory of '*abiogenesis*' it tries to explain the midn or states of consciousness also by matter and motion. The doctrine of the correlation of forces and the theory of evolution are as much applicable to the explanation of mind as to that of life. Mind is force, the highest development of force which is accumulated in the brain and nerves; and mental force is is exactly correlated. with vital force and with physical force as these are with other. Motion, heat and light may be transformed into sensation, emotion and thought, and these may be reconverted into motion, heat and light.

This form of materialism with regards mind or psychical processes as a distinct form of physical forces, that is, "which looks upon mental processes as really material in character" has been characterized by Kulpe as *Equative Materialism.*

But besides this, there is another form of materialism which regards mind as an occasional by-product or *epiphenomenon* of matter, though not identical with matter. Just as flashes of light are.struck out by friction of grinding machinery, or just as the liver secretes bile, so consciousness is only an occasional by-product of protoplasmic movements in the ganglionic cells. This form of materialism which makes mind an effect of matter is called by Kulpe *Causal Materialism.*

"According to *epiphenomenalism,* there is a causal relation between mind and body, but it holds only in one direction, is an off-shoot of brain activity, and so in a sense may be said to be caused by it, but mental processes cannot function as causes in relation to brain processes. Mind is an *epi-phenomenon* a phenomenon, that is, which is of a secondary importance only. It is produced by the brain, a halo dancing above the brain-cells as Bergson poetically puts it; but it is incapable of acting upon the brain in any causal manner." [Cunningham: *Problems of philosophy,* p, 303.]

Kulpe describes another kind of materialism which makes mind an attribute of matter. This form of materialism is called by Kulpe *Attributive Materialism.* Thus Kulpe recognizes three different kinds of materialism: "Attributive materialism, which makes mind an attribute of matter;, casual materialism, which makes it an effect of matter; and equative materialism, which looks upon mental processes as really material in character." *(Kulpe)* These are the three different materialistic conceptions concerning the relation of thought and movement, which are tangled into an extricable snarl in Buchner's *"Kraft* and *Stoff*".

(l) Thought *is* motion.
(2) Thought is the *effect* of motion.
(3) Thought is indissolubly *connected* with motion.

Thus materialism tries to explain the whole of Reality including life and mind by matter and motion. We may thus sum up the position of materialism. The material world is a mechanical aggregate or a fortuitous combination of material atoms acting and reacting on one another according to the laws of motion. The laws of matter and motion can account for everything in nature.

Life is nothing but a mechanical resultant of the physical and chemical forces in the constituent atoms of a protoplasmic cell, being spontaneously generated from lifeless matter. And mind or consciousness is either the function of the brain, or a secretion, or by-product or epiphenomenon of the brain, or an attribute of highly organised matter. "The universe is made of material atoms. All objects of sense perception and all things whatsoever in the world are combinations of atoms. There is no separate realm of mind or spirit. Nothing "happens by chance but all according to, the laws of nature; the reign of law is absolute and unrversal. There was no creation. since the atoms are eternal; they are in motion, through empty space. Ends or purposes do not exist in nature—nor freedom. Matter in motion under the operation of natural laws will explain the world and all that it contains." (Patrick; *Introduction to Philosophy,* pp. 200–201).

**The Arguments of Materialism**

"The reduction of psychical states to physical states forms the real thesis of materialism." The arguments in behalf of this view are as follows:

(1) "Experience discloses the fact that psychical processes occur only in most intimate connection with physical processes. As far as we can know, only organic, or rather only animal bodies are possessed of conscious states, and these appear to be connected particularly with the action of the nervous system. Hence it follows that science must seek the cause of the former states in the peculiar quality of these bodies. Psychical processes are to be regarded as functions of the nervous system." (Paulsen: *Introduction to Philosophy,* p. 61.)

Science seeks the cause of an event in its invariable antecedent and concomitant events. Hence science must seek the cause of psychic states in their invariable antecedents and concomitant phenomena, which are, as experience shows, physiological processes in the brain and nervous system. Hence psychical states, supposed to be peculiar and unparalleled states, are really nothing of the kind. "Psychical states as such, regarded objectively, are nothing but physiological processes." *(Paulsen),*

(2) This fact may be proved *logically* from the principle of the *Conservation of Energy.* It is a fact that movements in the molecules of the brain-cells are accompanied by psychical states *(e.g.,* sensations); and volitions too are accompanied by the innervation of the motor nerve-fibres. Now, if we look upon psychical processes as quite different from physiological processes, then there will be a violation of the law of conservation of energy. Peripheral vibrations conducted by the afferent or sensory nerves to the cortical centres will cease, according to this theory, in order that psychical states, *i. e.* sensations arise. Thus there will be loss of energy. Then, again, when volitions are manifested in the outward bodily actions, the Innervation of the motor centres in the brain will be creation out of nothing. This also is a violation of the law of conservation of energy. Hence psychical states must be regarded as modifications of physiological processes. Psychic force is nothing but a distinct mode of vital force, which, again, is convertible into physico-chemical force.

(3) The same materialistic conclusion is confirmed by *biological* and *cosmological* considerations. The doctrine of evolution by natural selection seems to add an additional evidence. There was a time, modern cosmology teaches, when no organic life existed on the earth. Life has gradually evolved out of matter, and mind or consciousness out of life, *i. e.,* highly organised matter. Hence cosmological reflections strengthen the materialistic position.

(4) The facts of *Comparative Anatomy* also lend support to materialism. They disclose a thorough-going parallelism between the development of the nervous system and soul-life. Brain and intelligence show a corresponding increase in their growth throughout the advancing stages of animal life. Man heads the animal kingdom in intelligence as well as in the size and internal development of his brain, especially of the cerebrum. The same parallelism occurs in the human race.

The development of the brain and the civilization of the races run parallel." *(Paulsen.)*

"An intimate connection between brain and mind is disclosed by *physiological* and *pathological* experiments and observations. Every disturbance or injury in the brain produces disturbances in mental life." *(Paulsen.)* A severe injury to the brain brings about a temporary extinction of all consciousness, while its dissolution produces the permanent loss of consciousness.

According to modern psychiatry, every mental disease is a brain-disease, be it disclosed by anatomical investigation or not. Therefore, the brain is the mind.

**The Practical Consequences of Materialism**

Before we proceed to criticise materialism, we should discuss the practical consequences of materialism for morality and religion. It is generally believed that materialim has consequences dangerous to morality and religion. "In destroying religion, it is held, it also destroys morality and faith in ideals; its practical conclusion is: Virtue is an empty dream, conscience a freak, and the moral law the invention of priests; true wisdom consists in enjoying life and getting what we can get." *(Paulsen.)*

But this view cannot be accepted in the form in which it is stated. Indeed, "materialism actually tends to undermine our belief in God and in the universal validity of our moral judgments. We tend to think that in a world of atoms governed wholly by purely mechanical laws, there is no room and no rational need for God, nor any basis for morality other than the chance working of physical forces that have given rise to certain moral instincts and sentiments in our brains." *(Marvin)*. Theoretically, materialism can have no morality or religion. According to materialism, the world is a mechanical aggregate of infinite number of self-existent atoms colliding and combining in various ways in self-existent infinite time and space; it does not require the authorship or guidance of a Supreme Spirit or God for its creation or evolution. So, theoretically, there is no room for God in the materialistic conception of the universe. Then, again, materialism regards the mind as a function, by-product, or epiphenomenon of the brain, and consequently, it does not, and cannot recognize freedom of the will which is the foundation of morality. Thus, theoretically, for materialism there can be neither religion nor morality.

But from this it does not follow that the advocates of materialism must be immoral and irreligious. "A man's conduct is not determined by his metaphysical ideas concerning the nature of reality, but essentially by natural impulses, temperament, education, and condition in life. If, however, there is any connection between theoretical and practical materialism, it is brought about, not because a man's metaphysics determines his life, but because his life determines his metaphysics. An empty and low life has the immediate tendency to produce a nihilistic conception of life; its features are a low estimate of life and its destiny, a depreciation and scorn of the nobler phases of man's nature, a loss of reverence for moral and spiritual greatness; disbelief and derision as regards all ideal aspirations. And such a nihilistic view of life natuarally tends to a materialistic philosophy. Conversely an active and honourably good and great life naturally tends. to an idealistic metaphysics. From the striving after great ends, grows the belief in the supremacy of ideas, in the goverance of Providence in the historical life of man, and this belief finds a theoretical basis in the thought that reality as a whole is founded on ideas, that the world is the work of God." (*Paulsen*). Thus it is not materialism which compels its advocate to be immoral and irreligious, but it is an empty "and low life that naturally leads to a materialistic philosophy.

**Criticism of Materialism**

According to materialism, the world is evolved by the random play of mechanical forces which attract and repel innumerable self-existent atoms, and combine and re-combine them in various ways in infinite time and space without the guidance of an intelligent principle. But can this view of mechanical evolution account for the unity, order, and harmony of the world ? Can this materialistic conception, of the world explain its cosmic nature and the wonderful adaptations that abound in the world ?

Materialism seeks to derive life from lifeless matter, organism from mechanism, vital force from dead mechanical forces. It accounts for the origin of life by the theory of *'abiogenesis'* or spontaneous generation of life from inorganic matter. None has yet been able to produce protoplasm in the laboratory from chemical substances. The protoplasm which has been prepared artificially is not living but dead protoplasm; and again, the protoplasm which can be analyzed and of which the chemical constitution is known, is not living but dead protoplasm. There are certain peculiar features of life such as assimilation, growth, self-reparation, self-reproduction etc., which can never be explained by mechanical forces.

Mind presents a still greater difficulty to materialism than life. It was regarded by the Greek atomists as made up of subtile material atoms. But mind or consciousness is never felt as material. Then, again, the mind or consciousness is regarded by some materialists as a function of the brain, just as locomotion is the function of legs, and manipulation is the function of hands. This view also is untenable. By the function of an organ, we mean the action or movement of the organ. So, by the function of the brain, we mean the movement of tha brain. But thought is never felt as motion. Consciousness is regarded by others, again, as a by-product or epiphenomenon of the brain. Just as intense friction of a grinding machine strikes out a flash of light, so intense friction of the molecules of the brain generates a flash of consciousness. This is called the *phosphorescent theory of consciousness.* But this theory contradicts the direct testimony of our experience. If the mind or consciousness were an occasional by-product or epiphenomenon of the brain, then it would have no power of free initiation, and no power of controlling the body, just as the shadow cast by a train can never control the motion of the train of which it is a by-product. But we are directly aware of the mind's power of free initiation or energizing in volition and of the mind's power of controlling the body. So we cannot regard the mind as a by-product of the brain.

Moreover, materialism cannot account for the unity and continuity of conscious life. The brain, of which the mind or consciousness is supposed to be a by-product, is composed of innumerable atoms and molecules, cells and ganglia, the actions of which can never account for the unity and continuity of consciousness.

"All the evidence.in favour of materialism shows at the most only an intimate relationship between mind and body, not an identity. That an absolute uniformity of co-existence obtains between the activities of our brain and mental states, no one will deny. But a relation of uniformity is not one of identity. Are mental states and brain motions identical ? The two seem worlds apart. By my thoughts, I mean my thoughts, and not gyrations of molecules." *(Marvin).*

Materialism contradicts the law of Conservation of Energy, According to this law, one kind of physical energy *(e. g.,* heat) can be transformed into another kind of physical energy *(e.g.,* light) without any loss of quantity, but physical energy can never to converted into non-physical or mental energy. How, then, can we account for the origin and disappearance of consciousness, if it is not transformed from and into physical energy ? Materialism contradicts the law of conservation of energy when it assumes that "motion is transformed, not into another form of motion, not into potential physical energy, but into something that does not exist at all physically. Transformation of motion or force into thought, into pure states of consciousness, would be nothing but the destruction of energy. Similarly, the origination of motion from a purely mental element, for example, from the idea of a wish, would in physics be equivalent to creation out of nothing." *(Paulsen).* The only logical conclusion of materialism is to regard mental processes as a special form of physical energy on the same level with chemical, electrical, thermal, or mechanical energy, and convertible into each other. But mental processes can never be regarded as a special form of physical energy.

Besides these ontological difficulties, there are two epistemological difficulties. The duality of the subject and the object is the indispensable precondition of knowledge. Hence, to reduce the subject to the object, to resolve mind into matter, is to make knowledge impossible. Just as the object or matter cannot be resolved into mind or a system of ideas, so the subject or mind can never be resolved into matter.

Moreover, matter and its qualities are known through mind; it is the mind that knows itself at first; and it is through the mind that it knows matter. How is it, then, possible to reduce mind to matter ? Is it not putting the cart before the horse ? Is it not a rgasoningn circle? Thus we must conclude that materialism can never be regarded as a satisfactory theory of ontology.

**Mechanism**

The term *Mechanism* has come into use since the beginning of the present century. The mechanical conception of the world is the same as the materialistic conception. The world is a dead machine composed of matter and motion, devoid of ends and purposes and final causes. and of vital and spiritual, forces. There is no God. The cool surface of the earth gave rise to *colloids,* very complex carbon compounds; colloids gave rise to cells, the units of life; cells were combined into simple organisms; complex organisms were evolved from simple organisms by chance variation, flatter, motion, force can explain the whole universe. There is no purpose in it. There is no mind to direct it.

**Naturalism**

In recent times the term *Naturalism* also has replaced the term Materialism. Materialsim makes too much of dead matter. Naturalism stresses the concepts of energy, motion, laws of nature, causal. determination. It is mechanical. It eschews ends, purposes, final causes. It is anti-teleological. It lays stress on physics and chemistry. It advocates a physico-chemical conception of the world. Physical and chemical laws can explain organic life and mind, human history and human institutions.

Naturalism stresses the concept of matter less and that of *energy* more. "It places great emphasis upon the law of *conservation of energy,* and regards the world as a redistribubion of energy, or of matter, or of both, and it relies profoundly upon the principle of *evolution* and adaptation as explaining the surviving. of structures and functions fitted to survive." *(Ibid,* p. 202). Naturalism in recent philosophical literature, recognizes the "levels" Nature and the emergence through evolution of new forms of reality matter, life mind, and moral values. Naturalism has become liberal.

**Idealism or Spiritualism**

It offers a spiritualistic conception of the world. If materialism reduces mind to matter, idealism or spiritualism goes to the other extreme, and resolves matter into spirit. There is nothing material in the world; there is no dead matter. Just as Materialism regards the world as rooted in matter, so Idealism regards it as grounded in mind. Materialism gives a mechanical interpretation of the world. It explains the world by matter, motion, and force or energy, mechanical and efficient causes, and conservation of energy. It reduces life to a complex physico-chemical forces. It reduces mind to an *epiphenomenon* of the brain. It makes mind an occasional by product of the brain which is composed of highly organised matter. "It makes mind an incident in the process of evolution, contingent upon a highly developed nervous system is the higher animals." *(Patrick)*. Idealism, on the other hand, regards mind as the primary reality, prior to matter. Matter is a phenomenon or appearance of mind. Matter is the axternalization of mind. Mind, reason, intelligence, personality, values, moral and religious ideals are the real entities. Physical forces are secondary. They are unmeaning apart from mind and its experience. They are products or manifestations of mind. "Materialism says that matter is real and mind an incident or accompaniment. Idealism says that mind is real and matter just an appearance." *(Patrick: Introduction. to Philosophy,* p; 211).

Idealism is spiritualism. It considers the world as grounded in spirit or mind. The term *Idealism* is more attractive and in more common use at the present time, though the term *Spiritualism* is more exact.

There are many forms of Idealism. Some are based on epistemological considerations. Others are based on metaphysical considerations. Subjective Idealism of Berkeley and Phenotnenalistic Idealism of Kant are based on epistemological grounds. Platonic Idealism, Monadism of Leibnitz. Absolute Idealism of Hegel. Voluntristic Idealism of Schopenhauer Panpsychism of Fechner, and Personalism of Howison and others are based on metaphysical grounds.

**Subjective Idealism (Berkeley)**

We have already discussed the view of Subjective Idealism held by Berkeley in the fourth chapter. So, here, we shall simply recapitulate the arguments of Berkeley in favour of his doctrine. Berkeley's idealism is called Subjective Idealism. Matter is made up of its qualities; it is known only through its primary and secondary qualities. As far back as Democritus, the father of atomism and materialism, we find that certain qualities of matter, the secondary qualities, are believed to have no existence except in the mind of the individual perceiving them. Descartes and Locke also held that extension, impenetrability and mobility are the true characteristics of matter, and the secondary qualities, *viz.,* colour, sound, smell, taste, heat and cold. are nothing but mental states, and are not true qualities of matter at all. Now, Berkeley argued that if the secondary qualities exist only in the mind, if they are nothing but mental states, there is nothing to warrant our drawing a different conclusion concerning primary qualities. They also exist in the mind as ideas.

Moreover, the objective world described by the materialist is a sheer abstraction. Can we picture any such world containing nothing but primary qualities ? No, Such a world is a mere abstraction, and therefore cannot be imagined. A bare extension without color cannot be pictured by the mind any more than a line without breadth or thickness." *(Marvin.)* If the world is nothing but a heap of primary qualities such as extension and motion, then such a world can never be pictured or imagined. The chasm that the materialism is trying to make between the primary and secondary qualities, is never seriously made in daily life. For in daily life the heat and cold, the sound and the colors, belong to the object as truly as their length, breadth, and thickness, their parts and their motions." *(Marvin.)* If both primary and secondary qualities are ideas of the mind, then there is no reason for the existence of matter, which is said to be the support of primary qualities.

The third argument of Berkeley represents his position most truly. According to him, the world as really apprehended by us, is made up of perceptions or mental states. His argument is the following: "If we know the world we know is an object of our perception. If it be an object of our perception, it is given to our minds, and so is known by us, only as the content of our perception, never as something not contained in our perception. If we declare that the objects which we perceive have an existence apart from our perception, what can we mean ?' Do we mean that objects exist that cannot be perceived ? Are we then to hold that there are distinct things apart from our perceptions and these things are without our minds ? If so, are they alike or different ? If they are alike, we must hold that the objects about us outside of our perception have color and sound, and heat and cold. But in spite of all this, they are not perceived. But what a ridiculous statement it is that there are coloured objects that are not perceived, or objects that are not felt, that there are noises that are not heard. Therefore, if things and qualities in this objective world be like our perceptions, they must be perceptions, and can exist nowhere but in some mind. Therefore, when we say that the world exists, we mean that some mind is perceiving.

According to Berkeley's cosmology the mind that always does this perceiving is the divine mind. The divine mind perceives the world in its fulness and completeness, and causes-finite minds, or spirits, also to perceive certain portions of it. The law and order of nature are ultimately then the law and' Order of God's perception and the law and order of the perceptions that God causes to exist in us. But the material world does not exist except as the content of perception. There is then no such thing as matter apart from mind. There is simply spirit and those manifestations of spirits which we today would call states of consciousness." *(Marvin),*

So-called external things are merely the perceptions of the percipient minds. They are merely subjective ideas. Thus, *God and* finite spirits alone are real. There are no real objects, independent of perceptions of the Infinite Spirit and finite spirits. So-called external things are *sensations* produced in the finite spirits by God according to some fixed laws. This doctrine is called subjective idealism, subjectivism, mentalism. psychism.

**Criticism of Subjective Idealism**

Berkeley's subjective idealism has been fully criticized in the fourth chapter. If the subject cannot be reduced to the object, the latter also cannot be reduced to the former. The distinction between subject and object is the fundamental condition of all knowledge. The reduction of any of them to the other would sap the very foundation of knowledge and make it impossible.

**Monadism of Leibnitz**

We have discussed monadism of Leibnitz under spiritualistic pluralism. Leibnitz holds that the world is made up of spirits. There is no matter at all. He defines a substance as that which exists by itself; and "that alone can exist by itself which has the power of action; so that force, self-activity is the essential mark of substance, and substance itself must be something immaterial, unextended. Leibnitz calls these substances,, the independent units of the sum of existence, *monads*. They are the true atoms as opposed to the phenomenal atoms of natural science; they are simple elements in everything complex, and therefore indivisible and indestructible; metaphysical points as opposed material or mathematical." *(Kulpe)*. They differ from material points or atoms, as they are spiritul in nature, and they differ frorn mathematical points, as they are not abstractions, but concrete objective entities. But if the world is made up of immaterial and unextended atoms or monads, why does it appear to us as extended and material ? Extension or space is nothing but the phenomenal appearance of the co-existence of monads; in reality there is neither matter nor extension.

Further, since the essence of the monads consists in self-activity, they cannot receive any impression from without. They are 'without windows', so that neither an influence can enter into them from the outside, nor can any pass out of them. How then, should we account for the apparent interaction of the objects of the world? Leibnitz explains it by his theory of *'Pre-established Harmony.'* According to his theory, God or the Monad of monads created the monads and pre-adjusted to them one another at the time of creation, in such a way as to make them correspond to one another without exerting any mutual influence, even as a watch-maker makes watches and sets them to the same time so that they keep the same time.

The activity of monads therefore, consists in their self-activity; and this self-activity consists in ideation or representation. Leibnitz holds that every monad ideates or represents the whole universe, and is this sense, a microsom, a mirror of the whole universe. And since ideation is a mental act, the essence of the monad is a psychical quality. "Things extended or corporeal are thus reduced to the level of mere phenomena, whose underlying reality is to be found in a multiplicity of. unextended substances. But not every monad mirrors the universe with equal clearness; there are as many monads as there are degrees of clearness of ideating activity." *(Kulpe)*. There is no matter.

**Criticism of Monadism**

There is no positive evidence to show that "there lies dormant and concealed in the elements of matter a peculiar existence which we must conceive of on the analogy of our own consciousness." *(Kulpe)*. Then as to the nature of the mental quality ascribed to uitimate spiritual atoms, no two spiritualists agree. Leibnitz holds that the capacity of representation or ideation is the inner aspect of natural phanomena. Schopenhaur holds that the universe as thing-in-itself is will; Herbert's reals, too, are incorporeal substances like Leibnitzian monads Wundt, too, regards a will-atom as the ultimate unit of all existence,

Psychology also does not lend its support to spiritualism. "It teaches that our personal mental life is connected with an *exteremely complicated part of the physical organism–not at all* that its packed away in the ultimate material particles of the body. And if we descend with the comparative psychologist to the lowest levels of animal life, where a last trace of mentality may be suspected or conjectured, we are still brought to a halt at the cell or the cell-nucleus; there is no warrant for placing the supposed rudiment of consciousness in the atom." *(Kulpe). Leibnitz's* is, a kind of panpsychism. Monadism suffers from all the defects of pluralism.

**(III) Panpsychism**

Fechner is an advocate of pan-*psychism.* The world is ensouled. The earth has a soul The world is a, great organism endowed with a soul God is the world-soul. Plants, animals, and men have souls. The body is the outer expression of the soul, which is its inner life. The physical world is the outer expression of the inner life of God. Paulsen is one of the most eloquent advocates of parallelism. After defending the theory of parallelism, he proceeds to deduce panpsychism as its logical conclusion.

Panpsychism is based on the argumentthat as all physical processes called physiological are connected with psychical processes, so all other physical, processes which resemble the former must also be supposed as connected with inner states of consciousness in some form or other. It argues in this way; it is an incontestable fact of experience that brain activities are attended with states of consciousness. Hence, only animals and human beings have inner states of consciousness, since they are, possessed of the nervous system, and especially the brain. But how far does the animal world extend ? Is it separated by a fixed boundary from the rest of the corporeal world, especially from the organic world ? Generally, the corporeal world is divided into three distinct kingdoms, *viz.*,- animal, vegetable, and mineral kingdoms. But modern biology has obliterated these fixed lines, and proved that these different kingdoms of nature are continuous. Though animals differ from plants in many respects, they closely reselmble each other, on the lower stages of development. There are numerous forms of life which have characteristics neither of true animals nor of true plants. The group of protista is an intermediate kingdom in which plant and animal meet. If there is no fixed boundary line between animals and plants, are we to extend psychic life to plants ? If there is no fixed line of demarcation between the animal and vegetable kingdoms, there is no fixed limit to psychic life which may extend over the entire organic world.

But should we stop here ? Or are we to extend psychic life to the inorganic world ? "The organic or inorganic bodies form, not two separate worlds, but a unitary whole in constant interaction. There is no difference in substance; organic bodies are composed of the same ingredients of which inorganic bodies consist." *(Paulsen)*. Both of them are composed of carbon, nitrogen, hydrogen, and oxygen. Organic life arises, according to modern biology, from inorganic matter by spontaneous generation. Should we not say that psychical life also arises out of the elements possessed by the inorganic ? But it may be objected that it is quite inconceivable that lifeless rigid matter should be the bearer of psychic life which is the invariable concomitant of spontaneous activity. Matter is always determined from *without* by pressure and impact; it is never determined from *within* by inner impulses. So matter cannot be said to have an inner psychic life. But this is an erroneous view. Matter is never devoid of spontaneous activity. "Spontaneous activity everywhere ! Your inert, rigid matter, movable only by impact, is a phantom that owes its existence, not to observation, but to conceptual speculation." *(Paulsen)*. Thus panpsychism tries to prove the existence of mind or conscious states in the whole world from inorganic to highly organised matter. It goes so far as to say that even our earth, the solar and sideral systems have a larger psychic life than our own. This view was first suggested by Fechner and has been adopted by Paulsen. (Paulsen: *Introduction to Philosophy,* pp. 87-111.)

**Criticism of Panpsychism**

Is the panpsychist argument justifiable ? It is based on the analogy of all physical things and their processes. But any analogy will not do. The analogous property must be necessarily related to the property at issue. Superficial similarity cannot be the ground of valid analogical argument. To apply this test to panpsychism we must be able to prove that "consciousness is necessarily connected with that element of brain-activity which is common to all physical manifestations." *(Marvin).* But we can never prove it. No doubt the physical concomitant to mental events is in some of its aspects similar to all types of physical, action, but this does not prove it to be similar in those aspects which are essential to it as a concomitant of mental events. Using the same argument we might prove that everything on earth is blue ! No doubt there is an analogy between all objects blue and not blue; but they are not necessarily analogous in the essential element in question." *(Marvin: Introduction to Philosophy).*

In short, panpsychism must show that the physical correlate of consciousness is invariably present in all physical events as such. But this is a problem for science, rather than for metaphysics. No amount of metaphysical speculation will give us the necessary information. At best panpsychism must be left as an open question.

**(IV) Platonic Idealism**

Plato maintains that the sensible world of individual things is a shadow and appearance of the transcendental world of Ideas. Ideas are eternal arche types of which the sensible individuals are copies and imitations. Individuals are born and die. Ideas are eternal. They are the real things. "They are eternal essences, forms types, or archetypes, serving as patterns, ideals, standards, for the things of sense." (Patrick: *Introduction to Philosophy,* p. 213). They are known by reason. The sensible things are known by experience. they are made out of the crude stuff of matter, which is a kind of non-being. Matter is a source of evil. The Ideas are a source of good. Matter is the cause of disorder. The Ideas are the cause of order and unity. They are known by reason. Sensible things are known by experience. The Ideas are unchanging. The things of sense are in constant flux. The sensible world of things adumbrates the intelligible world of ideas

**Criticism of Platonic Idealism**

Plato's idealism involves a kind of dualism of the Ideas and sensible things—the Ideas and Matter. It Ideas are the formative essences of sensible individuals, they must not transcend them, but must be immanent in them. The ideal forms must inspire the material things as their indwelling principles. Plato cannot bridge the gulf between the sensible world and the transcendental world is idealism does not recognize mind or spirit as the fundamental reality, but it affirms the superiority of ideals which guide the world of sensible things

**(V) Phenomenalistic Idealism (Kant)**

Kant's theory of knowledge has been discussed already. Its metaphysical implications are brought out here. Kant holds that there are noumena or *things-in-themselves* behind the sensible world of phenomena or appearances. They are unknown and unknowable. They act upon the noumenal self and produce impressions which are unconnected with one another. The self arranges them in time and space, which are the forms of perception supplied by sensibility. It subsumes the sensations arranged in time and space under the categories of the under-standing, substance, causality, number reality, negation, and the like, and reduces them to unity. The self arranges the categorized sensations under the regulative Ideals of reason, viz. World, Soul, and God, which reduce them to an unconditional totality. Thus, the self cannot know *things-in-themselves (ding-an-sich)* but only their *phenomena* or appearances through its own forms and categories. World, Soul, and God are not real, but merely Ideas of Reason, which help which help us reduce the manifold of sensations to a unity. Therefore, Kant's idealism. is called *Phenomenalism.* We can know only phenomena through ' theoretical reason."

But Kant holds that "practical reason" or will gives us a clue to reality. It gives us morality, which presupposes fredom of the soul, and the existence of God as Moral Governor. Kant believes in "the primacy of the practical reason."

His agnosticism is softened by his voluntarism. To our theoretical reason things in themselves are unknown and unknowable. But our practical reason or moral reason gives us a clue to the ultimate realities. viz., the human sould with its freedom and immortality, and God.

**Criticism of Phenomenalism**

Kant's philosophy is idealism in the sense that the sensible world is considered by hims as phenomena or appearances. It is not idealism which considers mind as the only reality. He believes in the reality of things-in-themselves.

Kant's philosophy leads to dualism of phenomena and not mena-appearances and thing-in-themselves. But phenomena are manifestations of noumena, which are their essences, apart from which they are unmeaning. Substance, causality, reality. number etc. are merely categories of the understanding. They apply to phenomena only. They cannot apply to noumena. And yet Kant holds that things-in-themselves are real in themselves, which produce sensations in the self. Sometimes he speaks of a "thing-in-itself", and sometimes of "things-in-themselves." Thus he applies the categories of reality, substance, causality, and number to the noumena. Phenomenalism is an unsatisfactory doctrine.

**(VI) Absolute or Objective Idealism (Hegel)**

According to Hegel, subject and object, mind and the world are correlative to each other, being the manifestations of the Absolute Spirit. The world is the material of God's thought and activity in and through which he raises himself from being an abstract power or potentiality into being a concrete self-conscious reality as subject and object and thereby as absolute spirit. Subjective idealism fails to give an adequate, explanation of knowledge by reducing matter to system of ideas. Objective idealism recognizes the existence of matter, independent of the finite minds but not of the Divine Mind. Objective Idealism differs from other types of spiritualism in that the former regards matter as *the other* of mind, its correlative and counterpart, while the latter conceives matter as analogous to mind. "A thoroughgoing idealism,"Edward Caird rightly remarks, "will not fear to admit the reality of that which is other than mind, and even in a sense, diametrically opposed to it, for it rests on a perception that these opposites are yet necessarily related, and that both are different and correlated aspects of one whole." *(The Evolution of Theology in the Greek Philosophers,* Vol. II, p. 27.)

The world is the externalization of the Absolute. The finite minds are finite reproductions of God. The world is intelligible to them because it is the expression of God. God is the Infinite Spirit. Finite minds are akin to God. God evolves the world from within himself according to the same categories through which the human mind knows it. The frame-work of thought is identical with the framework of reality The categories of knowledge are subjective as well as objective. The laws of thought are the laws of reality. The world is the divine thought process. "What we call nature is thought externalized ; it is the Absolute Reason revealing itself in out-ward form. But nature is not its final goal. Returning, it expresses itself more fully in human self-consciousness and in the end finds its complete realization in art, religion, and, philosophy." (Patrick : *Introduction to Philosophy,* p. 221).

**Criticism of Absolute Idealism**

Hegel makes too much of the Absolute. He leaves too little scope for human freedom. His emphasis on the Absolute has been misinterpreted as complete determinism, a block universe. His doctrine is called Panlogism. All is reason. Whatever is real is rational. Whatever is rational is real. But Absolute Idealism of Hegel contains important truths which must not be overlooked. He recognizes the reality of the external world, the finite minds, and God. He recognizes human freedom, which is not absolute, but limited by Divine freedom. He recognises the social nature of man, and looks upon society as the organisation of free spirits apart from which man is inconceivable. He regards God as a dynamic thought process, realizing higher and higher ideals.

### (VII) Personal Idealism or Personalism

Absolute Idealism makes too much of the Absolute and too little of, human freedom. It bases Ethics on Metaphysics. Personal Idealism is a protest against this tendency in Absolute Idealism. It lays emphasis on human personality, human freedom, human creation of new values. It limits tbe freedom of God by the freedom of finite spirits. It regards God as finite It does not identify God with the Absolute. It bases Metaphysics on Ethics.

Rashdall holds that the Absolute is the unity of God and the finite spirits, which is not self-conscious. The Absolute is the finite spirits plus God, who is finite. God realizes His purpose through the world, and reveals it to men who freely realize it. The Absolute is the unconscious unity of God, finite spirits, and the world. It is not personal. Evil is real. We fight out evil. Time is real. There is moral progress in time. Time is essential to morality.

Ward, holds that the world is made of self-active monads or egos. The finite egos are free. God is finite. He is *primus inter pares,* the Supreme among equals. He is limited by finite spirits. He is the Supreme Spirit like Leibnitz's Monad of monads There is a hierarchy of monads or egos at the top of which there is God.

Howison also holds that God is finite and primus inter *pares* (supreme among equals). He is the President of the republic of finite spirits. He is not their creator or efficient cause. He is their final cause. He is our ideal towards which we are moving. We are frqe. We create new values. God does not determine our freedom.

Personalism takes its stand upon human personality. "This philosophy emphasizes personality, freedom, self-determinism. moral responsibility, the existence of real evil in the world, and of a personal God, who struggles and strives with us for the overcqming of evil." *(Patrick)*. It has a pluralistice tendency. It is a reaction against monistic Absolutism. It satisfies our moral needs. Its philosophy is idealistic or spiritualistic. It lays stress on human freedom, moral responsibility, and the presence of real evil.

**Voluntaristic Idealism**

· Kant's Thing in-itself was converted by Fichte into Absolute Ego. It was converted by Schelling into the Absolute which is beyond ego and non-ego, subject and object, a neutrum.

Hegel converted it into the Absolute which expresses itself in Nature, and reduplicates itself in finite spirits, and realizes itself as a self-conscious unity. Hegel considered the Absolute as universal reason. His Absolutism is panlogism. Fichte, Schelling, and Hegel are advocates of Absolute Idealism. Hegel's Absolutism is intellectualistic.

Schopenhauer followed Kant who affirmed the "primacy of the will" converted Hegel's Absolute into the *Absolute Will*. The will is the essential quality of my self. The intellect is subordinate to it. The self is striving, struggling,, desiring activity. My body is the outward expression of my will. It is the externalization of my will. Likewise the world is the outward expression of the Absolute Will. The phenomenal world is the outer expression of the universal will, The world is not merely my idea. It has an objective basis. It has foundation in the Absolute Will.

But the Absolute Will is unconscious. It is neither conscious nor self-conscious. It achieves self consciousness in man. The world is dynamic. It is an active will groping in the dark to achieve something. There is unconscious finality or teleolggy in nature. Absolute will is blind and unconscious.

### Criticism of Voluntaristic, Idealism

Schopenhauer is right in stressing the will of the Absolute. But a blind unconscious will cannot be differentiated from brute physical energy emphasized by naturalism. The will must be a conscious striving to realize its purpose. Unconscious will is a contradiction in terms. It is unmeaning to call it Absolute. If the Absolute is a blind, unconscious tendency groping in the dark to realize unknown ends, it cannot be called Absolute. The conscious rational will of man is better than the so-called Absolute Will.

### Dualism

Both materialism and idealism are forms of ontological monism. Materialism regards mind alone as the fundamental reality, and reduces mind to mattey. Idealism or spiritualism regards mind alone as the ultimate reality, and reduces matter to mind. Materialism materializes spirit, while spiritualism spiritualizes matter. But dualism regards matter and mind both as fundamental and irreducible realities. The essential attribute of matter is extension, and that of mind is thought or consciousness. There is nothing in common between the two substances. They are radically opposed to each other. But they can interact upon each other. Descartes is an exponent of dualism.

### Criticism of Dualism

If matter and mind are absolutely heterogeneous, how can they be related to each other ? Their interaction is inexplicable. Descartes believes in the interaction of body and mind in the penal gland of the brain. But what magical property is there in the brain that it can bring two heterogenous substances like body and mind into relation with each other ? This will be discussed in detail in connection with the relation of body and mind.

## QUESTIONS

1. What is your conception of matter, and how do you apply

the conception to an explanation of the constitution of the world ? (1910).

2. Give an analytical exposition of modern materialism and criticize it as an ontological doctrine. (1912).
3. How far can materialism offer a satisfactory explananation of the universe ? (1914).
4. What do you consider to be the chief defects of materialism as an ontological theory ? Is it possible to establish a . system of morality on materialism ? (1915).
5. Examine critically whether Materialism can be accepted as an adequate and satisfactory view of the universe ? (1917).
6. How far can Materialism be a philosophical interpretation of the ultimate substances in the world ? (1936).
7. What is the main thesis of Idealism as distinguished from Materialism ? Distinguish between Kant's Phenomenalistio Idealism and Hegel's Idealism. (A. U. 1948).
8. Write short notes on
   (a) Panpsychism,
   *(b)* Personalism (A. U. 1948),
   (c) Monadism (A. U. 1948),
9. Distinguish between
   (a) Platonic Idealism and Kantian Idealism,
   *(b)* Subjective Idealism and Absolute Idealism. (A. U. 1946),
10. Write short notes on
    *(a)* Naturalism,
    *(b)* Materialism,
    (c) Voluntarist Idealism,
    *(d)* Phenomenalism.

## CHAPTER IX

# THE PHILOSOPHY OF THE SOUL

### The Nature of the Soul, Mind, or the Self

What is the nature and meaning of the mind, soul or self? The word 'self is used in three different senses. Firstly, it is used in the sense of the permanent spiritual principle of unity underlying thinking, feeling and willing, the permanent substance which lies behind and beyond the fleeting mental phenomena. This spiritual substance is called the mind soul, self. Secondly, it is used in the sense of an aggregate of mental states without any underlying principle of unity among them. Thirdly it is used in sense of a, concrete spiritual unity which is not above and beyond the mental phenomena *viz.*, thinking, feeling and willing, but realizes itself in them, without losing its unity and identity in them. The word 'self' thus, has three meanings, it means an abstract unity or substance apart from its manifestations; or an aggregate or plurality of mental states apart from their essence, or a concrete spiritual substance which realizes itself in its manifestations remaining identical with itself in the midst of changes. Thus, according to the first viw, the self is an abstract unity; according to the second, an abstract plurality; according to the third, a concrete unity-in-plurality or identity-in-difference. The first is the numental view of the self; the second, the empirical conception of the self; and the third, the concrete or idealistic view of the self.

### (1) Theory of Soul-substance

Plato and Aristotle conceived the soul as a spiritual substance. According to Plato, the soul is a mental or immaterial substance which expresses itself in three fundamental types of experiences, *viz.*, thinking, feeling and willing. Feeling and willing are baser functions of the soul which it owes to its connection with the body. Thinking is the essen-tial function of the soul. Reason is the divine element in the soul. The transcendental world of Ideas is the home and destiny of the soul. It has an intuitive knowledge of the world of Ideas or eternal archetypes through the divine element of reason. The soul is imprisoned in the body. Its earthly life is imprisonment in the body. Plato recognizes the pre-existence and immortality of the soul. It has personality and individuality. Its destiny is heaven or the world of Ideas.

According to Aristotle, the soul is the form (entelechy) of the body which is its matter. The soul is the purpose and perfection of the body. It is not imprisoned in the body. The soul is the *organisation of the body* in the sense that it is the organising, principle of the body but it is not identical with the bodily organisation. The soul is the non-bodily or *spiritual principle* or *substance* within the body, which is its organizing principle. The essence of the soul is the rational element. Both Plato and Aristotle maintain that the self is immortal because of the divine element of rationality in it.

This soul-substance theory of Plato and Aristotle was revived by Descartes, Locke and Berkeley in modern thought. Descartes conceived the soul as a spiritual *substance* whose essential attribute is thinking or consciousness. There is no mind or soul without consciousness, and there is no consciousness without the soul. But the soul is not to be identified with consciousness. It is a spiritual substance which *has* consciousness. I have an *intuition* of myself. *Cogito ergo sum : I think, therefore, I exist*. Descartes is an exponent of dualism. He recognizes matter add mind as. two fúndamental substances. Matter is extended, inert, and subject to mechanical laws. Mind is unextended, active conscious, and subject to teleology purpose. "The soul is unique, dynamic, teleological, and non-spatial. It is a simple, indivisible substance" (Patrick : *Introduction to Philosophy,* p. 244). Descartes insisted on the substantial character of the mind or soul. The mind is conscious, while matter is unconscious. The mind is unextended, while matter is extended. The mind is active and purposive, while matter is inert and mechanical. The mind is radically different from the space-time world of physics. Thinking is the essential attribute of the mind. It includes all mental activities, *viz.,* judging, feeling, willing and so on.

Locke also holds that the soul is a *substance* which *has* experiences. It is the *substance* which thinks, feels and wills. He borrows his doctrine of the soul from Descartes. We have according to him, an *intuitive* certainty of the self : we have an immediate and irresistible conviction of the existence of our own selves. We have an *intuition* of our own souls as mental substances. Locke regards the soul as a cogitative or thinking substance, and matter as a non-cogitative or unthinking substance.

Berkeley also conceives the soul as a spritual substance which perceives ideas and acts upon them. It is entirely different from ideas or experiences. Ideas are passive while spirits are active. Ideas are perceived while spirits perceive ideas. They are entirely heterogeneous : they cannot be identified with each other. The soul or spirit is an incorporeal or spiritual substance which can never be resolved into ideas. The soul can never be identical with "floating ideas". In the spirit of Locke, Berkeley also maintains that we have a *notion of our* own souls. The spirit is a *knower*; it can never be known as an *object* or a sensible thing. We cannot have an *idea* of the spirit. We can only have a *notion* of it. By "idea" Berkeley means sensuous knowledge and by "notion" he means rational intuition. Thus with Locke, Berkeley holds that we have an intuitive knowledge of our own souls. It will be considered in detail below.

**Criticism of the soul-substance theory**

In modern thought the traditional theory of the *soul-*

*substance* was severely criticized by David Hume. He argues that there is no evidence for the existence of the soul-substance. We have no impression of it. We can never perceive it. We can never "catch hold of" the so-called permanent spiritual substance. We perceive only feelings, ideas, and passions. These fleeting experiences constitute the soul. There is no permanent soul-substance. All we perceive are sundry experiences which are constantly changing. Hence they cannot be identified with that spiritual substance which is supposed to continue the same in the midst of changing experiences. Hume conceives the soul as a series of mental states. His conception of the soul is called the *empirical* conception of the self. It will be considered in detail below.

Kant also severely criticized the traditional theory of the soul as a spiritual substance. He did not argue like Hume that there is no evidence for the existence of the soul-substance. He argued that the traditional view is self-contradictory. "For this view holds in effect that each individual knows his *self* as he knows other objects, that he can make his *self* a direct object of knowledge, Now this is impossible, Kant maintains, since it is always the self that does the knowing ; the self is always *subject* of knowledge and cannot be made object of knowledge. I cannot know *I,* but only *me* ; myself as *subject* I cannot know, but only myself as *object*. But myself as object is precisely my various experiences that come and go with passing moments." *(Problems of Philosophy,* p. 258.) The *subject self* or Pure or Tranagendential Ego or *I* is beyond the reach of knowledge. The *object self* or Empirical Ego, or *Me* only is within the range of knowledge. This conception of Kant is called the noumenal conception of the self.

**II. The Noumenal Self. (Kant)**

By the expression 'noumenal self Kant means the Transcendental Ego or Subject which is behind and beyond mental phenomena, an abstract principle of unity which is unknown and unknowable, the knower being unable to know itself. It is purely an abstract analytical unity, which is above and beyond thinking, feeling, and willing transcending the plurality of mental states, as the permanent and abiding background and support of all these mental phenomena. Mental states are not the expressions of the self, but its phenomenal appearances. This is also called the Pure or Transcendental Self. The mental phenomena which are known constitute the empirical self. Kant holds that 'substance' is a category of the understanding. The self applies the category of substance to phenomena. It is the source of the categories. The categories are the synthetic principles by which the understanding can combine the discrete and unconnected impressions given by sensibility. Therefore the category of substance cannot apply to the self which is the source of the category. The self cannot be regarded as a substance. It is the Transcendental Ego or Subject which can know things as objects. It is the knower. It can never be known. It can. never be revealed in experience. It can never become an object of experience. It is always the subject of experience. Hume holds that impressions and ideas are connected with one another by the laws of association. But Kant urges that they point to a deeper function of unity. They refer to the unifying function of the self as the "transcendental unity of apperception." All knowledge of phenomena implies the "I think" which cannnot be accounted for by the laws of association. Kant emphasizes the essential unitary spiritual character of the mind or self as the knower or subject.

**Criticism of the Noumenal Self**

A noumenon apart from its phenomena or manifestations is an empty abstraction; unity without plurality, identity without difference, the mental substance apart from the mental phenomena is quite meaningless. The self must be regarded as a spiritual principle of unity underlying and supporting mental phenomena but not above and beyond them as an abstract analytical unity which does not express itself in the plurality of mental states, but as a concrete unity or a spiritual principle which realizes or manifests itself in them and connects them with one another, remaining permanent and abiding among them.

### III. The Empirical Self. (Hume, Mill, and James)

By the expression 'empirical self we mean the aggregate or series of mental states, the mass of sensations feelings and desires, without any principle of unity among them. "Mind is but the series of feelings and ideas, like a row of beads without any connecting thread. What atoms are in the theory of the physical world, feelings and ideas are in that of mind ; as the world is an aggregate of atoms connected together by gravitation, so self is an aggregate of feelings and ideas connected together by the forces of association." *(Problems of Metaphysics)*. Thus the empiricist denies the existence of an abiding substantial self behind the mental phenomena. It denies the sense of personal identity ; it explains it away as an illusion or a figment of our imagination. The self, thus, according to the empirical view, is nothing more than a series of mental states. "It is not anything that *has* the states; it is the states them-selves. We say, indeed, 'I feel, 'I think', 'I will', but the corrcet form of expression will be simply 'there is a feeling', 'a thought', 'a volition', or there is a series of feelings, thoughts, volitions. The pure essential self, considered as something that *has* the feelings and remains the same through them all is not a fact of positive experience, but a fiction of metaphysics, and must be rejected by positive science." *(Stephen)*. Hume, J. S. Mill and others are advocates of this doctrine.

The empirical account of the self has been given by different thinkers in different ways. Hume says, "No man is anything more than a bundle or collection of different perceptions, which succeed each other with inconceivable rapidity, and are **in** perpetual flux and movement.."

J. S. Mill says, mind is "nothing but the series of sensations and internal feelings as, they actually occur, with the addition of *possibilities* of feelings."

William James regards the mind as a "*stream of consciousness*" "The passing thought is the only thinker." This implies that consciousness instead of being a series of distinct states is a *continuum,* and flows on without interruption, without breaking up into discrete units as implied in the Humean conception of the self. Hume regards impressions and ideas as discrete and unconnected with one another. They are connected with one another by the laws of association. James regards them as flowing into one another and forming a "stream of consciousness" or a psychic continuum. Hume's conception of the self will be best understood when it is contrasted with Berkeley's conception of it.

**Hume's conception of the Mind, Soul—or Self contrasted with that of Berkeley. *Berkeley conception of the Self***

Berekeley holds that besides *ideas* there is "*something* which knows or perceives them, and exercises divers operations, as willing, imagining, remembering, about them." Berkeley says, "this *perceiving active* being is what I call mind, spirit, soul, or myself." Thus the self, according to him, is the mental or spiritual substance that perceives, imagines, remembers, wills, or acts in various ways. Berkeley emphasizes two functions of the self, *viz.,* perceiving and willing or acting. Berkeley defines the nature of the self or spirit as follow ; "A spirit is one simple, undivided, active being as it perceives ideas it is called the understanding, and as it produces or otherwise operates about them it is called the will." Berkeley holds that the self is a spiritual principle of unity or a spiritual substance, and as such is simple and indivisible. It is an intelligent and active substance. It has understanding and will. It perceives ideas and wills or acts upon ideas. "By the word spirit we mean only that which thinks, wills, and perceives."

The self or spirit is entirely distinct from ideas. The self perceives while ideas are pereeived. The self is active while ideas are passive. Ideas cannot exist if there be no self. They exist in, and are perceived by the self. Thus the self or spirit can never be regarded as a series of ideas. Berkeley says, "by the words (mind, spirit, soul, or self) I do not denote any one of my ideas, but a thing entirely distinct from them, wherein they exist, or which is the same thing, whereby they are perceived." "The words *will, soul, spirit,* do not stand for different ideas, or, in truth, for any idea at all, but for something which is very different from ideas, and which, being an Agent, can never be like unto, or represented by, any idea whatsoever." The soul or spirit is "a real thing (substance) which is neither an idea nor like an idea, but that which perceives ideas, and wills, and reasons about them." Thus Berkeley emphatically denies the identity of the soul with ideas. He says. "All the unthinking objects of the mind (ideas) agree in that they are entirely *passive,* and their existence consists only in *being perceived,* whereas a soul or spirit is an *active* being whose existence consists, not in being perceived, but in *perceiving* ideas and thinking.

**Hume's criticism of Berkeley's view and his conception of the self**

Hume believes in Berkeley's dictum *Esse* is *percipi,* the existence of an object consists in being perceived. He applies this dictum to the so-called mind, self, or spirit which is regarded as a *permanent spiritual substance* which thinks, perceives, feels, and wills, and which abides in the midst of changes in mental states. Hume denies perception of any such permanent spiritual substance distinct from ideas or mental states. "There are some philosophers," Hume argues, "who imagine we are every moment *conscious* of what we call our *self* ; that we *feel* its existence and its continuance in existence ; and so are certain, beyond the evidence of a demonstration, both of its perfect identity and simplicity. For my part, when I enter most intimately into what I call *myself,* I always stumble on some particular perception or other, of heat or cold, light or shade, love or hatred, pain or pleasure. I never can catch *myself* at any time without a perception, and never can observe anything but the perception." "The mind is a kind of theatre, where several perceptions successively make their appearance, pass, re-pass, glide away, and mingle in an infinite variety of postures and situations. There is properly no *simplicity* in it at one time, nor *identity* in different. The comparison of the theatre must not mislead us. The successive perceptions only constitute the mind." Thus, according, to Hume, there is no permanent and abiding spiritual substance apart from a series of feelings and ideas ; we can never perceive the so-called permanent self or spirit; whenever we try to perceive it we perceive only a series of feelings, sensations, or ideas ; we perceive nothing beyond them. The so-called spirit or self is a figment of imagination. Thus the self, according to Hume, is nothing but a series of mental states. It is not anything that *has* the states ; it is the states themselves. Hume says, "No man is anything more than a *bundle or collection of different perceptions,* which succeed each other with inconceivable rapidity, and are in perpetual flux and movement." *(Treatise of Human Nature, Book I, Part IV, Section 6.)* J. S. Mill also holds the same view. He defines mind as "nothing but the series of sensations view. internal feelings as they actually occur with the addition of *possibilities* of feelings." The empirical conception of the self is not satisfactory.)

Berkeley anticipated Hume's view of the self and vehemently opposed it. We have Berkeley's answer to Hume's objection (by anticipation) in the third *Dialogue between Hylas and Philonous.* Hylas represents the view of Hume, and Philonous, that of Berkeley. "It seems to me," Hylas objects, "that according to your own way of thinking, and in consequence of your own principles, it should follow that *you are only a system of floating ideas,* without any substance to support them." (This is the view of Hume.) "How often," replies Philonous (representing Berkeley), "must I repeat that I *know or am conscious of my own being,* and that *I myself am not my ideas, but somewhat else,—a thinking active principle that perceives, knows, wills, and operates about ideas."*

**Criticism of the Emperical view of Self**

Firstly, the empirical theory commits the fallacy of substantializing or hypostatizing abstractions. The states and processes apart from their substance or reality; are empty abstractions. There can be no mere thinking, mere feeling, or mere willing, without belonging to a particular self which thinks, feels and wills. But the empiricist makes the states and processes themselves to be substances, as Prof. James says, "the thoughts themselves are the thinkers" and thus makes consciousness impossible.

Consciousness implies an agent or substance which is conscious.

Secondly, the empiricist cannot account for the fact of self-consciousness which is the distinctive feature of mind. If the mind or self is nothing more than an aggregate or series of discrete sensations, feelings and ideas, how can a series know itself to be a series ? How can any one state understand itself as *before and after* other states, or know anything about other states ? How can one feeling or idea know itself ? And how can it know other feelings coming before or after it and its relation to them ? All these are possible, only if we suppose that there is a permanent thinking principle or self which is present in all the states and can, therefore, think them all in their relation to one another. But J. S. Mill speaks of one mental state as knowing another and of a *series* of feelings as being *aware* of itself as a *series,* and as past and future." But Mill himself acknowledges the paradoxical character of this empirical conception and admits that here "we are face to face with a final inexplicability."

Thirdly, the empirical theory cannot explain memory of the past and anticipation of the future. The self perceiving an object at one time and the self remembering it on another, must be one and the same. But if the self be nothing but a series of feelings and ideas, how can one feeling or idea at present remember another in the past? To meet this objection, Mill conceived mind as "a thread of consciousness consisting not only of present sensations, but likewise, in part, of memories and expectations"—or as "a series of feelings. which is aware of itself as past or future." But memory and expectation can never *be* explained without assuming a permanent principle of unity behind them.

Fourthly, the empirical view cannot account for the sense of personal identity and continuity. I am conscious of remain-ing essentially the identical person as I was five or ten years ago. The empirical conception of mind as a series of feelings and ideas cannot explain this personal identity, as feelings once come and gone never appear again. So Mill himself admits that sensations and ideas must include "a belief in something more than their own existence."

Lastly, the empirical theory of the self makes knowledge impossible both on epistemological and psychological grounds. In the first place, mental states have no meaning except in relation to something other than the states themselves, viz., to the thinking principle which experiences them, and the external word revealed in them; knowledge is possible only when there is the subject or the knower and the object or the known, Sensations, in themselves, are meaningless. They must be interpretod according to certain forms and categories, viz., space, time, substantiality, causality, etc., which are not contained in sensations themselves, but must belong to something beyond them, to a thinking principle which evolves them from within itself to interpret sensations. In the second place, the empircial conception of the self, makes knowledge impossible also on psychological grounds, as it cannot account for assimilation, discrimination and apperception without which knowledges impossible. One mental state cannot compare itself with the other preceding ones and assimilate itself to the like ones and discriminate it from disparate ones.

**To sum up** The empirical theory involves the fallacy of substantializing abstractions it cannot account for the facts of self-consciousness, memory and expectation, personal identity and continuity, and it makes knowledge impossible, as it cannot account for assimilation discrimination and apperception on which knowledge is based.

**IV. The Idealistic view of the Self**

The self, then, is neither an abstract noumenal principle of unity, above and beyond inental phenomena, nor an aggregate of mental states but a concrete spiritual principle of unity-in-plurality; in other words, the self is a single abiding subject manifesting itself a plurality of states and activities and in and through them realizes itself a self-conscious and self-determining spirit. The self, apart from its manifestations in particular mental states, is no more meaningless than the aggregate of mental states, apart from and without reference to the unity of the self. The self with its states and activities form one concrete reality or organic whole. A mental state means simply the self expressed in a particular way." Self-consciousness and self-determination are the characteristic features of the self.

Patrick says, "In the absolute or objective idealistic systems the whole Universe is rooted or grounded in mind or spirit, call it Absolute Ego, as did Fichte, or Absolute Idea with Hegel, or Absolute Will with Schopenhauer, or Absolute Experience with Bradley, or Absolute Self with Royce. The soul of man is thus intimate with, or participates in, or represents the very essence of reality. Mind is not something accompanying matter, or something generated in an evolutionary process, but something primordial and original ; it is the vecy stuff of the Universe." *(Introduction to Philosophy,* pp. 249-50).

"An element of difference", says John Caird, "enters into the very idea, or if we may so speak, into the very substance itself of mind. You cannot think of mind as one single substance beneath all diversities of powers and attributes; for when you chase this very substance back to its furthest retreat, you find it to be *not one,* not a bare unit, but complex unity which is the combination or interaction of elements distinct yet indivisible. We are debarred from thinking of a spiritual nature as a substance behind all diversities ; a unity which is and remains simple and unchangeable amidst all changes and differences ; for spirit cannot be conceived save as containing in it an element of diversity, and the only unity we can ascribe to, it is not a unity *beyond* differences, but a unity which manifests itself *in* them Mind or spirit cannot be thought of as a substance distinct from all other substances, for it has no reality apart from them

; or as an identity prior to all differences for its very life and being is *in* differences. It is not a unity behind differences, but it is a unity in differences, and of difference." (*Introduction to Philosophy of Religion,* pp. 211-215.)

A spirit is an essentially self-conscious being. "But self-consciousness is not a simple notion or one which can be thought of as excluding from itself all difference. It includes in it of necessity two elements, a self which is conscious and a self which is the object of consciousness, a self which thinks and a self which is thought of ; and these two not added to each other or in external contiguity but in inseparable correlation.

"Self-consciousness implies not only, if we may so speak, an internal dualism or difference, a self which is opposed to or object to itself, and so, distinguished from itself, but also an external difference, a self which knows or realizes itself only through its consciousness of that which is not self. You cannot define mind or spirit as a substance which exists by itself, prior to or apart from its relations to other substances, for its very nature and essence is to exist in and through its relations to other substances. They are a part of its being. It discovers or realizes its own nature only through natures that are foreign to or outside of itself. Its whole life *as* spirit consists in taking into itself that outward world which it at first opposes to itself. The very beginning, the earliest dawn of that life, is the awakening of the consciousness in one and the same indivisible act, of a self and a not-self, of a world without as opposed to a world within; and the whole subsequent development of that life consists only in the reclaiming or gathering back into the inner self of the rich content of that world which it first *posits* as foreign or external to itself, or in the unfolding or evolution of the consciousness of self, through the mediation of nature and other spiritual beings." (*Ibid,* pp. 212–215.)

This view of the self gives an adequate explanation of self-consciousness and self-determination, memory and expectation, personal identity, unity and continuity of consciousness, and the interpretation of sensations by assimilation, discrimination and apperception, according to the forms and categories of the mind.

**Personality**

Personality is the essential attribute of a person. What is, then, a person ? A person may be defined as an individual being considered as having the higher reflective or intellectual and moral attributes of man *e.g.*, self-consciousness, self-determination, sense of responsibility, and consciousness of having a function to discharge, and an end to realize in life. A person is a social being. He is a member of the social organism. A person has interests that carry him far beyond his life as an organism. But they depend on inter-personal intercourse which profoundly affects his being. His life is closely bound up with the social unity.

A person is an end in himself. He is not a means to an end. Kant and Hegel emphasize the sacredngss of human personality. Kant holds that a person is an end in himself. He is not a means to anybody's gratification. Hegel says, Be a person and respect others as persons." "Each individual has to regard himself at once as a lawgiver—*i. e.,* as an ultimate authority on what has supreme value—and as subject to the law which he himself sets up. Hence he can never regard himself as merely a means to an end that is foreign to himself. The end that he pursues is essentially his own end, a good that he himself recognizes as such. The self that is lawgiver is the self that apprehends what is ultimately good." *(Mackenzie).*

The person is inconceivable apart from the social group. He realizes his personality through social intercourse. "Even the lower animals become aware of themselves as belonging to a persistent group of partly competing and partly co-operating individuals. In human beings, this becomes more definitely developed. They imitate one another, they communicate with one another, guide one another, compete with one another, co-operate with one another, are conscious of common ends to which they adapt common means, and in many ways learn to think of their group or groups as a more comprehensive unity of which they are parts, and from which they are not entirely separable." *(Elements of Constructive Philosophy,* p, 269).

Self-consciousness and self-determination are the essential characteristics of the self. We have already brought out the implications of self-consciousness. We have found that it implies the two-fold opposition between the self and the not-self, and also between the self and its own mental states and processes. Self-conciousnss implies the distinction between self and the not-self, the subject and the object, the mind within and the world without and also the reconciliation of them with each other. It also implies the distinction between the self as a permanent spiritual principle which thinks, and the fleeting mental states and processes, such as, perceiving, remembering, feeling, thinking and willing which are thought of, and also the reconciliation of them with each other.

The self is not only *self-conscious* but also *self-determined.* "Self is known, not merely as Intelligence, but also as Power.I am a self-conscious, intelligent, self-determining power Personality thus involves self-conscious being, self-regulated intelligence, and self-determined activity." (Calderwood : *Hand-booh of Moral Philosophy,* p. 12.) Man, as a spiritual being, is not only self conscious, but also self-determined or free. But man is not absolutely free : his spiritual life has limits or conditions imposed upon it from without ; but these limits or conditions are converted by man into the means of his self-development and self-realization. Man freely determines his own activity. In this respect, he is quite different from material objects, plants, and animals. Material objects do not exist for themselves. They are made to be what they are by external forces. They are entirely determined from without. In plants there is the germ of self-activity. But they are not completely determined by themselves ; nor are they wholly determined from without. Plants can gather materials from external nature and absorb them into their systems. They can also, to a certain extent, counteract the hostile forces of nature. Animals differ from plants only in having the power of feeling and acting instinctively. But they also cannot wholly determine their own activity. They also are partly determined by themselves and partly by external forces. Plants and animals maintain and develop themselves by subjugating external forces. But they have *idea* of their own end ; are they *conscious* of the effort which they put forth to realize that end.

But it is the essential characteristic of a spiritual self-conscious being to have an *idea* of his own end, and to realize this end by *conscious* effort. The animal is a creature of impulses; it is absorbed in the gratification of each momentary impulse. The animal life is one in which there is no internal strife, no antagonism between higher nature and lower nature. The animal nature, therefore, is not divided against itself. But "it is of the very essence of a self-conscious nature to be divided against itself and to win its perfection, its ideal freedom and harmony, as the result of a fierce and protracted internal strife... The conflict of nature and spirit, of impulse with reason, of the lower with the higher self, is one from which, for a rational, self-conscious being, there is no escape. But it is just through this conflict that its spiritual development is attained. Moral and spiritual perfection does not and cannot come to us by nature, but only as a result of struggle and self-conquest." (John Caird : *Introduction to Philosophy of Religion,* pp. 251-252.) The spiritual life is developed out of the natural life when it is transformed) reason it does not consist in the total sup-pression or extinction of the natural life, but in its transforma-tion by reason. Both sensibility and reason have their place in the constitution of the self; but they are not equally supreme; Sensibility is to be subordinated to and transformed by reason. The true self is the *rational self.*

**The Individual and the Society**

We have seen that the moral life of man consists in transforming the natural appetites and desires into the means and materials of our higher rational life; the true self is the rational self. Here, we have to add that the true self is the *social self.* Self-realization is possible only through self-sacrifice. The true or ideal self is *universal* in nature. And we can live the universal life of the ideal self only when we transcend the narrow limits of our individuality, and identify ourselves with the wider life of the society. *Self-realization is possible only through the society.* The individual apart from the soeiety is inconceivable. Aristotle truly said that such a being must be "either a beast or a god." "Such a being could have no ideal self. He must either have realized his ideal like a god, or have no ideal to realize like a beast. For our ideal self finds its embodiment in the life of a society, and it is only in this way that it kept us before us. It is in relation to our fellowmen that we find our ideal life. The "I" or ideal self is not realized in any one individual, bub finds its realization rather in the relations of persons to one another. We can realize the true self or the complete good only by realizing social ends. In order to do this, we must negate the merely individual self, which is not the true self. We must realize ourselves by sacrificing ourselves. The more-fully we so realize ourselves, the more do we reach a universal point of view—*i. e.,* a point of view from which our own private good is no more to us than the good of any one else" (Mackenzie : *Manual of Ethics,* pp. 271-274).

"That I am capable of a universal life, a life transcending the limits of my own individuality, I learn practically in my relations to other human beings, when I find it possible so to identify myself with them as to make their life my own Morality or the moral life may be described as the renunciation of the private or exclusive self and the identification of our life with. an ever-widening sphere of spiritual life beyond us. That I am more than this self-contained individuality, capable of a larger and fuller life, I realize, in the first place, when my private, personal self expands into a self that is common to all the members of the corporate unity of the family. Here the latent capabilities of love and sympathy are liberated. If there is an escape from selfish isolation when the individual identifies himself with the larger unity of the family, or again, if his spiritual life is still more expanded and enriched when his happiness is implicated with the welfare and progress of the wider organism of the state, then most of all with the individual nature become enlarged when the love of kindred and of country expands into an affection yet more comprehensive, the love of humanity, and the life and happiness of the individual becomes Identified with the spiritual life and perfection of the race," (John Carid. *Introduction to the Philosophy of Religion* pp. 263-66). This is the view of Hegel and Neo-Hegelians.

In short, the self gradually realizes its higher nature Through the medium of social institutions, *e.g.*, the family, the community, the state, and the human race. The self can never realize itself in complete isolation from the corporate life of the family, the community, the state, or humanity. Thus, the individual is indissolubly bound up with the society.

### V. Materialistic theories of the Mind or Soul

Democritus, the Greek materialist, considered the soul to be composed of finer, smoother, rounder atoms. The German materialists considered thought as being a secretion of the brain, even as bile is a secretion of the liver. Hœckel considered the mind as a function of the brain. Huxley considered the mind as. an *epiphenamenon* of the brain. Mental processes are merely occasional by products of the physiological processes of the brain. They merely *accompany* cerebral processes without influencing then. They have no activity. They cannot do anything. They cannot regulate or modify cerebral processes. This doctrine is called *epiphenomenalism.*

### Criticism of the Materialistic Theories

The mind is conscious. It is incorporeal. It is subjective. It cannot be composed of material atoms. Function of an organ is in the nature of motion. Mind is not experienced as motion. The secretion of a material thing is material. Bile is secreted by the liver. It is material. But consciousness cannot be regarded as a secretion of the brain. Mind or consciousness cannot be regarded as an epiphenomenon of the brain. It has an initiative. It is a centre of free activity. It can control, regulate, and influence the organism, A mere epiphenomenon cannot have any power or activity. Mind is an active agency creative and appreciative of values. It cannot be a mere by product of the brain.

### VI. The Neo-Realist Theory of the Mind

Perry, an exponent of Neo-Realism, distinguishes three parts of mind. "First, the biological interests; second, a nervous system acting as instrument of the biological processes; third, those parts of the environment to which the nervous system specifically responds the so-called mental *contents.*" (Patrick: *Introduction to Philosophy,* p. 255).

The Neo-Realist considers the mind to be the nervous system with its biological needs responding to the environment. The mind is nothing but the brain in its selective and controlling aspects, selecting stimuli from the environment, responding to them, and moulding the environment to its needs. Those portions of the environment to which the organism specifically responds are called the *mental contents* Those portions of the environment to which the organism does not respond are called *physical.* Thus, the mental and the physical are made of the same neutral stuff. This doctrine is called *neutral monism.* The things in relation to the other things in the environment are called physical. The same things in relation to the nervous system which responds to them, are called mental. The distinction between matter and mind is effaced.

**Criticism of the Neo-Realist theory of Mind**

The mind, is conscious. Consciousness is subjective. The Neo-Realist ignores the subjectivity of mind. His pan objectivism leads him to reduce the mind to the nervous system with its biological needs. It leads him to regard portions of the environment to which the organism responds as *mental contents.* This is pan-objectivism with a vengeance ! What about the biological interests ? Evidently, they are organic needs, hunger, thirst, sex, likes and dislikes, striving, and so on. Do they not presuppose a mind, or, at least, a conation, or mental activity ? *Interests* are *felt* tendencies. They cannot be non-mental. The Neo-Realist theory has the merit of novelty ! But it is sheer muddle-headednes.

**VII. The Pragmatist theory of the Mind**

The Pragmatist does not speak of the soul, or the mind, or very much of consciousness. He approaches, like the Neo-Realist, the problem of mind from the objective standpoint. His approach to the mind problem is biological and evolutionary. The organism has to adapt itself to the environment. It is confronted with a complex situation. It has to master the situation. It has to mould the environment to its organic needs. It makes experiments. Experience is experimenting. As the organism moulds the environment to its biological needs by experimentation, it gathers experience. At first, it has non-reflective experience characterized by mere liking or disliking, and striving. It is determined by pre-organised mechanisms in the organism. Then, a more complex situation arises; conflicting stimuli are presented; conflicting responses are apt to be evoked by them; thus a perplexing situation arises. A necessity arises for re-adjustment. "The new situation has to be integrated; the response has to be adapted to a new situation. Experimentation follows, and selection; conduct is to be controlled by its consegüences; future consequences become transformed into a stimulus for behaviour. Now, such adaptive behaviour is called *reflective, conscious, mental. The mind,* therefore, is *instrumental,* serving biological ends; and Pragmatism of this kind is sometimes, called *Instrumentalism.*" *(Ibid,* p. 258).

**Criticism of the Pragmatist theory of the Mind**

The Pragmatist approach to the mind problem is objective like that of the Neo-Realist. So the objections to the Neo-Realist theory equally apply to the Pragmatist theory. The mind is subjective. The *subjectivity* of the mind is ignored by the Pragmatist. He seeks to evolve *intelligent* behaviour from non-reflective behaviour. He seeks to evolve mind from vital processes. Mental processes are regarded as organic functions which adapt the organism to the complex environment. Again, the non-reflective elements of experience, the biological interests, the organic needs, impulse, craving, desire are *mental,* rather than vital. Pragmatism speaks of "dynamic personalities striving, struggling, achieving," fighting out evil. They cannot be mere tools or instruments of the organism, serving biological ends. They are free, spiritual *agents,* centres of activity, remembering the past, forecasting the future, moulding the environment according to their ideals.

## VIII. The New Psychological Theories of Mind

### (a) Behaviourism

Waston, the founder of Behaviourism, holds that psychology is a science of behaviour. He banishes the soul, the mind, the consciousness, mental processes from psychology. He dispenses with introspection. Observation and experiment are the only psychological methods. Behaviour only is the proper subject matter of psychology. It is the response of the whole organism to a stimulus or a stimulus-pattern. Psychology is the science of stimulus-response. Psychology should not make a fetish of the brain.

Thinking is sub-vocal speech or implicit speech movements. Memory is neural habit. Sensation is response of the receptors or sense-organs to stimuli. Emotion is a pattern of visceral responses. Personality is a behaviour-pattern. It is a totality of reactions as assets and liabilities. There are no inherited tendencies. The organism is entirely moulded by the environment. Behaviourism believes in environmentalism.

### Criticism of, Behaviourism

We are conscious of mental processes. They are subjective. They cannot be reduced to objective behaviour. Experience is not mere response of the orgasnism. Behaviourism, like Neo-Realism. and Pragmatism ignores the *subjectivity* of mind and mental processes. It ignores the activity of the mind and its free moulding of the environment. It reduces the mind to the organism which is entirely moulded by the environment. It ignores heredity and overrates the environment. It commits the absurdity of reducing thinking to sub-vocal talking. It is pan-objectivism run mad! Behaviourism does not give us a theory of mind.

### (b) The Gestalt theory of the Mind

The Gestalt theory stresses experience or behaviour as a *gestalt,* a whole a configuration, a pattern. It is not a mosaic of physical atoms. Experience is not an aggregate of sensations. Behaviour is not an agregate of reflex actions. The Gestalt psychology is a revolt against associationism and reflexology. It defines the mind as "the structural correspondence of excitatory fields in the brain with the experienced contents of consciousness." "Kohler postulates a psycho-physiological correspondence between experienced order in space and time and the underlying dynamical context of physiological processes." (*Ibid,* p. 261). The Gestalt theory is antimechanistic and anti-vitalistic.

**Criticism of the Gestalt theory**

The Gestalt theory does not clearly define the nature of mind. The mind is a unique centre of consciousness, a subject experience, a free, active agent recting on the environment and moulding it to its needs. It cannot be regarded as mere correspondence between the space-time order and the physiological processes in the brain. The Gestalt theory explains experience and behaviour in terms of physiological processes in the brain. It makes too much of the tension in the brain and its equilibrium. But physiological processes cannot adequately account for mental processes. The former are objective, while the latter are subjective. The Gestalt theory rightly stresses the configurational character of experience and behaviour. Experience is a *whole.* But it is a whole because it embodies a *purpose.* It fulfils the purpose of the mind, or active agent. Experience is the mind's experience. Organisation of experience and behaviour is due to the *purposive activity of the mind which* is ignored by the Gestalt " psychology. It ignores the *subjectivity* of the mind and its experience. Its approach to the mind problem is objective. It is entirely a wrong approach. The configurational character of experience and behaviour can only be explained by the purpose of an active, psychic principle.

**(c) The Aniministic theory (McDougall)**

McDougall, the founder of Hormic psychology, holds that the mind or subject is a unitary and distinct psychic principle animating the organism. It is an immaterial or incorporeal principle endowed with certain enduring capacities for psychical activity, sensation, perceiving, remembering, imagining, thinking. feeling, emotion, and willing. It guides nervous energy in such a way as to counteract its tendency to dissipation. The mind interacts with the body, controls and guides it. Mc Dougall calls his theory *Animism.* The distinct; reality different from the body. He revives the old dualism of Plato and Descartes.

**Criticism of McDougall's theory**

The dualistic theory of mind and body cannot adequately explain the relation between the two. It believes in interaction which contradicts the Law of Conservation of Energy. McDougall's theory is more sound than the objectivist theories of mind advocated by the Behaviourist and the Gestaltist. His central concept is *purpose* and striving to realize a purpose. This is an important truth emphasized by McDougall.

**(d) The Freudian theory of Mind**

Freud stresses the dynamic character and the unconscious motives of the mind. He makes too much of sex desires *(libido)* The desires which are banned by the society are *repressed* and driven to the unconscious. The unconscious motives do not lose their activity. They form "complexes" and well up into conscious life in the form of dreams, day-dreams, and the like. The unconscious repressed desires form the *Id*. The Ego is partly conscious, and mostly unconscious. As conscious it reacts to the social environment and follows the realily principle or the social code of morality. As unconscious it follows the pleasure principle or the direct or indirect fulfilment of the anti-social repressed desires. The Censor does not allow the repressed desires to come to the level of consciousness and seek direct fulfilment. So they assume various forms of disguise and indirectly fulfil themselves in dreams. Dreams are symbolical expressions of regressed desires in adult life.

**Criticism of Freud's theory of Mind**

Freud has stressed important truths about mental life; He has laid emphasis on the active nature of the mind and its unconscious and irrational impulses, cravings, desires But he hardly gives a clear and consistent account of the mind. His concepts of Ego, Id, Censor, Super-Ego, Conscience, Complexes and the like are mere hypotheses to explain certain actual facts. He does not explain them adequately.: nor does he show their inter-relation to one another. Freud hardly gives a philosophy of the mind.

## XI. The Emergence Theory of Mind

Evolution is emergent. It displays a series of *levels*. At each new level a higher reality emerges due to organization or creative synthesis. *Novelties* emerge at each new level. Atoms are organised into molecules; molecules are organised into living cells; cells are organised into organisms; simple organisms are organised into complex organisms; *mind* emerges from the organization of vital processes. "The world is a process of *realization,* of progressive achievement, Aristotle had the right idea when he thought of the mind as the form or the realization, or the fruition, or perfection of the body and the brain are stepping-stones to the higer reality of the mind. Mind is an *achievement,* a fruition, perhaps a goal," *(Ibid,* pp. 282–83). "Mind is an activity, a power, a capacity, and in evolution it is a new power and a new capacity, crowning the whole evolutionary movement. In mind, nature reaches a higher level, issues in a new reality. Not only has mind the power of envisaging the future and then of controlling the present to realize the future, but it is also at home in the field of values; it creates these values, then overcomes all obstacles to realize them; its field is the field of science, philosophy, art, literature. It not only knows and studies the world, but dominates and controls it. The forces of nature are subservient to mind. It changes the direction of energy, subverting to its own ends every form of energy, molar, molecular, chemic, thermic, and electric, and by means of these modifying its own environment. Not only does the mind have the power of dominion; it has the final faculty of appreciation. It discovers something in nature which we call beauty. In morals, again, it vision: higher ideals of conduct and controls itself to realize these ideals." (*Ibid*, pp. 279–80). The mindis called *spin* because it appreciates and creates values, truth, good, beauty and the Holy.

**Criticism of the Emergence theory**

This theory regards the mind as the highest achievement of the evolutionary process, Evolution is orderly gradual change. Order and organization presuppose a Mind which organises the pre-existing elements into a new and higher reality. Lloyd Morgan admits that there is an *Activity* which is the *nisus* guiding the evolu-tionary proeess. He calls it God. The Cosmic Mind or God is the guiding and controlling force, the evolutionary, urge, the root cause of higher and higher powers of organization Without a guiding spiritual principle, a purposive agent, emergent evolution of different levels of reality cannot be adequately accounted for. Evolution is transformation of the implicit into the explicit, the potential into the actual.

**Freedom of the Will**

We have already seen that man as a spiritual being is self-determined or free. He determines his own activity. He is not determined by external forces. Though he is not absolutely free, though his freedom has limits, yet he can transform even his limits into the means and materials of his self-development and self-realization. But this is not admitted by all.

The question of "Freedom of the will" has raised a hot con-troversy among the philosophers of different ages. In ordinary usage, the expression "freedom of will" means freedom to do what we *will* to do, without any compulsion or restraint. But here the question is, whether we are free *to will what we will,* and how we come to will it, whether we are free to choose between alternative possibilities *i. e.* possible lines of action or compelled to choose one of them by something other than ourselves. In other words, does our willing a line of action depend essentially upon ourselves alone and is therefore *autonomous* or *self determined,* or does it depend upon any other things extraneous to the self and is thus *heteronomous* or other-determined?

Some are advocates of the doctrine of freedom of the will. They are called **Libertarians**. Others deny freedom of the will and are called **Necessarians**.

The question of freedom of the will may be considered from different points of view–psychological, ethical, metaphysical and theological.

**Necessarianism** or **Determinism** denies' freedom of the will and puts forward the following arguments partly psychological, partly metaphysical, and partly theologieal. in its defence.

**(I) Psychological grounds**

**(a) Psychology of voluntary action.**

Our volitions are determined by motives and desires. When there is a single motive, (*e. g.*, in a simple action), this motive determines the volition and the consequent action. When several motives are simultaneously present (e. *g*., in a complex action), there arises a 'conflict of motives' and the *strongest* prevails, inhibits and represses the rival motives, and determines the volition.

In other words, volition is determined by the *strength* of the motive. The strength of a motive again, is determined (i) partly by the environment or external circumstances influencing the individual from without, *(ii)* and partly by the mental character and constitution of the individual himself, which, again, is determined *(a)* partly by inherited tendencies of his ancestors, and *(b)* partly by the structure of his brain and organism.

Thus our volitions are rigidly determined by a series of causes and antecedents, and if all the antecedents of human volitions and actions were accurately known, the future actions of men could be predicted as infallibly as the movements of the planets, the tide of rivers, etc.

**(b) Possibility of prediction of human conduct**

We can not only predict future physical events *(e. g.*, eclipses, rainfall, famine etc.), as they are rigidly determined by their antecedent circumstances and inevitably follow from their natural causes, but we can also predict the future actions of men, if all their antecedent circumstances are known beforehand. And this possibility of prediction is confirmed by the statistics of marriages, crimes, suicides and other voluntary actions, upon which the civil and criminal legislation of a country greatly depends. So there can be no freedom of the will.

**(II) Metaphysical grounds**

First, the *Law of Causality* contradicts the doctrine of freedom of the will. A volition not determined *by* antecedent circumstances, the so-called free volition, would be an event without a cause which is impossible. For, according to the law of causality, every event, physical as well as mental, must have a cause; there cannot be any uncaused phenomenon either in nature or in mind. Indeterminism flatly contradicts the law of causality. "The will of man is made by this theory an exception to the law of causation. Determinism, on the other hand, stands in harmony, with the postulate; the act of will is, as this view conceives it, like every other event in the world enmeshed in the causal nexus." *(Problems of Philisophy,* p. 395.)

Secondly, The Law *of Conservation of Energy* also contradicts the doctrine of freedom of the will. By freedom of the will or free energising of the mind, we create a new or fresh energy in the body in the form of motor innervation and, through this energy of the body, produce a change in the external world. Thus, by our free volitions we add fresh energy to the; total amount of energy in the universe. But, according to the law of Conservation of Energy, the amount of energy in the world is constant *i. e.,* can never be either increased or diminished.

Thirdly, the materialistic and naturalistic conception of the world as a chance combination or a mechanical aggregate of material atoms operating according to the laws of matter and motion naturally leads to the denial of freedom of the will, According to materialism, mind is only a by-product or epi-phenomenon of the brain and as such it can have no causal power and consequently no freedom of the will.

Fourthly, the extreme form of the monistic view of the world (e. *g.*, the abstract monism or pantheism of Spinoza), necessarily leads to determinism. If God alone is real, the world and the mind become only illusory appearances. We think our volitions free, Spinoza said, simply because we are conscious of the volitions without being conscious of the causes which determine them. Stones, too, might think themselves free in ignorance of their causes, when they are thrown at a person.

**(III) Theological ground : Fore-knowledge of God**

Divine fore-knowledge is inconsistent with human freedom. God, to be God, must design and foresee all things and actions. God not only foresees the future phenomena of (nature but also the future actions of men. And prevision *or foreknowledge implies pre-determination.* God's foresight implies that God has determined beforehand the course of the world and the actions of men, so that man has no power of determining his own actions.

Martineau denies God the foresight or fore-knowledge of human volitions and actions to save them from predetermination by God. But this limitation of God's knowledge, Martineau argues, is not inconsistent with his infinitude and absoluteness, since it is a voluntary self-limitation on the part of God. God willingly denies himself the prevision or fore-knowledge of the human volitions and actions to leave them free. But this is an artificial device to reconcile the divine fore-knowledge with human freedom.

## SUMMARY

Necessarians or determinists deny freedom of the will and appeal

(1) To the *psychology of volition,* according to which volition is not free but is determined by the strongest motive.

(2) To the *possibilitiy of prediction of human actions.* If human actions were absolutely free without being determined by antecedent circumstances, they could not be predicted, as they generally are.

(3) To the *materialistic theory of the world,* according to which, mind is a function, by product or epiphenomenon of the brain, and as such has no causal power and freedom.

(4) To the *monistic and pantheistic theory of the world,* according to which, God is the *only* reality and the human mind has no independent reality of its own and consequently, no freedom of the will.

(5) To the *Law of Causality,* according to which, nothing can happen without a cause,—there can be no uncaused phenomenon in the world, hence no freedom of the will.

(6) To the *Law of Conservation of Energy,* according to which, the amount of energy in the universe is constant, but freedom of the will implies creation of *new* or *fresh* physical energy and consequent increase of the total amount of energy in the world.

(7) To the *fore-knowledge of God* which implies that God, in foreseeing the future actions of men, has determined them beforehand.

## The Doctrine of Free Will

### (a) Criticism of Determinism or Necessarianism

Firstly, the psychology of will on which determinism is based is erroneous. Volition is, no doubt, determined by the strength of motives; but the strength of motives depends essentially on the self itself, and not on antecedent circumstances. "Volition is determined from within the mental principle itself, and not by impulsion from without. It is not external determination by cause, but internal self-determination according to a reason." *(Stephen.)*

Secondly, the possibility of prediction does not necessarily imply that volition is rigidly determined by antecedent circumstances. It is also consistent with freedom of the will. For, by freedom of the will we do not mean capriciousness of will, so that prediction of human actions may "become quite impossible. Repeated free volitions lead to the formation of a character which acts in the same way under the same circumstances. If different persons of the same nature be placed in the same circumstances, their wants or needs will be very much the same. Hence their desires and motives also will be very much the same, and they will act in the same direction as they have the same reason for doing so. Thieves must steal whenever they get an opportunity. So, freedom of the will, too, leads to the formation of a *uniform* character which may be predicted to a certain extent. Mackenzie says, "The moral life means thg building up character, *i.e.*, it means the forming of definite habits of action. And if a habit of action be definite, it is, uniform and predictable," *(Manual of Ethics,* p. 75.)

Thirdly, materialism cannot be taken as the satisfactory theory of the universe and consequently mind cannot be regarded as an occasional by product or epiphenomenon of the brain, since if is conscious of its causal power in self-activity and volition.

Fourthly, abstract monism and pantheism cannot be regarded as an adequate theory of the world, since it denies the reality of the world and human mind. Concrete monism may be taken as the most satisfactory theory of the world, which does not deny the reality and freedom of the finite mind. Fifthly, the Law of Causality is not inconsistent with freedom of the will. Freedom of the will does not imply that volition is an event without a cause. The self itself causes it and it does so freely without being determined to do so by anything external to it, but by the conception of its own good. Sixthly, the Law of Conservation of Energy does not contradict freedom of the will, if we take it in a wider sense and apply it also to mental energy. In that case, the loss of mental energy in volition would be compensated by the creation of its equivalent physical energy in motor innervation. The answer is sometimes given that free volition does not create any new energy but only *changes the direction* of physical forces; so the law of conservation of energy does not contradict, freedom of the will.

Lastly, the fore-knowledge of God is not inconsistent with human freedom. God knows the future not because he infers the future as effects are inferred from causes, but because the past, the present and the future are all present to him, intuitively in one Eternal Now. Therefore he *sees* the future *as* present; he does not *infer* it from the past. He therefore foresees the future actions of men without himself determining them beforehand; he knows how they will act though they act freely. St. Thomas said that just in memory we know the past without determining it, so God knows the future actions of men without determining them beforehand. Provision or fore-knowledge does not necessarily mean pre-determination.

**(a) The positive arguments in favour of freedom of the will**

**(i) The evidence of self-consciouness**

In willing we are always conscious of willing freely, or determining the course of our actions from within ourselves and for our own good, without being determined by anything antecedent to, or external to ourselves. And the consciousness of freedom is specially distinct in the process of deliberation and resolution.

**(ii) The evidence of moral consciousness**

Kant argued that freedom of the will is a postulate of moral judgment. In moral judgment there is a sense of 'oughtness or 'moral obligation'; this moral obligation implies freedom of the will,– Thou *oughtst,* therefore thou *canst.*" Duty and responsibility, morality, justice, accountability, merit and demerit, virtue and vice would be quite meaningless, if there were no freedom of the will.

**(iii) Scope for human freedom in Absolute Idealism**

A true and adequate metaphysical theory of the world *(e. g.*, concrete monism or absolute idealism) confirms the doctrine of free will. According to it, the human soul is a finite reproduction or reduplication of God and as such it shares in the ultimate self-determining power of God, which produces and determines the series of outward events in time without itself being determined by them. Thus, the human, soul shares in the freedom of God but the freedom of man is not absolute but relative, since it is limited, to a certain extent, by the physical forces of Nature, by his relations to other men, and by the freedom of God.

### Indeterminism and Self-determinism

Freedom of the will either means indeterminism or self-determinism. Indeterminism, liberty of indifference or libertarianism holds that the mind can determine its own volitions without any cause, motive or reason. It can arbitarily choose between alternative possibilities without being determined guided by any reason. Cunningham says "Indeterminism is the view that man's will is free in *the* sense that it is *uncaused.* At the moment of action, so the indeterminist holds, there are real alternatives before the will; one or the other may be chosen indifferently. He finds freedom in a genuine spontaneity of the will that expresses itself in an undetermined choice within a limited field of possibilities." *(Problems of Philosophy,* pp. 390-391).

But this is inconsistent with our rational nature. The mind is free in the sense that it is determined not by anything external to it, but by itself for its own good. Thus freedom of the will does not mean indeterminism but self-determinism. "The self determines its own volitions according to its ideal of its highest good; but its highest good is its own highest self; therefore, to be thus determined is to be self-determined." *(Stephen).*

The self-determinist maintains that "the agent's will is always determined in the moment of willing, not by wholly external forces as the fatalist claims, but by the tendencies, the impulses and purposes, that belong to the agent's character. The act of choice is not uncaused; like any other event, it is always an element within a causal situation. It is the result of conflicting forces, namely, the motives present in the moment of choice. These forces are not external to the agent's character, but are elements within it. Hence the individual is in a sense free—free, that is, to follow the bent of his own nature and to express in conduct tendencies that belong to him as a rational being. Freedom is not to be sought in an uncaused spontaneous act of choice among alternatives, but in the capacity inherent in each moral agent to determine the bent of his own character;

Freedom, in short, means not indelerminism, but selfdeterminism—self expression and self-development." *(Problems of Philosophy,* p. 391.)

**Future Life or Immortality of the Soul-Martineau gives the following arguments**

**(i) Death in its Physiological aspect**

Death, in its physiological aspect, presents simply a case of transformation of energy. On death, the forces, of the organism are dissipated, and consequently the organism is dissolved. But these forces are not totally lost, according to the law of Conservation of Energy.

Now, the law of Conservation of Energy either includes mental energy or excludes it. If it applies only to physical energy, then mind stands as something independent of matter, and hence the human soul max continue after death. If the law applies to physical as well as to mental energy, then just as physical energy is never absolutely lost, but retained in some form or other, so mental energy, too, is not absolutely lost after death, but continues in some form or other even after death. Thus the immortality of the human soul is not inconsistent with the law of Conservation of Energy.

**(ii) Death in its Metaphysical aspect**

Every finite soul has its place and function as a factor in the evolution of the world. We may conclude, therefore, that the soul will continue to exist so long as it cannot perfectly fulfil its function for which it is needed as a factor in the world-system. And there is every reason for believing that the soul cannot exhaust its function and fulfil its purrpose completely in the present life; so it must continue to exist even after death and fulfil its function in the world-system.

**(iii) Death in its Moral aspect**

In the very constitution of our own mind we find strong suggestions and unmistakable indications of our future life. Our intellectual and moral constitution gives us certain indications (or predictions as it were) of the existence of a future life after death. These indications have been called by Dr. Martineau 'vaticinations of the intellect,' 'vaticinations of the conscience' and 'vaticinations in suspense.' *The* rational nature of the human self guarantees its immortal life.

**(a) Vaticinations of the Intellect**

Our intellect is limited by time and space. The development of intellect consists in gradually transcending the limits of time and space. As the mind gradually develops its powers of remembering the past, anticipating the future, conceiving the distant and discerning the inner causes and relations of things beyond the reach of sense, it gradually oversteps the bounds of time and space. But in the present finite life, the mind cannot completely transcend the limitations of time and space. So we may reasonably hope that there is future life after death, where the intellect will attain its full development and completely transcend the limits of time and space.

**(b) Vaticinations of the Conscience**

The moral ideal cannot be fully realized in the present life. The greater the moral progress, the higher the moral ideal. The conflict between desire and duty cannot be completely reconciled in the finite life. So Kant argued that there is a future life continuous with the present life, where too personality of the human soul will persist and the conflict between desire and duty will be finally reconciled.

**(c) Vaticinations in Suspense**

Kant also argued that the demand of the conscience for justice and equity points to the existence of a future life. We have an ineradicable conviction that virtue must be rewarded with happiness and vice punished with pain. But the virtuous are seldom found to be happy in this world. So we believe that there is an after-life where there will be a perfect coincidence of virtue with happiness and vice with pain. The physical sufferings and the public opprobrium are not sufficient punishment for the vicious; they must have their proper retribution in a future where their sufferings will be exactly proportionate to their sins.

## UNIVERSITY QUESTIONS

1. Explain the distinction that is made between the empirical and the noumenal self. What do you consider to be the true doctrine of self ? (1910).
2. Explain precisely what you mean when you speak of your "self". What reason have you for speaking of your "self" as a permanent reality ? How can you reconcile the permanent reality of your "self" with the changes which you are conscious of as going on within it ? (1913).
3. What reasons have you for believing in the personal identity of the human soul ? (1915).
4. When you say 'I will do it myself, what precisely do you mean by Self ? Are there any other senses in which the word 'Self is used ? Explain and illustrate your meaning fully. (1916).
5. What is meant by Liberty, and what is meant by Necessity, in relation to the Human Will ? What evidences can be advanced in support of Liberty of Will ? Give your own opinion, with reasons. (1916 Hon.)
6. What is your conception of Immortality ? (1917).
7. Explain the meaning of Self and the Identity of Self, and state what reasons there are for thinking that the Self will continue to exist after the present life. (1918).
8. Discuss the questions of Free will and Necessity. Is absolute indeterminism tenable ? (1920).
9. Analyse the idea of Self as you understand it, and state any idea of Self different from the one you have given, with some criticism. (1921).
10. Discuss critically the concept of Self. (1921).
11. What decision can be arrived at as to the particular problem of the continuance of Self after death on metaphysical grounds ? (1921).

12. Are there apy metaphysical grounds of believing in the continuance of the Soulh after death ? (1921).
13. Explain and examine the Empirical theory of Self or Mind (as held by Hume or Mill), pointing out its bearing on the questions of Morality and Future Life. (1923).
14. Explain the meaning of Personality, and show how the idea of a Person leads to the ideas of Personal Eights and Moral Law. (1923).
15. State the principal meanings of the term 'self. Give a critical estimate. (1924).
16. What reasons are there for thinking that the human mind continues to exist after the dissolution of the physical organism? (1927).
17. Discuss the conception of Necessity. Give a critical estimate. (1924).
18. Give any *one* reason for believing in the Future Existence of the Soul. (1925).
19. State what you mean when you speak of your own Self analysing the idea fully. Is there any reason for believing in the continued existence of the Self after death ? (1926).
20. The actions of finite beings are subject to necessity. Explain the meaning of this statement, and the grounds on which it is based. What is your own view with regard to it ? (1927).
21. Discuss the question of freedom of the will. Is absolute indeterminism a tenable hypothesis ? (1928).
22. What is the nature of the self ? Do you think that the self will continue to exist after death ? (1928).
23. Discuss the question of freedom of the will. Is absolute indeterminism a tenable hypothesis ? (1928).
24. Do you think that there are sufficient reasons for the belief in a future life of the self ? (1930).

25. Exhibit the relation in which the individual stands to society. (1932).
26. Expound the concept of 'personality' and show what light it throws on the distinction between the empirical and noumenal selves. (1933).
27. State and examine the main grounds for a belief in the future life of the individual self. (1933).
28. Trace the growth of the idea of personality. Discuss the question as to how far the personality of man is consistent with the pantheistic conception of the Deity. (1935).
29. Explain the conception of the soul. Give your reasons for belief in the future existence of the soul. (1936).
30. Discuss the problem of freedom of the will from the point of view of human personality. (1937).
31. State your view of the nature and origin of the self. (1946).
32. Explain the concept of 'Personality'. Has it any connection with a belief in future life ? (1947)
33. Give a critical account of the views of the Self held by Descartes, Hume and Kant. (A. U. 1948).
34. Explain the theories of the Self held by the Neo-Eealist, the Pragmatist, the Freudian, and the Behaviourist. (A. U. 1946)
35. Distinguish between
    *(a)* Plato's view of the self with that of Aristotle, and
    *(b)* Descartes' view of the Self with that of Hume. (A. U.)
36. Contrast Berkeley's theory of the Self with Hume's theory.

# CHAPTER X

# MIND AND BODY

## Mind and Body

There is correspondence between processes and physiological processes. There is correspondence between cerebral processes and mental processes *(e.g.* sensations). There is correspondence between mental processes *(e. g.,* volitions) and physiological processes *(e. g.* muscular movements). How can we explain this correspondence ? We may regard body and mind as two independent substances interacting each othar. This is the theory of Inter-action. Or we may regard their correspondence as the result of the occasional intervention of God. This is the theory of Occasionalism. Or we may regard the correspondence between mind and body as due to the pre-established harmony between them. This is the theory of Pre-etablished Harmpny. Or we may regard mind and body, or thought and extension, as the parallel attributes of the same substance, God. This is the theory of Parallelistic Monism. Or we may regard mind as an epiphenomenon of the body. This is the theory of materialism or Epiphenomenalism. Or we may regard body as a system of ideas in the perceiving mind. This is the doctrine of Subjective Idealism or Mentalism. Or we may regard mind as the entelechy of the body, its fruition and perfection, a higher reality emerging from the body. This is the theory of Emergent Evolution... Or we may regard the body as the necessary medium or instrument of the Absolute Spirit for its manifestation as a finite mind. This is the theory of Absolute Idealism.

## Interactionism

Descartes is an exponent of dualism. He regards matter and mind as two heterogeneous substances. Matter is extended.

Mind is unextended. Matter is unconscious. Mind is conscious. Matter, including body, is subject to mechanical law. Mind is subject to purpose and teleology. Body and mind have nothing in common. Descartes holds that body and mind act upon each other in the pineal gland of the brain, which is the seat of mind and the animal spirits which guide the body. There the animal spirits act upon the mind, and the mind acts upon the animal spirits. This is the theory of interaction or Interactionism.

According to Interactionism, the body acts upon the mind in sensations, and the mind acts upon the body in volitions. The body and the mind act upon each other.

**Criticism of Interactionism**

Interactionism holds, that brain events affect mind-events, and that mind-events affect brain-events." *(Types of Philosophy* p. 224.) But two quite heterogeneous substances cannot act and react upon each other. Action and reaction presuppose a certain homogeneity in nature among the things which act and react upon one another. Qualitative likeness is the invariable precondition of causal connection.

Dualism contradicts the law of Conservation of Energy. According to this law, the total amount of physical energy in the universe is constant, and one kind of physical energy can be transformed into another kind of physical energy without any loss of quantity but no physical energy can be transformed into non-physical or mental energy and *vice versa* as dualism supposes. For, in that case, the total amount of physical energy in the universe would not be constant, but it would be constantly increased and deoreased. For example, in sensation, physical energy (in the form of cortical vibration) is transformed into mental energy, and in volition, mental, energy is transformed into physical energy (in the form of motor innervation); thus in the former case there is a loss of destruction of physical energy, and in the latter there is an increase or creation of physical energy.

Hocking observes: "Will the brain use some of its energy

in producing thought or emotion in which case, some physical energy will appear to vanish ! Or will the mind, in deciding to move a muscle, impart some impulse to a brain-event which the previous brain-events do not account for ? in which case physical energy will appear to be created ?" *(Ibid,* p. 224.)

**Occasionalism**

To avoid the difficulties of the theory of interaction, the followers of Descartes, Geulinex and Malebranche resorted to the hypothesis of occasional cause *(or occasionalism).* According to this theory, mind and body are opposed to each other and consequently cannot interact upon each other: but still there is a correspondence between the two; and this correspondence is brought about by God, who upon the occasion of certain changes in the one, intervenes to bring about corresponding changes in the other;—whenever changes arise in the body, God intervenes and produces corresponding sensations in the mind, and whenever there are desires and volitions in the mind to move the body, he produces corresponding movements in the body.

**Criticism of Occasionalism**

This theory is quite, inadequate as a scientific explanation of the relation between mind and body. It makes too large demands upon pious credulity. To bring down God at every moment to produce changes in the one on the occasion of the corresponding changes in the other is quite absurd; it reduces God to a *Deus ex machina.* It believes inperpetual miracle.

**The Theory of Pre-established Harmony**

Leibnitz tried to explain the relation between body and mind by his theory of *Pre-established Harmoy.* According to this theory, God at the time of creation harmony between mind and body pre-adjusted them to each other in such a way, that they always correspond to each other without calling of his constant intervention as occasionalism supposes. Body and mind, thus, may be regarded as two clocks which once constructed and set to the same time, go on keeping the same time without either of them having any effect upon the other.

Leibnitz spiritualizes and mind and considers them to be composed of monads. Monads spiritual atoms; they are active perceiving forces. They are self-centred, self-contained, self-active substances of different degrees of complexity. The body is a cluster of lower unconscious monads. The mind is a self-conscious higher monad. It is a dominant monad, a queen monad. The body and the mind correspond to each other because God established a relation between them, adjusted them to each other after creation. Their correspondence is due to pre-established harmony.

### Criticism of Pre-established Harmony

The theory of pre-established harmony involves the same difficulty as occasionalism, but only has the merit of 'parsimony of hypothesis'. While the latter lends support to perpetual miracle, for it asserts constant intervention of God, the former admits of on miracle only at the time of creation. But Leibnitz does not go to the root of the matter and cannot explain how even God could establish harmony between two entirely heterogeneous substances like matter and mind.

Besides, body and mind both are composed of monads. Monads are self-contained entities. They cannot act upon each other. How, then, can God, the Monad of monads, act upon other monads, and adjust them to one another ? How can he establish harmony among them ? Causation is transeunt action. Leibnitz denies it in the monads. How, then, can he admit it in God ? In order to solve the difficulty of interaction between body and mind, he makes the hypothesis of the interaction of God upon monads. This is pushing the difficulty further back, but not solving it.

### Parallelism

To avoid the difficulties of Dualism and Interactionism. Spinoza started the hypothesis of universal parallelism of parallelistic monism, according to which mind and matter are not two distinct and independent substances but are only two parallel attributes or of one and the same substance, God. Mind and matter are the correlative aspects, internal and external, of one and the same ultimate substance *(viz.,* God), which is, in itself, neither mind nor matter, but appears in its two parallel attributes of thought and extension; hence for every unit of extension in the universe there is a corresponding unit of consciousness, and *vice versa;* for every change in the body, there is a corresponding change in the mind and for every change in the mind, there is a corresponding change in the body. There is a thorough-going correspondence between thought and extension, mind and body mental processes and physiological processes. Thus parellelistic monism explains the relation between mind and body by their co-substanbiality or co-inherence in one and the same substance; hence it effects a compromise between dualism and monism, by combining the dualism of attributes with the monism of substance. There is the identity of the divine substance behind parallelism of thought and extension.

Herbert Spencer adopted the parallelistic theory of Spinoza, but held that the ultimate substance, which appears in the two parallel series of mental and material phenomena, is unknown and unknowable. The ultimate reality is neither mental nor material but something unknown and unknowable which manifests itself in both mind and matter. The brain is not the mind. The brain follows its own laws. The mind also follows its own laws.

## Psycho-Physical Parallelism

Spinoza's doctrine of Universal Parallelism has been modified by some modern psychologists into *Psycho-Physical Parallelism.* Stout is an advocate of this doctrine. There is no causal connection between psychoses and neuroses mental processes and neural processes. There is mere concomitance between them. There is no psychosis without neuroses.

Psychoses and neuroses are equally real. Certain brain processes always accompany all psychical processes.

**The Mind stuff theory**

Clifford holds that corresponding to every atom of matter-stuff there is an atom of mind-stuff attached to it, so that when the material atoms combine into an organism, the corresponding atoms of mind-stuff combine into mind.

**The Double Aspect Theory**

Warren holds that conscious processaes and neural processes constitute *one single series of events.* They are two aspects of the same thing. Mental processees are the *subjective* aspect, while neutral processes are the *objective* aspect. This is called the Double-Aspect theory

**Neutral Monism**

The Neo-Realist holds that there is a neutral stuff which appears to be physical and mental in different contexts and relations. A thing is called *a physical thing* in relation to other things in the space-time word. It is called a mental content in relation to the nervous system which responds to it. Those parts of the environment to which the, organism specifically responds are called *mental contents.* The other parts of the environment to which the organism does not specifically respond are called *physical things.* This theory is called *Neutral Monism.* There are neutral entities, which become both physical and mental in different relations.

**Criticism of Parallelism**

This theory has certain advantages over Dualism and Monism. "Parallelism asserts that brain-events and mind-events run along in perfect correspondence each to each without interference from either side." *(Types of Philosophy,* p. 224.)

It neither reduces matter to mind nor mind to matter like spiritualism or materialism, but regards both of them as real. Spinoza regards them as parallel attributes of the divine substance, not as independent substances. He deduces their concomitance from their identity of substance.

But Spinoza's doctrine ends in panpsychism. He holds that wherever there is thought there is extension, and wherever there is extension there is thought. But this is not confirmed by scientific evidence. Consciousness is found in a highly organised nervous system. It is not found in stocks and stones. It is not found in organic matter. It is found in a living organism endowed with a nervous system.

The weakness of Parallelism lies in the denial of the efficacy of mind. The mind is not parallel to the body as it supposes. The mind is a higher reality than the body. It controls and regulates the body. It has freedom. It has the power of initiative. It cannot be regarded as on the same level with the body.

Parallelism contradicts the clear testimony of consciousness. Just as the body acts upon the mind so the mind also acts upon the body. The mind feels pain when the body is wounded when the mind is overwhelmed with grief, the body becomes weak and emaciated. The mind can withstand the influence of the body. (A soldier can defy hunger and thirst, cold and heat, and forge ahead in the field of battle. He can control his body. A martyr embraces death and gets burnt with a smiling face ! He makes his body the fit instrument of his mind. These facts cannot be explained by Parallelism.

Parallelism is a statement of fact. It states the mere concomitance of mental processes and neutral processes. It tries to explain it by the hypothesis of Identity. This is no explanation. Identity is the denial of duality. But mind and body are not the same thing. Parallelism points to causal connection.

The mind-stuff theory is some kind of panpsychism which is not supporbed by scientific evidence. The double-aspect theory and neutral monism are cheap solutions to the problem. They tend towards pan-objectivism. Psycho-physical parallelism is a statement of mere concomitance of mental processes and neural processes. It does not explain the concomitance.

**Epiphenomenalism**

Materialism reduces mind to an epiphenomenon of the brain, —an occasional by product merely accompanying cerebral processes without influencing them. Consciousness is, a phosphorescent light emitted by intense friction of brain molecules which are composed of phosphorous substances.

This theory contradicts the clear testimony of consciousness. We are conscious of the reality of mind. We and conscious of its *efficacy.* It is not a mere halo cast by the brain which cannot influence its activity. The mind can control the body. The mind is a centre of energy which prevents bodily energy from dissipating. It directs, regulates and controls bodily energy.

**Subjective Idealism**

Berkeley holds that finite spirits and God constitute. the universe. There are no material things. They are clusters of sensations produced in finite spirits by God according to fixed laws. They are not extramental realities. They are not independent of perceiving minds. So the body is a group of sensations or ideas. This is the doctrine of Subjective Idealism.

Berkeley evades the mind-body problem by reducing body to a system of ideas existing in the perceiving mind, just as materialism evades the problem by reducing mind to matter.

Mind and body both are real. Mind and matter, subject and object, are necessary for experience. Knowledge presupposes the duality of subject and object, none of which can be reduced to the other.

**Emergent Evolution**

Lloyd Morgan, the exponent of Emergent Evolution, holds that matter, life and mind are three levels of reality. Life emerged out of matter when it was organised. Mind emerged out of life when the cells were organised into a nervous system. Life is a higher reality than matter. Mind is a higher reality than life.

Life is governed by higher laws than those of life. Mind and body are not on the same level. They are not-parallel to each other. Mind is a higher reality that emerges out of a living organism on account of its organisation, is governed by higher laws, and acts upon the body and controls it. A ladder represents emergent evolution of higher and higher realities owing to creative synthesis or organisation. Mind is the fruition or perfection of the body. "Mind and bods do. not interact, a Dualism teach, The mind is not a form of the mechanical interplay of atoms, as Materialism teaches. The body is not a phenomenon or appearnce or externalization of mind as Idealism teaches. Mind and body are not parallel, as Psychophysical Parallelism teaches. Neither are they two sides or aspects of the same reality, as the Double aspect theory teaches. Mind is something which the body achieves, or which nature achieves by means of the body. When nature achieves the molecule, the atom ceases to be of primary importance. When nature achieves the cell, the molecule is eclipsed. When the organism is achieved, the cell is eclipsed. When mind is achieved, the body is eclipsed. Mind is a new reality, gained, achievd, won. It is, in Aristotelian phrase, the form of the tody." *(Introduction to Philosophy,* p. 298).

**Criticism of the Emergence Theory**

It is true that mind is a higher reality than life, and that life is a higher reality than matter. But how can mind emerge from life, if does not exist in an implicit form in life ? Again, how can life emerge from matter, if it does not exist in a potential condition in matter. What is the evolutionary urge? What directs the evolutionary process? Lloyd Morgan holds that there is an Activity, a Mind, which is the *nisus* of the process of evolution. He calls it God. But he does not fully work out the implication of this fruitful suggestion. Evolution is forward-looking. It is emergent. It is not merely repetitive. But what evolves newer and newer realities, achieves higher and higher values to realize higher ends ? Lloyd Morgan does not explain it clearly.

**Absolute Idealism**

Hegel holds that the body is the medium or instrument through which the Absolute Mind reveals itself as the finite-mind. The Absolute manifests itself least in matter, manifests itself more in life, manifests itself most in mind. The Absolute Mind is present in matter, life, and mind, in less and greater degrees. If mind is not implicitly present in matter and life, it cannot emerge from them. Matter is the lowest stage of the manifestation of the Absolute Mind. Life is a higher stage of its manifestation, Mind is the highest stage of its manifestation. The Absolute Mind is the evolutionary urge. It guides the process of evolution to realize its immanent purpose. Therefore, mind can aot upon the body, direct control, and regulate it. This truth is implied by Emergent Evolution.

## UNIVERSITY QUESTIONS

1. Explain the theories of Interaction and Parallelism in connection with the relation between mind and body. Which theory appeals to you as preferable and on what grounds ? (1911).
2. State clearly the principal hypotheses with regard to the relation between mind and body. Which of them do you consider to be the most satisfactory, and why ? (1916).
3. State the principal hypotheses as to the connection between Soul and Body, and give your own conclusion, with reasons. (1918).
4. Explain fully the doctrine of Parallelism in Philosophy, and examine the view that Parallelism supplies a sufficient explanation of Mind and body, referring briefly to the history of the theory. (1918 Hon.).
5. Explain the different views as to the relation of Mind to Body. Which of them offers a satisfactory explanation of the relation? (1920).
6. What do you consider to be the most reasonable account of the relations of Body and Mind ? (1921).

7. Explain what you consider to be the nature of Soul and the relation between Soul and Body. (1925).
8. What, in your opinion, is the relation between Mind and Body ? Examine critically the different theories bearing on the problem ? (1931).
9. Explain the different theories of the relation between Mind and Body. (1934).
10. Examine the Parallelistic theory of the relation between Mind and Body. (1936).
11. Explain the theory of parallelism between Mind and Body. How far is this consistent with the facts of interaction revealed in our ordinary experience ? (1937).
12. Discuss the relation between Mind and Body. (1947).
13. Estimate the value of Interactionism and Parallelism as theories of the relation of Mind and Body. (A. U. 1947).
14. Show how the Emergence Theory explains the relation of Body and Mind, and compare it with Interactionism and Parallelism. What are its limitations. (A. U. 1948).

## CHAPTER XI

# THE PHILOSOPHY OF GOD

### Different conceptions of God

The different theories of the world have a close bearing on the different conceptions of God. Corresponding to the pluralistic, dualistic, and monistic theories of the world, there are the pluralistic, dualistic and monistic conceptions of God. "The various theological beliefs are pretty closely related to the more general metaphysical theories. Theism ordinarily goes along with spiritualsm and spirituslism and dualism pantheism has an affinity to monism; and atheism is a natural consequence of materialism." (*Kulpe*). We may represent the different conceptions of God in the following way:—

**2. Atheism.**—Athesim holds that the world is made up of matter and motion and that there is no intelligent First Cause of the world. Atheism is the complete negation of theism.

The theological doctrine of atheism is the logical consequence of the metaphysical doctrine of materialism. Atheism takes different forms, dogmatic atheism, sceptical atheism, critical atheism and practical atheism.

(1) Dogmatic atheism absolutely denies the existence of God.

(2) Sceptical atheism does not deny the existence of God, but denies the capacity of the human mind to know his\ existence.

(3) Critical atheism neither denies the existence of God nor the capacity of man to know his existence, but it simply asserts that there is no valid proof of the existence of God.

(4) Practical atheism asserts that the existence or non-

existence of God has nothing to do with our life". Life is possible even at its best, without belief in

**Criticism**

Atheism has never succeeded in proving the non-existence of God. It has maintained that the existence of God cannot be established; it has tried to justify its unbelief, but it has not sought to lay a foundation. for disbelief.

Atheism is affiliated to materialism, and hence involves all the difficulties of materialism. It cannot explain the order, unity, beauty and harmony of the world. If it explains every-thing of the world by matter and motion, it cannot account for their existence; it only assumes matter and motion andtheir laws to be self-existent. It fails to explain the properties of vegetable and animal life, and human mind and its moral principles and religious convictions. It not only fails to satisfy our intellect, it also fails to satisfy our heart. The pure forms of Truth, Beauty and Virtue without being supported by God cannot satisfy our heart.

**Theism (in a wider sense)**

Theism is opposed to atheism. The word 'Theism' comes from the Greek word *'Theos'* which means 'God'. Thus the term 'Theism' literally means belief in God. In this wider sense, theism is the opposite of atheism. Atheism denies the existence of God, while theism asserts the existence of God. We may use the term 'Theism' in the widest possible sense to mean belief in any number of gods. Thus theism, in its wider sense, may assume three forms,—polytheism, ditheism and monotheism. Polytheism believes in many gods. Ditheism believes in two gods. Monotheism believes only in one God Monotheism, again may take four different forms *viz.,* deism, (in its narrower sense), gantheism, and panentheism. We shall discuss all these different conceptions of God—pluralistic, dualistic and monistic—in the following sections.

**Pluralistic conceptions of God—Polytheism**

Polytheism assumes the existence of many gods. It not

only believes in many gods, but also regards them as finite beings limited and resisted by one another. The forces of nature are regarded as endowed with vital powers. There is a diversity of opinion as to the origin, of polytheism. According to Herbert Spencer, the idea of spirit originated in the dreams of those who were dead, and the worship of ancestral spirits gave rise to polytheism. The spirits after death were believed to inhabit different planets rivers, woods and mountains, and thus was evolved the belief in many gods or presiding spirits over the, different departments of nature. In opposition to this doctrine which is called animism, Max-Muller and others hold that fetishism is the primitive form of religion which consists in the worship of stalks and stones, trees, rivers mountains etc.

As a matter of fact, polytheism passed through two stages – animism (or hylozoism) and spiritism (or fetishism).

**(i) Animism**

Wherever there is life, there is movement. So, the primi-tive people thought that whenever there are movements in nature, – specially regulated movements, there are vital powers. At first, no distinction was made between life and soul. Hence whenever there was an appearance of regulated, motion 'of unity and order in nature, the people thought that there was life and intelligence there. Thus all departments of nature, specially those abounding in movements, seemed to be alive with life and intelligence. The sun and planets, the sea, mountains, rivers, springs, hurricanes etc. were conceived as living beings, controlling and guiding their own movements. This doctrine is called animism. It corresponds to the metaphysical doctrine of *hylozoism* according to which all substance is alive.

**(ii) Spiritism**

In the stage of animism, the living and feeling powers of nature could hardly be conceived as personal gods or spirits in the human sense of personality. But in course of time the idea of life developed into that of *soul* or *spirit*. The tree had now its personal Dryad; the sea, its Neptune and Triton; the sun, its Phoebus and Apollo; the moon, its Diana etc. In this way the gods became distinctly personal beings, composed of a finer and subtler stuff than men, and having thoughts, frassions and motives, analogous to those of men, but freed from all human limitations. Thus polytheism arose out of the anthropomphic tendency of men to personify the forces of nature. Thus primitive animism grew, in course of time, into spiritism, and thereby into polytheism of the anthropomorphic kind.

**Criticism**

But polytheism is more mythological than philosophical. It cannot satisfy the legitimate demands of reason and explain the unity, order and harmony of the world-system. So it gradually gave way to monotheism. The more the unity, order and harmony of the world was revealed, the more a connection and organization was found among gods, the lower gods being subordinated to the higher, and the higher gods to still higher ones, thus yielding an organised form of polytheism. And finally, the knowledge of the complete unity of the world as a system of inter-connected reals gave rise to monotheism—the hierarchy of gods being subordinated bo one supreme ruler of heaven and earth. Thus monotheism was finally evolved from polytheism. But before we study monotheism or monistic conception God. we must study the dualistic conception.

**Dualistic conception of God : Ditheism**

Dualism is an intermediate position between monism and pluralism. The unity and harmony of the world points to the existence of one God who evolves and sustains the world. But if God is the author of the world, how can we explain its evils and imperfections? They are inconsistent with the perfection and benevolence of God. So dualism arose out of the difficulty of monism to explain the evils and imperfections of the world.

So, it was assumed that there must be two self-existent principles, one tending towards good, and the other resisting and producing evils as a result of the conflict—there must be two rival gods with opposite tendencies, always in strife and conflict with each other. This doctrine of two rival gods is called *ditheism.*

Thus the early Persians believed in two rival gods, one the source of good, called Ahura Mazda, and the other, the source of evil, called Ahriman. The former strives to make a world perfectly good like himself; but the latter always strives to frustrate his benevolent designs; and thus, as a result of their simultaneous activity and conflict, the world is full of evils and imperfections.

**Criticism**

Ditheism is more mythological than philosophical. It originated in the difficulty of monotheism to explain the evils and imperfections of the world. But monotheism can explain evils without the help of an evil principle. So we must not fall back upon ditheism.

Ditheism cannot explain the organic unily, order and harmony of the world-system. If there be two absolutely independent and self-existent rival gods,it is inconceivable how they could come together and interact with produce this unity of the world-system.

The conflict between two opposite principles presupposes a higher principle of unity to overcome the conflict and decide the issue of the strife. The conflict and interaction between two rival gods presupposes a higher god to whom they are subordinate, since we can understand interaction only between correlative members of the same ultimate reality included within the unity of one system.

**Monistic conceptions of God: Monotheism**

We have discussed the pluralistic and dualistic conceptions of God. Now we proceed to study the different monistic theories which agree in affirming the existence of one God. We use the term 'monotheism', in its literal sense, to mean a belief in one God. But monotheism has different forms. Though many believe that there is one God, there is a wide divergence of opinions to the nature of God and his relation to finite things and beings. This diffrence among the monotheists has given rise to different forms of monotheism *e.g.* deism, theism (in its restricted sense), pantheism and panentheism.

### Deism

Deism maintains that God existed alone from all eternity without the world, and created it out of nothing at some point of time and invested it with the necessary forces and after creating it left it to itself, so that the world now goes on of itself by the operation of those forces, which were implanted in it by God at the time of creation and now have become "second causes". But when the world will tend towards decay, God will intervene and set it right. Thus before creation God was without a world and after creation God withdraws himself from the world.

**Deism makes the following assumptions:**

#### (i) Creation in time

"The world was created in time: prior to which its Divine cause existed from eternity without it. In course of time it will perish, like everything which has a beginning; after which its Divine cause will exist to eternity without it." (Martineau: *Study of Religion, Vol. II, p. 135.)*

#### (ii) Distinction between First or Primary Cause and Second Secondary Causes

God created the world at a point of time and invested it with all the necessary forces. These forces implanted by God at the time of creation operate as secondary causes after creation and withdrawal of God from the world. Thus God is the First cause of the world and its inherent forces axe the "secondary causes."

#### (iii) Occasional Divine Interference

After creation God withdraws from the world and leaves

it to itself. But in times of emergency God intervenes to save the world from decay or to remove its evils and imperfections. Divine interference suspends or overcomes the operation of natural forces or secondary causes by the creation of a divine force and thus produces miracles.

**(iv) Complete Divine Transcendence**

After creation God withdraws from the world leaving it to itself and ocasionally interferes with its operations when necessary. Thus God is wholly transcendent *i,* e. external to, above and beyond the world.

**Criticism**

(i) In deism the world is conceived as created in time. But why did God create it, if he had remained without it ? Was he imperfect without the world ? If so, why did he not realize the imperfection before and why did he spend an eternity without it ? Why did God create the world at a particular point of time ? What need had God for a world at this point ? Why did he create this world and no other ? So we cannot uphold the theory of creation in time but must pass over to the idea of perpetual creation. [ See other criticisms above, Ch. VI]

(ii) Deism supposes that God is the First Pause and the material forces are the second causes. But how can the energy of God be divorced from Him and act of itself ? If God created the world, he must sustain and maintain it by his own energy. Why should God, whose very essence is ceaseless activity, should go to sleep, as it were after creating the world and investing it with his causal power ? "To an Eternal Being, Eternal life *i. e.* Eternal action, must be an essential element of perfection: all cosmic power is Will and all cosmic Will is His.... He is the One cause in Nature acting in various modes." Martineau: *Study of Religion, Vol. II, p. 139.)*

*(iii)* Deism believes in occasional Divine Interference, and this is too anthropomorphic in tendency. It makes God to be like, a human artificer who interferes with his machine to mend it at time. But why should God interfere with his work? Why should divine tend towards decay 'Why should it not continue perfect to all eternity ? What accounts for the seeds of decay in

the world? So instead of occasional divine intervention from without, we must uphold the doctrine, of immanent Natural Providence or government of the world from within.

*(iv)* Deism conceives God to be wholly transcendent. But the complete transcendence of God is inconsistent with his infinitude. If God is above and beyond the world, he must be limited by it and become finite.

*(v)* Deism supposes God to have existed without a world through all eternity, and yet as a self-conscious and thinking being. But consciousness presupposes a distinction between the subject or thinking principle and the object or material of thought. Therefore, God's eternal thought required material for it. What, then, was the object of Divine thought before creation ? "The eternal reality of God as thinking principle involves an eternal content of God's thought, and, therefore the eternal correlativity of subject and object of what thinks and what is thought, of absolute and relative, of God and world." *(Stephen.)*

**To sum up**

*(i)* Creation of the world at a particular point of time is quite inexplicable,

*(ii)* The so-called secondary causes, *viz.*, the natural forces of the world cannot act of themselves without the support and guidance of God. The energy of the world is the divine energy.

*(iii)* Deism, believing in the occasional interference of God, makes him to be anthropomorphic, like a human artificer,

*(iv)* Deism, holding the doctrine of complete transcendence of God, makes him to be finite and limited by the world,

*(v)* Deism, believing in the existence of God without a world before creation, makes him to be unconscious, as consciousness requires the material of thought, and this material was wanting before creation. These difficulties led to pantheism as a reaction against deism.

**Pantheism**

Pantheism arose as a reaction against polytheism and pluralism, on the one hand, and deism, on the other. Polytheism believes in many gods presiding over the different departments of nature. Pantheism believes in one God and identifies Him with the universe. Pluralism ignores the one *i. e.* the ultimate unity of the world and ascribes reality only to the plurality of finite things. Pantheism or abstract monism ignores the many individuals, and thinks mainly or wholly of the One; while pluralism sacrifices unity to plurality or one to many; pantheism or abstract monism sacrifices plurality to Unity, or many to one. Deism conceives God as wholly transcending the world in space and time, and thus regards God as infinite and eternal, and the world as finite and temporary. Pantheism goes to the other extreme and conceives God as wholly immanent in the world and identifies God with the world.

According to Pantheism, all is God and God is all (Pan—all; *Theos*—God): God and the world are identical. Only God is real; the world of finite things and minds is an immanent modification or an unreal appearance of God. It has no reality of its own; it is real in the reality of God: it has an illusory existence. The One, in its abstract unity, is the only reality, the plurality of finite things and minds are illusions or unreal appearances, possessing no independent reality of their own. The One, in its abstract self-existent unity, is sufficient in itself; the infinite needs no finite; the absolute, no relative; the unconditioned, no conditioned. The One is all in all. The world of the many is only an accidental and inessential appearance. God alone exists *(pantheism)*, but there is no real world (acosmism). According to this view, therefore, God (as the absolute one) is the only reality; the world of finite things is unreal apearance. It is not *atheism* (that there is no God), but rather *acosmism* (that there is no world), or *pantheism* (that God is all). It is abstract monism in the sense that it takes the one in abstraction from the many and regards it as constituting all realitv by itself." (*Stephen.*) "Pantheism is diametrically opposed to deism. So far from separating God from the world as the deist does, the pantheist identifies God with the world-process. Everything is in God, God is in everything. God is all, all is God. The pantheist wholly denies transcendence. God for him is entirely *immanent* within the space-time order...God equals everything, everything equals God–this is pantheism." (Cunningham: *Problems of Philosophy,* p. 401.) Spinoza and the Eleatics are the, typical exponents of pantheism.

**Criticism**

*(i)* Pantheism, in making God to be one and all, having no need of the world, reduces him to an abstract power or a blank colourless substance, an impersonal principle devoid of feeling and attributes, which cannot satisfy our religious cravings.

*(ii)* Pantheism, regarding God or the abstract One as the only reality, fails to account for the world of plurality; unity without plurality, the one apart from the many is an unreal abstraction. A pure being is equivalent to nothing. A being which is not the becoming of anything in particular, a unity which is not expressed in plurality, an Infinite, Absolute, and Unconditioned which does not reveal itself in the finite, related and conditioned things of the world, is an unmeaning abstraction.

(iii) Pantheism denies the reality of the world, and thus leads to *acosmism.* But the world cannot so easily be merged in God, We feel it to be real, and as such it must be explained.

*(iv)* Pantheism does not altogether deny the existence of the world, but assigns an illusory existence to it. It is an illusory appearance of God. Thus acosmism leads to *illusionism.* But the world cannot be explained away as an illusion. Illusion has an existence. What is the cause of the illusion ? Illusion is an unreal appearance. But to whom is it an appearance ? Is it an appearance to the finite minds? No–the finite minds themselves have no reality; they also are illusions. How, then, do illusions appear as illusions to illusions themselves ? This is absurd!

*(v)* Pantheism identifies God with the world, and so may easily lapse into naturalism and materialism.

*(iv)* Pantheism contradicts the testimony of our general self consciousness. We are clearly conscious of ourselves as distinct, individual persons having the power of self-determination. But pantheism regards the finite minds as immanent modes or modifications of the one substance, viz., God, having no independence of their own.

*(vii)* Pantheism, by taking away personality, freedom and independence from man, and doing away with the distinction between right and wrong (as all of them are illusions), strikes at the root of morality. "If human personality and freedom are illusions, then must obligation, guilt and retribution be the absurdest-fictions." (Flint.)

**To sum up**

*(i)* Pantheism reduces God to an impersonal abstract power or a blank colourless substance which cannot be the God of religion with whom we can hold religious communion.

*(ii)* Pantheism reduces God to an abstract unity without any element of difference in it and thus cannot account for the plurality of finite things.

*(iii)* Pantheism denies the reality of the world and thus leads to acosmism.

*(iv)* Pantheism explains away the world of plurality as illusory appearances and thus leads to illusionism. But this is no explanation of the world.

*(v)* Pantheism identifies the world of material things with God, and thus may easily lapse into naturalism and materialism.

(vi) Pantheism denies the personality of man and thus contradicts the testimony of consciousness.

*(vii)* Pantheism, by denying the freedom and personality of man and doing away with the distinction between right and wrong, saps the very foundation of morality.

**Merits of pantheism**

"Pantheism, is superior to atheism as it satisfies to a certain extent our religious cravings; it is superior to polytheism as it affirms the unity and infinity of God: it is superior of Deism as it does not believe in creation independent of God." ("R*eligion in modern light."*) The difficulties of pantheism have led some thinkers to theism.

**Theism**

As pantheism arose as a reaction against deism, so theism arose as a reaction against pantheism. Deism conceived God as wholly transcending the world. Pantheism went to the other extreme and conceived God as wholly immanent in the world. The conflict between deism and pantheism is the conflict between the complete transcendence of God and the complete immanence of God. When pantheism merges the world in God who is immanent in it, there is no very serious objection to it, but when it absorbs the human will in the divine will, it makes morality impossible. But this is revolting to our moral consciousness. No system of metaphysics, no doctrine of theology must deny the freedom and personality of man and undermine morality. So the legitimate demands of our moral consciousness. The unambiguous verdict of conscience dictated a reaction against pantheism in the form of theism.

According to theism (as maintained by Martineau, Lotze and others), God is immanent in the world, but *not in the finite minds*. The opposition between pantheism and theism is, to use the language of Martineau, the opposition between "*All-immanency*" and "*Some-transcendency*. Theism agrees with pantheism in holding that God transcends the finite minds which are external to, and outside of God, and are free to act of themselves. Theism holds that finite minds have been created by God and have been endowed with freedom of the will, so that they may be regardedas secondary causes" having the power of free initiation.

"Theism is in no way committed to the doctrine of God external to the world, but is at liberty to regard all the cosmical forces as varieties of the method assumed by his conscious causality, and the whole of Nature as the evolution of his thought." "The whole external universe we unreservedly surrender to the Indwelling Will which it is the organised expression." But "the voluntary nature of moral beings must be saved from Pantheistic absorption, and be left standing as, within its sphere, a free cause other than the Divine, yet homogeneous with it." (Martineau: *Study of Religion.)*

"In order to secure a consistent Theism, this Immanency of God must be subject to two reservations: (1) it must not annex and absorb the faculties of created minds, but leave room for their personality: (2) though pervading the rest of the world, it must not stop at the cosmical limits, but spread beyond them as an infinite sea of possibilities, other than the realized legislation of reason, righteousness and love." (*Martineau.)*

**Characteristics of Theism**

*(i)* God is immanent in the world; the cosmic energy is the divine energy.

*(ii)* But God is not wholly immanent in the world; his infinite powers and potentialities are not fully exhausted in this finite world; so God also transcends the world in the sense that, his powers are infinite and as such beyond the cosmical limits.

*(in)* Though God is both transcendent, and immanent in the world. He wholly transcends the finite spirits, to save-their freedom and independence.

**Criticism of Theism**

*(i)* Theism is right, when it affirms that God evolves and sustains the world by his divine will and transcends it as an infinite power extending far beyond the limits of the world.

*(ii)* But it is wrong, when it holds that God wholly transcends the finite spirits to save them from pantheistic absorption in the divine will. For, if finite spirits are excluded from God, either they must limit God or God must voluntarily limit himself. In the former case, God would become finite and limited, whereas, in

the latter, God would voluntarily impose limits upon himself and by this voluntary self-limitation would make room for the finite wills, as Martineau supposed. But Matiineau's hypothesis of God's voluntary self-limitation is quite an arbitrary makeshift for the explanation of human freedom. Infinite God cannot, by his very essential nature, be limited either by himself or by something else. Hence the total exclusion of finite spirits from God or God's complete transcendence over finite minds is inconsistent with the infinitude of God.

*(iii)* Finite spirits are not absolutely free. The theist (*e. g.* Martineau) admits that human wills are *second causes* "We are *second* because there is a first (*viz.* God), in relation to whom we are *effects:* we are causes, because, in spite of this, we are not *only* effects, but are constituted with a will and directing faculties, which have a store of power at their disposal to be thrown on the line of this possibility or of that; and are not therefore mere implements or media for executing the volitions of another." [ *Study of Religion.*]

According to theism, then, human freedom was derived from God at first, but after its origin it is quite independent of the divine will and absolutely free. In other words after the creation of human wills God wholly transcends them, throwing them outside the sphere of his own work, to says them from absorption in the all embracing divine will. But human wills cannot be absolutely free and quite independent of the divine will, after they have derived their existence from God. Human wills are limited by the physical world and by one another, and consequently are finite and limited. They are limited also by the divine will, as they cannot, even with the abundance of their freedom, go beyond the plan of God and frustrate the divine purpose. The divine will is partly immanent even in the human wills, which restricts the scope of their operation. This is admitted even by the theist himself (*e. g.* Martineau) when he says that God may be "the cause of all our *possibilities* without being responsible for our actualities,". He has determined the *general* outlines of our actions, but not their concrete details. God is partly immanent in man also in another sense: He reveals himself to man as the *Moral Law* or the *Moral Ideal;* the voice of conscience is the voice of God in man. Martineau himself admits that the "Moral Law first reaches its integral meaning, when seen as impersonated in a Perfect Mind, which communicates it to us, and lends its power over our affections sufficient to draw us into divine communion." But the difference between the theistic view and our view is this: Whereas Martineau

takes the Moral Law as the command or behest of God "who is outside our minds and thus imposes the Moral Law from without, we take it to be the voice of God who is not outside our finite minds, but is immanent in us as our Ideal Self, and inspires our Moral Ideal, since "moral obligation must be essentially self-imposed," the Moral Law must be imposed by the self upon itself, by the Ideal Self (which is the finite reproduction or revelation of the Divine Self) upon the actual self.

**Summary**

*(i)* Theism rightly holds that God both transcends the world and is immanent in the world,

*(ii)* But it erroneously excludes the finite spirits from God to secure their freedom and personality. For, the exclusion of finite wills from the divine will is inconsistent with the infinitude of God, even if it be supposed that God voluntarily limits himself and his voluntary self-limitation and self-abnegation does not compromise his infinitude.

*(iii)* Finite spirits are not absolutely free; the divine will is partly immanent even in the human wills, determining the *possibilities* of their actions, but *not their concrete actualities,*—restricting the scope of their operation to a limited field; and God is also immanent in finite minds, as he reveals himself to them as *Ideal selves* and inspires their *Moral Ideal.* Thus God is not only transcendent and immanent in his relation to the world, but also in his relation to

man. This is the view of panentheism as advocated by Hegel and his followers.

**Panentheism (Deism, Pantheism, Theism and Panentheism compared)**

The conflict among different types of religion arises out of the difference of opinion as to the transcendence and immanence of God. *Deism* makes God wholly transcend the world and finite minds. *Pantheism* makes God wholly immanent in the world and finite spirits. *Theism* makes God both transcendent and immanent in his relation to the, world, but wholly transcendent in his relation to finite spirits. *Panentheism* reconciles the conflict among all these different types of monotheism and holds that God both *above* the world and in the world, *above* the finite spirits and in the finite spirits. In other words, all is *in* God, *(pan*−all *en*−in *Theos*-God), but God is not all (pan−all, *Theos*−*God)*. "It is more correct to say that; all things are in God *(panentheism)* things are in God (panentheism than that God is outside of things (deism), or that God is the-whole of things (pantheism)." *(Stephen.)*

**Deism and Panentheism compared**

*(i)* Deism conceives God as wholly transcendent and denies any necessary connection between God and the world. According to deism, God was without a world before creation and withdraws from the world after creation so that there is no necessary connection between God and the world. Panentheism establishes a necessary, vital and organic connection between God and the world. God is necessary to the world as it is the self-manifesta-tion of God, while the world also is necessary to God as it is in and through the world that God realizes itself.

*(ii)* Deism makes God wholly transcendent, while Panentheism makes God both transcendent and immanent.

**(B) Pantheism and Panentheism compared**

*(i)* Pantheism is abstract monism, while Panentheism is

concrete monism. Pantheism sacrifices the many to the one, while pluralism sacrifices the one to the many. Panentheisia reconciles the two and regards the ultimate reality or God as unity-in-plurality or identity-in-difference." The God of Pantheism is an abstract power without concrete embodiment in the world while the God of Panentheism is a rich concrete reality which realizes itself in the world of finite things and minds.

*(ii)* Pantheism makes God wholly immanent in the world Panentheism makes God both transcendent and immanent. God transcends the world in two senses:

(1) as Infinite, God's inexhaustible potentialities are never fully realized in the finie world, and

(2) as a Self-conscious Spirit or Divine Personality he transcends the world which is the material of his thought. He knows himself in distinction from the world and realizes himself as a self-conscious spirit.

*(iii)* "The attraction of Pantheism and of pantheistic systems of philosophy lies in this, that they meet the cravings of the religious mind for absolute union with God and of the speculative mind for intellectual unity. But what Pantheism gains by the sacrifice of individuality and responsibility in man, by depriving thefinite world of reality and reducing Nature, Man and God, to a blank, colourless identity, a true philosophy attains in another and deeper way. It gives us a principle in the light of which we can see that God is all in all, without denying reality to the finite world and to every individual human spirit, or without denying it except in so far as it involves a life apart from God—a spurious independence which is not the protection but the destruction of all spiritual life." (John Caird: *Introduction to the Philosophy of Religion,* p. 221.)

**(C) Theism and Panentheism compared**

*(i)* Panentheism agrees with Theism in that God is both

above and in the world both transcendent and immanent and both agree in holding the doctrine of "*perpetual creation*". Some. however, hold that theism believes in the theory of creation. According to this version of theism, God created the world at a, particular time, but after creating it he did not leave it to itself as Deism supposes, but maintains it by his own energy immanent in it. But we take theism in another sense, as represented by Martineau, Lotze and others.

*(ii)* But Panentheism differs from Theism in that the former makes him both transcend the finite spirits, while the latter makes God wholly transcendent and immanent not only in relation to the world but also to man. For, the exclusion of finite spirits from God is inconsistent with the infinitude of God. Martineau's hypothesis of voluntary self-limitation and self-abnegation of God to make room for human freedom is an arbitrary assumption. God, as infinite, can be limited neither by himself nor by anything else.

Thus, according to Panentheism, God and the world of finite things and minds are neither outside of each other nor in each other in the same sense as finite things. "Thieir relation involves both identity and diversity, internality and externality, in a way which we cannot adequately picture to ourselves. The world of finite minds and things is real in relation to God in the sense that without the energy of production in evolving and sustaining a world of things, God would not be a living God; and God is real in relation to the world, in the sense that without the evolving, co-ordinating, unifying, sustaining power of the absolute, there would be no world." (*Stephen.*)

## Transcendence and Immanence of God

By the transcendence of God we mean that God is above the world of finite things and minds. By the imtrianence of God we mean that God is *in* the world of finite) things and minds. Is then God transcendent or immanent ? There are different views as to the transcendence and immanence of God as we have fully discussed in the preceding section.

*(i)* **Deism** maintains that God is wholly transcendent, being *above* the world, of finite things and minds; he lived from all eternity without the world; he created the world of material things and finite minds at a point of time and invested the former with natural forces and the latter with freedom of the will. then left them to themselves.

*(ii)* **Pantheism** holds that God is *wholly immanent* in the *world* and fonite spirits, so that the plurality of finite things and minds have no reality of their own, but are immanent modes or modifications (or illusory appearances) of the absolute one or God. The world and God are identical.

*(iii)* **Theism** holds that God is both *transcendent* and immanent in his relation to the *world,* but *wholly transcendent* in relation to *man.* The energy of the world or cosmic energy is nothing but the immanent energy of God; but the energy of the human will though originally created by God, is not a part and parcel of the divine will: God completely "transcends the human wills.

*(iv)* **Panentheism** holds that God is both *transcendent* and *immanent* not only in relation to the world but also to man. God manifests himself in the world and sustains it with the divine energy so that God is immanent in the world; but God is not wholly immanent in the world (as pantheism holds) so that the world can be identified with God and God with the world; God also transcends the world as the infinite and as a Self-conscious Spirit.

God reproduces or reduplicates himself, in a finite manner, in the finite souls, so that the divine spirit is the immanent essence of the finite spirits, or the Absolute Self is the inner life of the finite selves. But though immanent in finite spirits, God is not wholly immanent in them, to save human freedom and Personality; God also transcends the finite spirits and gives them *relative freedom* to realize their own ends their own way with in the sphere of the divine will, plan and purpose.

Thus. God is both *in* and *above* the world of finite things and minds.

## The Relation of God to World and Man

The question of the relation of God to man and the world is the same question as that of transcendence and immanence of God which we have elaborately discussed in the preceding two sections. Let us sum up the different theories once again.

### (A) Relation of God to the world *i.e.* physical things

Physical things can be regarded only as means and materials, not as ends to themselves; but only self-conscious mind is really *for* itself and consequently an *end-to-itself.* So physical things are only passive products or instruments for the self-realization and self-expression of the Absolute. God evolves and sustains the world of physical things and forces as means and materials of his own self-realization; the so-called material atoms are the "standing volitions" of God and the so-called physical forces are nothing but the divine will *(Martineau).* God is immanent in the world, but he also transcends the world, as *(i)* an end to himself to whom the world is the means, *(ii)* as the infinite of which the world is a finite expression, and *(in)* as a self-conscious spirit of which the world is the object.

### (B) Relation of God to man *(i. e.* finite spirits)

A human being has his *physical, rational* and *moral* sides. He is a finite self-conscious and self-controlled rational spirit embodied in an organism. So the relation of God to man involves his relation to all these three aspects.

### (i) The relation of God to the Physical aspect of man

It can be unhesitatingly affiermed that human body is on the same level with other physical things of the world,. and as such is a Passive product or instrument of God (or the Infinite Spirit,) as a finite self-conscious spirit in man. It is evolved by God as the means and material of his self-reproduction as a finite spirit, so that all the actions and movements of the human body other than voluntary, *e. g.,* instinctive actions, reflex actions, random or spontaneous actions and automatic actions of the vital organs immanent volitions of God, being absorbed in the Divine Will (*Martineau.*)

**(ii) The relation of God to the Rational aspect of man**

Physical things are not ends to themselves they are only passive products or instruments for the realization of an absolute end. The human body, too, as a physical thing, is not an end in itself. But the human mind is a self-conscious and self-controlled or self-determining spiritual being; self-conscious mind realty is for itself; so the human mind is not on the same level with physical things, but to some extent, an "end-in-itself". it exists for itself and has an end of its own.

So the human mind cannot be regarded as an immanent mode or modification of God having no reality of its own, as pantheism supposes. As a free and self conscions spirit, it has an indepen-dent and substantial existence in and for itself. The human mind, in so far as it is self-conscious, shares in the universal life of the Absolute and re-thinks what has already been thought out by God. Thus the Divine Thought may be held as immanent in the human consciousness. God thinks in the finite mind not as the Infinite Spirit but *as a finite* spirit. But God is not wholly immanent in the human thought, as the Divine Thought goes far beyond the range of finite thought and has far more comprehensive and adequate categories than the human mind. (See Dr. Haldar's "*Hegelianism and Personality*", Ch. III.)

**(iii) Relation of God to the Moral aspect of man**

Man, as a rational being, is not only self-conscious but also a self-regulating, self-controlled or self-determined being. He has *freedom of* the *will* by means of which he can work out his own destiny in his *own* way. Is this human freedom a part and parcel of the divine will ? Is it a portion of the divine freedom ? Is God immanent in the human will ? There is a difference of opinion. According to Deism and Theism, God wholly transcends the spirits so that they are left absolutely free. But the theist *(e. g.* Martineau) admits that God determines the *possibilities* of human actions, but *not their actualities* or actions in their concrete details. But the exclusion of *the,* finite apirits from God is inconsistent with his infinitude. [ See above 10.] So God both transcends the finite spirits and is immanent in them; the divine will is the source and origin of the human will, immanent in the form of the Ideal Self or the Moral Ideal, but transcends it and leaves it free to realize this moral ideal as revealed by God to man and thus realize the infinite potentialities of the Ideal Self. Thus (*i*) "man is a personal being, self-conscious and self-controlled, and is therefore an end to himself, a spring of free spontaneous activity. He shares in the productive and self-regulative power of the absolute itself." (*ii*) "But he is a finite and relative beign at the same time. He shares indeed in the nature of the absolute in so far as he is self-conscious, self-regulating power having a good and end of his own. But his end and good can be realized only in correlation with the goods of other finite persons, and as a factor of the one absolute good in which all relative goods are contained. Thus, though he is a free, personal, self-determining reality, in so far as he reproduces in himself the absolute power, and purpose; yet, in so far as he is determined by his relations to other personal beings and to physical things, within the absolute, he is finite, relative, conditioned and instrumental; his own good consists in his contribution to the universal good." (*Stephen.*)

*Summary*—(*i*) The *physical* aspect of man, *viz.*, the human body is a physical product or instrument for the revlation of the infinite spirit in man.

(*ii*) The *rational* aspect of man, *viz.*, his self-conscious thought is a part and parcel of the divine thought; man shares in the nature of the absolute as a rational self-conscious spirit; he *re*-thinks what has already been thought out by God, but in his own way, as a *finite* spirit, according to his own categories: the human experience is a part and parcel of the Absolute Experience which incorporates it into itself and transcends it in its all-embracing unity and resolves all the antinomies and-contradictions of the human experience by means of far more comprehensive and adequate categories.

The *moral* aspect of man, *viz.*, his freedom and

independence, though ultimately derived from God is partly free from the divine will. Man is free in producing in himself the freedom aad productivity of God. But man's freedom of will is not infinite (or unlimited) and absolute; it is limited by the divine will and by other finite minds and physical things in nature. Man cannot do anything contrary to the divine plan of the universe. He can work freely and independently only within the sphere of the divine will; his own end or good is a part and parcel of the absolute end or good. Hence man has a relative and limited freedom, A master gives his servant ten rupees to purchase whatever articles he likes. The servant can buy anything he likes with that amount; but he cannot spend more than ten rupees. So God has given man a limited freedom. Man can work freely in his own sphere; he cannot depart from the plan of the universe and revolt against God himself.) .

**Theistic objection to Panentheism considered**

The theist takes a serious exception to the panentheistic conception of man or the finite self as a partial reproduction of God, As a physical being, indeed, man is a part of nature and thus holds the same kind of relation to God as other objects of nature. But does he hold exactly the same relation to God in so far as he is a spiritual and moral being ? Is his moral and spiritual life a mere manifestation or partial reproduction of the divine life ? This is one of the most disputed questions in philosophy. Some writers (*e. g.* Andrew Seth, in his "*Hegelianism and Personality*") charge panentheism with absorbing human, freedom and personality into the divine. If man, they say, is merely a factor or element in the divine life, a mere manifesta tion of God where is the room for his personality, which: implies his freedom, independence and externality, and where is the scope for morality and religion ?

The reply to this objection is that it is based upon the wrong conception of the terms, 'freedom', 'independence' and externality'.

(i) The true meaning of freedom is not "preferential choice" and "unmotived action" (as Martineau and Seth suppose) but self-determination or subjection, to the laws of ones own true self, and the true value of freedom is determined by the nature of the self as conceived by the agent. The rational self is the highest self in man, and the subjection to the laws of this rational self constitutes the highest freedom. But the rational self is the divine self in man realizing itself under the limitations imposed by his finite organism. Hence a man is more free, the more does he follow the laws of the divine self. Hence there is no real contradiction between the freedom of man and the fact of his being a factor or element in the divine mind.

*(ii)* Similarly, the independence of man does not mean absolute independence. Man is independent, in so far as he has a function and position in the world system. We have seen that as a factor in the reality he is distinct from and correlated to God. He is distinct from God, because he is his manifestation and reproduction. His independence is based upon his distinction from God. He is not absolutely independent; he is limited by physical things and other persons, and finally, by the plan and purpose of God. Thus man is only relatively independent. Hence his independence is not inconsistent with the fact of his being a mere factor or element in the world-system.

*(iii)* Likewise, again, man's externality is relative. As a physical being, he is external to other physical things; but he cannot be external to the Absolute Being or God, for a part can be external to another part but not to the whole; the whole cannot be external to the parts. Moreover, externality is a condition of knowing physical objects, and it cannot, therefore, be an attribute of mind which evolves that condition from within itself; mind is not in space and thus cannot be external to anything; mind is in its essential nature, all-inclusive, and is, therefore, universal, When we speak of a finite mind, we speak of a universal mind working under limitations imposed by the finite organism of man. The universal and infinite mind

working under specialized limitations is designated a finite mind.

Thus we find that man's freedom, independence, and externality, clearly understood in their proper sense, in a word, his personality constituted by these attributes, are not in any way inconsistent with his organic relation to God of whom he is a partial reproduction. Morality and spirituality of man are thus saved, and saved in a way which gives them true dignity and significance.

## Contents of the idea of God (or the true conception of God)

### God in human experience

"What does the word *God* mean to us ? What most people *mean* when they use the word *God* is a supernatural being, spoken of as a spirit, who is righteous and supremely powerful, who has a certain control over our destiny, and with whom we may come into friendly relations, if our own character and attitude are right. They regard him as the creator of the world, and as moral law-giver and judge, and believe that he is everywhere present in the world as an indwelling presencg". (Patrick: *Introduction to Philosophy,)*

### The Idea of God in Philosophy

Plato conceived God as the *Idea of the Good.* Aristotle conceived him as the *Prime Mover.* The Stoics conceived him as *Providence.* The Neo-Platonists conceived him as the *Ineffable One.* Spinoza conceived him as *one substance* endowed with the attributes, thought and extension. Fichte conceived him as Absolute Ego. Schelling conceived him as the *Neutrum* or the Absolute beyond subject and object, ego and non-ego. Hegel conceived him as *Absolute Idea,* Universal Reason, Infinite and EternaI Spirit or self-consciousness: Herbert Spencer conceived him as, the *Unknown and Unknowable,* Infinite and Eternal inscrutable Energy. Bradley and Royce conceived him as *Absolute Experience.* Patrick says, "God is the soul of the world, an indwelling spiritual presence, a creative, organizing and perfecting power, the source of our moral, religious, and aesthetic ideals, God means to us a spiritual presence, a creative power, an exponents of righteousness, beauty, and love." *(Ibid*, p, 394).

### (i) God as the First Cause

The finite conditioned and relative things of the world depend upon higher causes; these, again, depend upon still *higher* causes and so on; *but* we cannot go on in this way *ad. infinitum,* and consequently, we are compelled to stop at some point and think of a first pause, which is the cause of everything, without itself being caused by anything, being a *causa sui* or self-caused being.

### (ii) God as the Ultimate Season

Everything in the world has a ground or reason for its existence; all things of the universe are connected and correlated with one another; so their reasons too are connected and correlated with one another in a systematic unity. But to say that the world is a unitary system of correlated things, complete and sufficient in itself as a whole is equivalent to assuming that it is the product of a single self-sufficient power, which evolves everything of the universe from within itself, containing the ground of its existence within: itself, and gives unity and connection, correlation and co-ordination to all the things of the world.

### (in) God as the Absolute and the Unconditioned

God is absolute and unconditioned. He is absolute, as he is self-existent, self-complete and self-sufficient, and hence is not related to and conditioned by anything outside himself, but comprehends all relations and conditions of things within himself. God is unconditioned, in the sense of being (self-conditioned or conditioned by himself, not by anything beyond himself).

### (iv) God as Infinite and Eternal

God is an infinite power which realizes its infinite potentiaities in the world of finite things and minds, not being limited or resisted by any other reality outside of itself, but free to evolve itself with inexhaustible power without end God must be conceived as *infinite* in this sense. God is infinite also in the sense of transcending the limits of space. God is also eternal, as he transcends the limits of time.

### (v) God as the Absolute Self or Personality

God exists for himself and for his own sake and is therefore, aware of himself and of his own activities and products. God, thus, must be conceived as "universal self awareness or self-conscionsness – a self conscious subject evolving the object-materials of its consciousness from within itself." (*Stephen.*) We must conceive God as an Infinite *Personality* – controlling his own activity to realize his own end, and distinguishing (not indeed from other things outside and independent of himself as finite persons do), but from his own activities and products, the self-evolved contents and materials of his own life and consciousness. "*We* are led, therefore, to the idea of the absolute as a self conscious, self-distinguishing, self-controlling power, evolving and, coordinating all finite things from within itself, as means to end, *viz.*, the complete realization of its own infinite nature." (*Stephen.*)

### (vi) God as the Moral Governor

God is not only the Ideal of Truth, but also the Ideal of Good and the Ideal of Beauty. He satisfies our head, heart and conscience. God is the living embodiment or incarnation of our moral ideal; he is the ultimate source or Authority of our moral obligations; he is the Judge and Arbiter of all our actions, from whom we draw our inspiration and to whom we are ultimately responsible for our actions; He is the Moral Governor or Moral Providence of the universe.

### (vii) God as the source of ideals

At the present time we lay greater emphasis on God as the source of our moral, religious, and aesthetic ideals than as an omniscient, omnipotent Being. God is the source of Truth, Good, Beauty and Holy. History is a process of the realisation of ideals. Our present social, economic and political conditions are better than they were in the past. But we are dissatisfied with them because we have higher ideals. Ideals always go beyond the actual conditions prevailing at present. Whence do the ideals come ? Do we create the values ? Or, are they eternal types or patterns. "Is there a system *of ideal values,* in which our ideals *subsist. We* may think of these ideal values as not only real, but as possessing agency or efficiency" *(Patrick).* Ideal values exist in God. They inspire us to strive and struggle for the realization of them. "The conception of God as the soul of the world, an immanent a spiritual power. a creative and perfecting agency, the source of our ideal values, may give us a helpful notion of God, which will be consistent both with science and philosophy and with the meaning of the word *God* in common speech." *(Ibid,* pp. 397-98).

God is not merely an Infinite, Omniscient, omnipotent Power, but the squrce of the ideal, values. The ideal values are not merely efficient energy. They are power of the integrating, harmonizing, and perfecting type. "God is not a ary urge the creator in the sense of a constructive, integrating, and perfecting power, the power which makes for wholeness and beauty and truth and righteousness, for love and co-operation" *(Ibid,* p. 399).

**The Personality of God (or Divine Self-consciousness)**

God is conceived as an infinite and absolute personality, a self-conscious and self-controlled being. But many have denied the personality and self-consciousness of God.

**Objection to the Personality of God**

Consciousness presupposes a distinction between self and not-self, subject and object. Consciousness of the self arises only when it is acted on by the not-self, so that the conscious self must be conditioned, limited and acted on by the not self; but God being absolute. embraces evervthing within himself, so that there is nothing external to him or over against him, to resist and affect him and thereby produce self-consciousness in him. In other words, the finite self knows itself in distinction from the not-self which is external to its and resists, limits and acts upon it from the outside; but God is not resisted, limited or acted on by anything external to him; so God cannot be self-conscious.

**The objection considered**

The essential condition of consciousness is the possibility of contrast and discrimination, and therefore the existence of a plurality of objects and materials which can be contrasted with, and discriminated from one another and the thinking self. But the externality of these materials or objects is not at all essential and indispensable to consciousness. The externality of the materials or objects is an accidental condition of the finite consciousness. And even the immediate materials of our finite consciousness are really our own sensations, feelings and ideas which are imposed on us from without by external objects. Thus, just as the finite self can know itself in contrast with, and in distinction from its own contents, *viz.*, sensations-feelings and ideas so the infinite and absolute self knows itself in contrast with and in distinction from its own thoughts and volitions; but in the former case, *i. e.* in the finite consciousness, sensations or the materials of knowledge are imposed upon it from without by external or extra-mental things; whereas in the latter, e.g. in the absolute consciousness, the thoughts and volitions which form materials of the divine consciousness are not imposed from without by anything external to God, but evolved from within by God himself in distinction from his own nature. God is thus conscious of himself in distinction from his self-evolved products and activities, thoughts and volitions.

In the divine consciousness the materials are evolved from within, not imposed from without; is therefore of the nature of "intellectual intuition", and not of "sense-intuition" in which there is an element of other-consciousness, *i. e,* consciousness of something other than and external to the self.

The diving consciousness, again, transcends the limitations of time and space. Things are presented to our finite consciousness in a piecemeal fashion, in different points of time and space. But to God everything is present in one intuitive grasp: the past, the distant and the future are present in one Eternal.Now, in an Absolute Moment, which transcends the limits of time and space. God views things *sub specie aeternitatis. i.e.* from the standpoint of eternity,

## Proofs for the Existence of God

Various arguments have been advanced to prove the existence of God, *e. g.* cosmological argument, teleological argument, ontological argument and moral argument.

### Cosmological Argument

#### (a) The common form

The argument from the world as an effeet to its First Cause: The world is a system of effects: these effects have causes; these causes, again, are effects of other causes, and so on. But we cannot go on indefinitely backward from effects to causes. There can be no *regressus ad infinitum.* So, we must stop at a point and suppose the existence of an absolute First Cause or *Causa Sui* which does not depend upon any other cause. The cosmological argument took the form of causal argument in Martineau.

#### (b) Martineau's Causal Argument

Causal argument consists in the argument of the existence of God from the very nature and idea of causality. A cause is a power or force or energy which produces an effect. There is the idea of production and necessary connection between the cause and the effect. We are conscious of energy and causality, not in our outward perception of the external world, but in ourself in self-conscious volition and resolution. Causation implies not only the existence of energy but also its *direction* or *regulation*. A cause produces a particular effect, to teh exclusion of others. The cusal energy, therefore, must be regulated in a definite direction so as to produce a definite result. The origination and direction of energy are only possible in a mind; all energy we all directly conscious of is mental energy; all causality immediately known to us is *will-causality.* We extend this idea of causality to Nature by analogy. So the energy in Nature too, must not be a brute and blind energy, but the energy of a mind, *viz.*, of the Infinite Mind or God ; the causality in Nature is Will causality or the causality of God. The cosmic energy is nothing but Divine energy immanent in the world.

**Teleological Argument**

The argument consists in arguing the existence of an intelligent designer from the marks of design in Nature. Dr. Martineau points out that *selection, combination* and *gradation* are the marks of an intelligent design. An intelligent being selects his means, combines them together, and places them in an order of gradation. In Nature there are innumerable evidences of selection, combination aind gradating. So they point to the existence of God as an Intelligent Designer in Nature.

**Moral Argument:**

**(a) Kant's moral argument**

According to Kant the existence of God is a postulate of morality. Our moral consciousness demands that virtue must be rewarded with happiness. But it, is a fact of common experience that the virtus are seldom happy in this world. So, Kant argues that there must be a Supreme (viz. God) who will reward virtue with happiness and punish vice with pain in a future life.

**(b) Martineaus moral argument**

Martineau argues the existence of God from (i) moral obligation and *(ii)* the moral ideal, *(i)* Moral obligation presupposes the existence of two perons, a porson who is under moral obligation, and a person who imposes moral obligation. The person under moral obligation must be a finite person; but the person to whom our moral obligation is due *i. e.* to whom we are morally responsible neither ourselves, nor the society, nor tho state, but God. He is the Moral Governor and ultimate Judge to whom all our moral obligations are ultimately due. *(ii)* Then, Martineau argues the existence of God from the moral ideal or the ideal of moral perfection. Is the moral ideal merely an *ideal,* and *not real ?* If is not real, it cannot have any influence upon our character; but it can influence, inspire and elevate us, because. It is already real, beings realizad in God. God, then, is the eternal embodiment or living incarnation of our moral ideal, of whom it is a faint echo or dim reflection in our moral consciousness.

## Ontological Argument

It consists in arguing the *existence* of God from the *idea* of God in our minds. It assumes several forms.

### (a) Anselm's argument

We have in our minds the idea of an infinite, absolute and all-perfect Being: if this ideal is real, such a Being must exist; because existence is an essential element of perfection an existent being is more perfect than a non-existent being. Hence an all-perfect Being must exist.

### (b) Descartes's argument

Descartes substantially repeated the same argument of Anselm, but offered another form of ontological argument. It consists in arguing from the idea of the infinite being as an effect to its cause. We have the idea of an infinite Being in our minds. What is the cause of this idea ? No finite thing in the world can produce the idea of an infinite Being ; we ourselves being finite, cannot be the author of this idea. Hence an infinite, all-perfect Being *(viz.* God) must be the cause of this idea. Hence God must exist.

### (c) Hegel's argument

An idea or thought does not necessarily imply its existence in reality. The idea of a hundred dollars in my pocket, Kant truly remarked, does not prove the actual existence of the amount there. But Hegel pointed out that there must be a point in thought where thought carries with it its objective certainty, where thought and reality,, thinking and being are identical. In thinking of the self and the not-self, we imoplicitly rise to a universal point of view—to the conception of universal consciousness which comprehends both self and not-self, in its all-embracing unity, so that ultimately thinking and being, thought and reality are identical.

## Moral Government and Providence

The word 'Providence' means the power of fore-seeing what will happen in the future, and making arrangements before hand which will prevent foreseen evil and bring about good'.

By "Nåtural Providence" we mean that God watches over the operations of nature and arranges, directs and regulates the natural forces in such a way as to make them subservient to the realization of his own end viz., the final triumph of good over evil. By 'Moral Providence" or "moral government of the world" we mean that God watches over the actions of men and controls and regulates the operations of nature and development of the human society in such a way as to ensure the ultimate triumph of virtue over vice, and of good over evil.

We may suppose that Providence works in such a way that virtue is rewarded with happines, vice punished with pain in the present life". Or, we may suppose that Moral Providence works in such a way that virtue is rewarded and vice punished in a future life. Such equity cannot be fully realized in this life. The world is a sphere of moral education andprobation. The question of moral providence brings in the problem of evil and future life.

## The Problem of Evil

If God is the moral Governor and Providence of the world, how can we reconcile the existence of evil with the perfection of God ? How can we account for the existence of evil on a theistic basis ? Different answers have been given by different schools of thinkers.

Evil is of two kinds, natural moral. We shall consider them separately.

## I. Natural or Physical Evil

*(i)* **Pantheism** denies the reality of evil as of every other thing of the universe except the reality of God. Spinoza takes the so-called evil to be an illusory appearance.

## Criticism

You cannot explain away an evil by calling it an illusion. An illusion itself demands explanation. Besides, evil is a *positive* fact of experience and ai such cannot be denied.

Others admit the existence of evil, but offer different explanations of it.

*(ii)* **Dualism** seeks to explain evil either by a rival evil power or by matter.

(a) **Ditheism** believes in two rival gods, the god of good and the god of evil. For example, Zoroastrians believed in the existence of two gods, Ahura Mazda, a good god, and Ahriman the evil one.

*(b)* According to **Manicheism** or conditional *Deism* God, did not create the world out of nothing, but out of pre-existent primordial matter which was co-eternal with God. Matter being opposed to spirit resists the power of God and frustrates his good and holy design. Thus the evil in the world is not due to God, but to *matter* which resists the activities of God.

**Criticism**

Such dualism of two rival gods or two self-existent principles like God and matter is unthinkable. It is inconsistent with infinitude and absoluteness of God.

The explanation of evil, then, must be sought not in any other foreign power or principle external to God, but in God himself.

*(iii)* **Schelling** tries to avoid the difficulty by saying that God is not responsible for evil, but there is a *ground* in the divine nature which ia the cause of evil. But this is no explanation at all. It is simply disguising the difficulty.

(iv) **Theism** offers another solution. The world is finite and everything in the world is finite; but finitude means limitation; limitation means imperfection: and imperfection is an evil. Evil, then, is a necessary consequence of finitude. God, in creating a finite world, cannot but bring about evil, because evil is a necessary consaquence of finitude. But evil serves a good purpose; it offers a scope for the moral education of mankind. This is the view of Leibnitz, according to whom, this world is the best of all possible worlds.

(v) **Panentheism** holds that evil is a necessary step to good; nothing is absolutely evil. Viewed *sub specie* *aeternitatis i. e.* from the eternal point of view, what appears to us as an evil, is nothing but a means for the realization of the good in the universe. Everything is good in its own place from the absolute and eternal point of view. "Whatever is real is rational." It is owing to our limited understanding and imperfect apprehension that some things appear to us as evils. This is the view of Hegel.

**Moral evil or sin**

(i) **Pantheism** denies the existence of moral evil too and takes it to be merely an illusion. It cannot be due to man's freedom of the will, for according to pantheism (*e. g.* Spinoza ) human freedom is an illusion.

*(ii)* **Deism**, Theism and Panentheism all agree in holding that man's freedom of the will is the cause of moral evil. Man is endowed with free will; hence he is free to choose between good and evil. If he were compelled to chpose what is good, and thus if he were completely shut out from evil, he would be no better than a machine. God is a moral being; so he has created moral beings with freedom of the will to hold communion with them and impart them his own bliss and perfection. "It is *because He is Holy* and cannot be content with an unmoral world where all the perfection is given and none is earned, that he refuses to render guild in possible and inward harmony mechanical." *(Martineau.)*

## UNIVERSITY QUESTIONS

1. Discuss critically the arguments in proof of the existence of God. (1919),
2. Enumerate the theistic arguments known as the proofs of the existence of God, and examine any one of them in detail. (1914).
3. What is your conception of God ? Is He absolute and infinite ? State your reasons. (1919).

4. What is your conception of God ? What are your reasons for adopting it ? (1928).
5. What is meant by saying that the world is subject to Moral Government ? What arguments may be advanced against this belief ? Give your own conclusion with reasons. (1918). The conflicting moral aspects of the world *e. g.* evil, in and death are apparently inconsistent with the Moral Providence. Consider these in general and reconcile them withmoral governmment of the world. For this see 18.]
6. What is meant by saying that the world is pervaded by Universal Reason ? What grounds are there for believing that it is so ? What arguments may be advanced against this belief ? Give your conclusion. (1918). [The causal, teleological and ontological arguments prove that the world is pervaded by Universal Reason. See 16. The existence of evil, useless adaptations, hurtful adaptations etc., are arguments against our belief in the all-pervading Reason in the universe. But a deeper reflection shows that they are not inconsistent with the Universal Reason. See 18.]
7. Discuss critically the problems of 'Transcendence' and 'Immanence' in their bearings upon the questions of Ethics and Theology. (1917).
8. What is meant by saying that God is 'transcendent' and by saying that God is 'immanent' ? What different forms of Theology does this distinction lead to ? State your own conclusion as to the transcendence or immanence of God, giving reasons. (1913). [See 11; the different views as to the transcendence or immanence of God lead to different forms of Theology *e. g.* Deism, Pantheism, Theism and Panentheism. See 7, 8, 9 & 10.]
9. What is the place of Self in Reality, and how is the finite Self related to the absolute Self ? (1917).
10. "The world is for us not a bare succession of eventsion necessary order; it has character.' "The world is the revelation to us of God." What is the proof and what are philosophical implications of the above? (1912). [See the causal argument of Martineau, which shows that the world

is; not a bare sequence of casually connected phenomena, but is the product of the Divine Energy. It is subject to Moral Providence. See 16 and 17.]

11. The chief axiom of religion is: "The world as a whole deaerves our absolute reverence." Elucidate-this axiom. (1911). [The world is a revelation of God to us and as such it expresses His character. It is subject to Moral Providence; hence religion assumes that it deserves our absolute reverence. Fully elucidate these points. See answer 10.]
12. Give a philosophical explanation of the idea of God. (1912).
13. How would you reconcile the presence of death, evil and sin with the moral government of the universe ? (1910).
14. Give a brief account of the relation in which you consider man to stand to God man being regarded on his physical, rational and moral sides. (1909).
15. Write short notes on the following:ṭImmanence (1909), *sub specie aeternitaties*. (1909).
16. What is meant by the Absolute ? What is meant by saying that God is the Absolute ? Has God ever been other than Absolute ? Do you consider non-absoluteness to be really consistent with the idea of God ? Give your reason. (1913). [See 14. Polytheism, Ditheism and Manicheism deny the absoluteness of God. Criticize these conceptions and show that non-absoluteness cannot be consistent with the true conception of God.
17. Explain what is meant by 'Theism'. (1914).
18. Write short notes on Pessimism and Optimism. (1915). [Optimism holds that this world is "the best of all possible worlds," that pain is only a *negative* feeling, consisting in a want of pleasure, and that the evils of life will be gradually overcome and good will ultimately come out of evil. According to Pessimism, conscious life is essentially painful,ṭpain being the only *positive* feeling and pleasure being a *negative* feeling of a momentary relief from pain. The world, according to it, is full of evil. Leibnitz is a

typical exponent of optimism. Schopenhauer and Hartmann are typical exponents of pessimism.]

19. Give a critical exp osition of the doctrines of Transcendence and Immanence as applied to the ultimate Reality. (1910 Hon.)
20. How would you distinguish the conception of Personal God from that of the Absolute ? Examine the bearing of each of these conceptions on human personality. (1912 Hon.)
21. Explain the meanings of Transcendence and Immanence in relation to God. If God be conceived as transcendent, what then will be the relation of God to the world and to men ? If God be conceived as immanent, what will the relation be ? (1916 Hon.)
22. What reasons have you for believing in the existence of the Absolute ? What would be the relation of finite individuals like men to the Absolute ? ( 1915 Hon. )
23. Can evil be regarded as a positive conception, and is the existence of evil incompatible with the perfection of the universe ? (1913 Hon.)
24. Explain the relation between the individual person and the Absolute. Does the idea of the Absolute involve Necessarianism ? (1918 Hon.)
25. Analyse fully the idea of the Absolute, and state and examine the difficulties which stand in the way of conceiving God as Absolute Being. (1918 Hon.)
26. 'The world is pervaded by a Universal Eeason'—explain the meaning of this statement. On what grounds can it be maintained ? Can any considerations be advanced against it ? Examine them. (1916 Hon.)
27. What is your own conclusion as to the Transcendence or Immanence of God ? (1921).
28. Analyse your idea of God and of the relation between God and the world. (1922).
29. Distinguish between a Monistic, a Dualistic and a Pluralistic conception of Deity, and give one prominent type of each. (1922). [Discuss Polytheism, Ditheism and Monotheism.

30. What is meant by saying that God is the Absolute Being ? How can Absoluteness in God be reconciled with Evil in the world ? (1923).
31. What do you understand by the term Absolute ? What are the principal forms of Absolutism ? (1924).
32. Analyse the Idea of God and the relation between God and the world, as you conceive them. (1925).
33. What is meant by saying that God is the Absolute ? What do you consider to be the relation between God as absolute and the finite things and events of nature and history ? (1926).
34. What is your conception of God ? What are your reasons for adopting it ? (1918).
35. Consider fully the nature of Causality, and indicate its bearing on the question of God's existence. (1929). [See the Causal Argument for the existence of God.
36. Discuss the deistic and theistic conceptions of God, indicating their main differences. (1929).
37. God as Absolute cannot be a self-conscious person. Fully discuss this view. (1929). [See 14 & 15.]
38. What is your view of God ? How do you explain God's relation to man and the world ? (1930).
39. Develop the implications of the idea of the Absolute, and show that it is not necessarily inconsistent with the idea of God. (1931).
40. What view of the relation of God to man would you propose consistent with the *free will* of man and Divine Providence?
41. State some of the chief reasons for belief in the existence of. God. (1932).
42. What do you understand by God as the Absolute ? Does God's absoluteness leave any room for man's individuality and freedom ? (1933).
43. Distinguish between Deism and Pantheism, and estimate their value as religious theories. (1933). [See 10, 7 & 8.]
44. Explain the relation of God to Man. How does the

pantheistic conception of God affect our idea of this relation ? (1934).

45. Analyse the concept of the Absolute. Can the Absolute be known ? (1934).

46. Explain clearly the meaning of the transcendence and immanence of God. Which of these two views is, in your opinion, more consistent with the common notion of worship ? (1936).

47. What do you understand by the transcendence and immanence of God ? What is in your opinion the correct; theory ? (1937).

48. Explain the pantheistic conception of the relation between God and the world. (1947).

49. What do you understand by the immanence and transcendence of God ? (1947).

50. What do you understand by God as the Absolute ? Can the concept of the Absolute be independent of the knowing mind ? If not, in what sense is the Absolute so-called ? (1945)

51. Analyse the idea of the Absolute. How do you reconcile the idea of God as Absoluts with the idea of a Personal God ? (1946).

52. What is, according to your view, the relation between the human self and God ? (1946).

53. Write short notes on the following:

    *(a)* Deism;
    *(b)* Pantheism;
    (c) Theism.

54. What are. the proofs for the existence of God ? (A. U. 1946).

55. Analyse your idea of God. How do you know that God is the source of ideals ?

## CHAPTER XII

# VALUE AND REALITY

### Nature of Value-Judgments.

Judgments of value are appreciative judgments. They appraise the worth of objects. But judgments of fact are descriptive judgments. They merely describe the nature of objects. If we judge that a flower is. beautiful, or an action is right, we appraise its worth and consider it valuable. But factual judgments are different. They do not evaluate, but only describe a given environmental situation.

### Objectivity of Value-Judgments

Values are some times said to be purely subjective. They are said to be wholly relative to individual preferences. There is an element of truth in it. Values depend upon the human mind for their existence. But there is an element of untruth also. 'When we judge that an object has value, that the flower is beautitul or the deed is generous, we feel that the judgment is by no means an arbitrary one and that there is something in the objects so judged which makes the judgment necessary. Values lie in objects; values are beyond (he preferences of individual human beings." *(Cunningham)*. Valuejudgments describe those qualities of objects, which evoke the appreciative response. They do not fundamentally differ from judgments of fact. Both deal with actual facts. The difference between them is primarily a difference of emphasis. Value judgments emphasize appreciation. while factual judgments emphasize *(description)*

## Instrumental Values and Intrinsic Values

Bodily values such as health and efficiency of the body, recreation values such as games, sports and physical exercise, economic values such as wealth and property, and, social values such as social co-operation and comradeship are regarded as instrumental values.

They are not ends in themselves. They are means to higher ends. But truth, good, and beauty are regarded as intrinsic values. They are the highest ends. They are not means to higher ends. Truth is the ideal of knowledge. Good is the ideal of volition. Beauty is the ideal of feeding. Just as there is a unity of knowing, feeling, and willing in the self.

## The nature of Beauty or Aesthetic value

Some hold that beauty is *objective;* it exists in things and will continue to exist independently of any minds to appreciate it. Beauty is a quality *inherent* in objects. It would exist in objects whether any mind perceived it or not. The locus of beauty is in the environment, not in the mind which appreciates it, There is an element of truth in it. There is something objective in real things in the environment, which is appreciated by the human, mind. It is not an arbitrary creation of human imagination.

Some hold that beauty is *subjective.* The locus of beauty is in the individual mind which appreciates it. Beauty exists not-in the environment, but wholly in the mind. There is, an element of truth in it. Beauty is relative to tradition, training and social heredity. The Chinese used to see beauty in limping ladies with crippled feet. The Europeans see beauty in golden hair. The Indians see beauty in black hair.

Beauty is *subjective-objective.* The locus of beauty is neither exclusively in objects nor exclusively in the mind; it is in the enyironment and in the mind of man, in the mind as a special sort of reaction to the environment. 'Beauty is neither totally dependent upon the person who experiences, nor upon the thing experienced; it is neither subjective nor objective, neither the result of purely intellectual activity, nor a value inherent in the object, but a relation between two variables— the human organism and the object." ( Langfeld*)*. "The values of beauty are the objects of the aesthetic judgment; and every judgment is precisely the reaction of mind to an environmental situation These objects are beautiful which are of sach qualities as to arouse in an observing mind that particular response called 'aesthetic'—the judgement of beauty." (Cunningham: *Problems of Philosophy,* p. 360).

**What are the Objective Conditions of Beauty ?**

Unity in variety is a principle of beauty. The unity, harmony, or order is the essence of beauty. The unity is expressed in unity of consent, unity of form, and unity of form with content. These are the objective conditions of aesthetic judgment.

**The Aesthetic Judgment**

The aesthetic response is neither purely intellectual nor purely emotional. It is a *judgment;* it expresses an intellectual point of view and grows out of an intellectual background. Intellectual background and point of view are necessary for the perception of beauty even in natural objects, and still more so for the appreciation of objects of art. There is also an immediate feeling in the aesthetic response. The beauty of the object is directly experienced. That is the primary fact. Thus the sesthetic response involves both intelligence and feeling, both reason and emotion. It is a judgment with a prominent feeling-tone.

**The Absolute—the embodiment of Truth, Beauty, and Good**

Truth is coherence. Beauty is harmony or unity in variety. Good is moral perfection. These are completely embodied in the Absolute. They are revealed to us as *ideals* in the finite minds. "The Absolute contains all finite existence, and contains it as a perfectly harmonious system. And therefore all finite aspiration must somehow be realized in the structure of the

Absolute whole, though not necessarily in the way in which we, as beings of limited knowledge and goodness, actually wish it to be realized. The Absolute whole is thus the concrete individual reality in which our ideals have actual existence. As all our ideas themselves are but so many expressions of our place in the system and ou relation tin the rest of it so the system itself is their concrete harmonious embodiment. (Taylor: *Elements of Metaphysics,* p. 394 ).

Some thinkers hold that ideals or values are in the nature of *Ought,* not in the nature of *Is,* always transcending the real and objective, incapable of complete realization. They were not foreseen by any mind, human or divine. They were not planned by any mind. They are known when they appear Values transcend reality.

Others hold that values are ideals towards which Nature has been consciously striving. They have been foreseen, planned, desired, and willed by God, the cosmic mind. This view is held by theistic idealism.

Others hold that moral and, aesthetic values are products creative evolution which is in the nature of a process of *realization.* Truth, beauty, good, justice, righteousness, love are the "eternal values", the ends in themselves, which deter-mine the means of their realization, the various steps in the evolutionary process being indispensable to the ends, the means and the process of achievement being controlled by the values or ends themselves,, The ideals or values are regulating powers, alluring causes rather than efficient causes-

Values or ideals without relation to a mind are inconceivable and meaningless. Values as ends in themselves, unrelated to a mind, guiding and directing the process of evolution as alluring rather than efficient causes, are not satisfactory. Values as ideals realized in God, the eternal embodiment of truth, good, beauty, righteousness, justice, and love, informing the world and inspiring mankind to strive and struggle to achieve a better order, seem to satisfy our intellectual, moral, religious, and aesthetic aspirations. Pringle Pattison rightly says, "Truth, Beauty, Goodness have no reality as self-existent (abstractions; they have no meaning apart from conscious experience. They carry us therefore to a primal Mind in whose experience they are eternally realized. God himself is at once the supreme Reality and the supreme Value. And *the* highest conception we can form of perfect personality is Love, the self-giving Love which expands itself for others and lives in all their joys and sorrows. Such lòve is the ultimate value of which the universe is the manifestation. The inmost being of God is not 'solely the realization of eternal. Truth and the enjoyment of perfect Beauty, but pre-eminently the exercise and fruition of his nature as Love." *(The Idea of Immortality,* p. 190).

## UNIVERSITY QUESTION

1. Discuss the nature of Value and the relation in which it can stand to Reality. (1945).

# INDEX